'*Second Half First* offers a diaphanous and nuanced vision of the layers of a life, and of life writing. Its magnificent collective portrait reveals Modjeska's life as part of those it intersects with, including the women writers she lives with and reads . . . [a] luminous and captivating work' *Australian*

'Modjeska's memoir *Second Half First* is warm, intelligent and open-hearted, and provides a rarely captured perspective . . . Like Italian novelist Elena Ferrante, Modjeska takes the reader to the close grain of an older woman's life . . . Also examined are the complexities of the literary form, including those of the memoir' *The Monthly*

'[A] thoughtful and thought-provoking memoir . . . blending stream-of-consciousness with passionate argument and astute self-reflection' *Sydney Review of Books*

'*Second Half First* is a beautiful, sometimes profound, and always engaging memoir by a great writer' Mark Rubbo, Readings Magazine

'*Second Half First* is on my shelf near the poet Elizabeth Bishop, who also wrote despite tragedy and liked travelling in remote, unmapped regions . . . Modjeska's work, with its unanswered questions, is a beacon' *Sydney Morning Herald*

'This enthralling memoir . . . is a remarkable literary work . . . Modjeska's eloquent reckoning not only of her own history, but of her intellectual life, reaffirms her as a lucid, formidable thinker . . . Wise, vital and relayed in Modjeska's restrained, sophisticated prose [the book is] a major contribution to a literary lineage traceable to Virginia Woolf, one of Modjeska's own heroes, herself a constant presence throughout this remarkable book' *Books+Publishing*

'With an amazing lightness of touch [Modjeska] takes her reader on a journey across continents and centuries . . . a deeply crafted narrative, not only in its weave and structure, but also in the ways in which Modjeska invokes the visual arts to articulate her concerns . . . *Second Half First* has a soul. It is both solid and expansive. Modjeska assembles her stanzas masterfully to create a poem of great insight, intelligence, and beauty' *Australian Book Review*

DRUSILLA MODJESKA

Second Half First

VINTAGE BOOKS
Australia

A Vintage book
Published by Penguin Random House Australia Pty Ltd
Level 3, 100 Pacific Highway, North Sydney NSW 2060
www.randomhouse.com.au

Penguin
Random House
Australia

First published by Knopf in 2015

This edition published by Vintage in 2016

Random House Books is part of the Penguin Random House group of
companies whose addresses can be found at global.penguinrandomhouse.
com.

National Library of Australia
Cataloguing-in-Publication entry

Modjeska, Drusilla, author
Second half first/Drusilla Modjeska

ISBN 978 0 85798 981 9 (paperback)

Modjeska, Drusilla
Women authors, Australian – 20th century – Biography
Authors, Australian – 20th century – Biography

A823.3

Cover design by Nada Backovic
Cover image: *Citrus-citronier* by Pierre Joseph Redouté, courtesy of the
New York Public Library
Text design by Jenny Grigg
Typeset in Galliard by Midland Typesetters, Australia

Printed in Australia by Griffin Press, an accredited ISO AS/NZS
14001:2004 Environmental Management System printer

Random House Australia uses papers that are natural, renewable and
recyclable products and made from wood grown in sustainable forests.
The logging and manufacturing processes are expected to conform to the
environmental regulations of the country of origin.

Contents

Of course I may be remembering it all wrong after, after – how many years?

Elizabeth Bishop, 'Santarém'

The House on the Corner

The night before my fortieth birthday I told him I couldn't go on. I can't go on, I said. Not like this, not over the line to another decade. I hadn't intended to say it though it was long overdue and I'd been thinking it all day, and the day before. When he opened the door and walked up the hall into the room with the table, the words arrived – and there they were, brittle in the air around us. That's ironic, he said, as I've just told Elena that I owe it to you, a time of monogamy. *A time of monogamy*, what does that mean, I thought, but beyond that it didn't register; the tears had started again, and we were due at dinner. I don't remember much about the dinner, though it was for my birthday. We came home, and sometime during the night he left and I slept, and woke alone in the house. He came back again, I don't remember how often, and I wept, and hoped, and wanted him, and didn't, and then he left for good. Gone. He's married to Elena now, and has been for twenty years or more. They live in Brooklyn and they have a son. Elena was beautiful, and also rich

I was told by the friend of his who told me that what Ross meant by a time of monogamy was that he was going to get me settled back down and then pick up with Elena again. As if that would have worked. For a long time I put everything down to my lack of beauty, or of wealth, or of both, but Lynne, a friend of mine who was once a lover of his, said that no, it wasn't that. Unlike me, Elena had got Ross's measure. The balance of insecurity had tipped his way. He, it seems to everyone's astonishment, has become utterly uxurious. There are stories of him watching her at meals as others claim her attention; stories Lynne and I have returned to sometimes, for she was once stung by his infidelities, though not to the state of misery I found myself in. When he slept with someone else, he didn't lie, which he thought made it okay as he wasn't deceiving anyone. It was the tail end of an era, a sub-era, of free love and sexual revolution, so back then, in that world, it wasn't as brutal as it sounds; there was a certain political rectitude to his position, not just a strategy that removed an arena of guilt, though it was certainly that. The problem became my insecurity rather than his infidelity.

Lynne had known Ross at Sydney University, students together before she went to London. Leaving Sydney didn't have anything to do with him. An extremely conservative professor told her he'd make sure she never got ahead; even that wasn't the reason, not on its own, but it made a good story, for in London Lynne had done well. That winter of 1986, before I turned forty in October, she was back in Sydney, just for a few months, on a fellowship at Ross's university. She stayed with me, as I did with her, and sometimes still do, when I'm in London. I was trying to get pregnant with Ross. Don't ask what I thought I was doing; the clock was ticking, I was in love, and it was a love that seemed at the time to exorcise the grief that had come with my mother's death, so shocking and unexpected, just two years before. What better salve than love? And imagine, a baby to secure it, to bed it all down, so to speak; why would I not want to get pregnant? Imagine was all I did, a sleepwalker in the grip of longing.

I'd first met Lynne a decade earlier when I'd turned up on her London doorstep in the company of another man who'd known her at Sydney University. Are you sure it's okay? I'd asked George when he'd said he had a place we both could stay. Of course, he said, it's a communal house, as if that explained everything. Are you sure? I asked again as we stood with our cases on the steps of the tall house in Highbury. When Lynne opened the door and George lugged the cases in, I could tell at once that Lynne had no idea we were coming, let alone that we were in London for a whole semester.

George was my first experience of a man unfaithful by principle and I didn't like it, and as soon as Lynne spotted the tension between us she said I could stay but he could not. She, it turned out, found him exhausting with his pipe and his political certainties, always at the kitchen table, always talking. Communal, in her mind, didn't mean anyone, anytime, could lob in without warning. So George moved out and I carried the vacuum cleaner up two flights of stairs to the small room where we'd been sleeping. I changed the sheets, found a bright Indian bedspread and bought a bunch of flowers, most of them for Lynne, a few for a vase for the desk in the room upstairs. I was there for six months.

So that's how I met Lynne, and despite the mode of arrival it was a good beginning. She was a few years older than me, with plenteous dark-red hair. She wore loose clothes, layered in colours and shapes, jumpers several sizes too large slipping off her shoulders: not a hippy style; more how a nineteenth-century pre-Raphaelite might look transported to the 1970s. I learned to shop at markets with her, for vegetables, and for clothes made by the artisans of a new age: colour and flair. And I went with Lynne to a women's centre in a basement in Essex Road, Islington, where we raised our consciousnesses – which is easy to make fun of from this distance, but was in fact a significant passage in the lives of many of us. It was on cushions in rooms like the one in that basement that we learned we weren't alone in our humiliations, our longings, our crisscrossing, aberrant desires. At a time of sexual liberation and communal living, a great deal was said about the infidelities of men. As we wanted, or partly wanted, our own freedoms, the question became whether, and how, such liberations might work for us, and not leave us without control. Were there models of women who'd succeeded? Simone de Beauvoir? That was a tough standard. What about rosters? Agreements and limitations? There were women at those meetings who arranged their sexual lives along those lines, some with remarkable success – if only in the short term – and though I was awed, I couldn't imagine it for myself, at least not with a man I loved. Which makes it all the more strange that it was Ross I chose at that moment of grief and dread in the wake of my mother's death. In every way, it was just about the worst possible choice.

When Lynne had the fellowship at Ross's university that winter before my fortieth birthday, where else would she stay but with me? At first it was good to have her there, borrowing my clothes and my books as I did hers when I stayed with her. Every morning Ross would drive off with her to his university, and in the evening they'd return full of stories of their day, and little by little, as days went by, weeks, I could see they were enjoying themselves, having far too happy a time, while I was trudging into my university to do my classes and trudging home again on the bus, stopping to buy more food, mopping the kitchen floor. Ross said I was being possessive even to raise the question, and in response the tears came pouring. Lynne said, He's a friend going back years, and besides James would soon be arriving from London; it was no threat. And then of course I assumed the inevitable had happened and they'd ended up in bed, though maybe they hadn't, but I thought they had, and Ross equivocated, and whether they had or whether they hadn't didn't much matter as the effect was the same.

A veil of tears usually refers to grief, and maybe that's what it was; I saw the world through salt and tears: a stream, a veil, a *pour*, that was beyond will or control. Lynne sat beside me, her face concerned, and even though I knew that for her whatever it was that had, or hadn't, happened with Ross was a making good of her own youthful experience with him, I had no words. It made no sense. I made no sense. When James arrived, Lynne moved out of my house and into Ross's, and Ross moved into mine. Not that he was there much; he'd come back late after meals with them, or with Elena, who flew up from Melbourne each week to teach at the same university, and also needed lifts back and forth. His car filled up with women with shiny hair, who smiled and laughed and flirted. Little wonder he preferred to be with them than with me and my tears. When Lynne and James went back to London, I didn't say goodbye.

Many years later, in 2003, I spent a year watching artist Janet Laurence work with her large veiled glass works. She, it turned out, had been living in London around the time I was living in Lynne's Highbury house. She'd read Virginia Woolf's *The Waves* there – I'd read *A Room of One's Own* – and it had set her thinking and experimenting with the idea of washy veils: washes of paint, like waves, partly obscuring, partly revealing. She wanted to get away from the clarity with which we think we see: not to be rid of clarity but to challenge us into another way of seeing. 'A way of looking within the world rather than at it.' 'What do we see when a veil falls?' she wrote in a notebook back then. What do we see if the layers open and we step between the veils into the hidden or partly hidden places?

'Is it

Still space?

Slow space?

A membrane?

The resistance?

The hesitation?'

It didn't occur to me to think of Ross or my veil of tears while I was watching Janet work. Why would I? It was long ago, and besides I was working, preparing an essay for a book on her art.[1] There was nothing in Janet's studio to take me back to that distant time, and I didn't then make a connection between her veils and my tears. Yet, writing here, the images that come to me, insistent and repetitious, are of veils and pours, occlusions and opacities. I used to say that Ross had been a mirror in which I'd seen not him, or even myself, but an image of what I thought I wanted, an imagined future that would make good all that lay unresolved with my mother's death in England, and me here, alone, on this far side of the world. A distorting mirror with its reflective glitter peeling away underneath. A mirror? Or a veil? And if a veil, rather than a reflection in an ill-chosen mirror, was it – as I thought at first – proof of the misery I'd been reduced to? Or was it, as I came to think, a hesitation, a resistance, a necessary slowing?

One night not so long ago, I looked up Ross on the internet. I rarely hear of him any more, and it's years since I saw him, he's been away so long. Occasionally someone I know visits him and Elena in Brooklyn and reports that he enjoys the life there. They both have positions at prestigious universities. They are a fashionable pair, I'm told; they write papers together and he is still devoted. When I hear these reports I feel almost entirely nothing, though I do occasionally have dreams that come unbidden and that invariably take the form of lying in bed with Ross. He gets up and leaves, he kisses me, not erotically, just sadly, and he goes, back to her. There's a house where they live in these dreams and he walks back to it, and sometimes I walk past it, or even into it. In the dream it is in a street in Glebe, down towards the point, but it is unlike any house ever built in that part of Sydney. It has a long, narrow dream garden in front rather like a garden in a Glover painting, a garden belonging somewhere else, more a garden my father might have, but he was in England and knew nothing of any of this. In the morning when I'd wake after one of these dreams, I'd lie there sad, but not as I was: a wistful sort of sad that says, Who was he? Who was I?

And when I look back to my young weeping self, I say to her that it had to happen, a tough way to find whatever it was I had to find, which I suppose was myself: my not-rich, oddly shaped self who left England way too young, didn't find what she thought she wanted, but found a good deal else: wealth of other kinds, a life that has gone on to shape itself in words and in forms of love I couldn't have so much as imagined from behind that obscuring

veil. And if I have painted an unfair picture of Ross and
Elena, which I almost certainly have, it is because I never
knew them. I only met her once. She came to my house,
a corner terrace in (then) unfashionable Enmore one
weekend afternoon – I've no idea why she was in Sydney
seeing as she had a husband and a son in Melbourne –
when I was watering the tubs in my garden: parsley,
rosemary, a lemon tree. I heard Ross's car pull up in the
street along the side of the house; the gate opened, and
there they were in my garden. We were going to Bondi,
the three of us. I sat in the front, so that's an indication of
the state of things. It must have been the summer before
the winter Lynne stayed, that clear blue day when we
went to Bondi with Elena. We lay on the beach, with Ross
and my towels touching, and hers a little distance away
on the other side of him. We walked across the grass, up
to the Gelato Bar, the best gelato in Sydney in those days,
maybe still today. And I remember walking back to the car
in that sweep of parking along the front where you now
have to pay, but then was free. And this is the odd thing.
It came back to me afterwards as if it were a clue, though
at the time I thought it was merely odd. Elena went into
the toilets at the Pavilion to put on her make-up. Ross
and I, salty and dishevelled, stood in the sun and talked
and joked and kissed, and he put his foot on the back
fender of the car, which was a Jackaroo we called Jill, a
four-wheel drive before its time. He pressed down on the
fender and when he took his foot away the car bounced
in a solid, earthy kind of way, and we laughed, and oh

I was happy, and eventually Elena returned. We got in the car and drove to Newtown, where Ross's house was, and I don't remember what happened after that. A snapshot of memory, that's all.

The weird thing about looking Ross up on the web was how old he looked. There's a photo of him sitting on a chair in front of a window. There's a cat beside him, and a radiator on the wall to the side. His hair is thin, but it always was so that's not odd. His face is longer than I remember, and the skin is slack. He doesn't look at all like the Ross of memory, which he isn't, of course; that's the disconnect. If he were to look me up, I'd look old and not at all the girl he knew, or – more accurately – didn't know. I came across an old staff card from the 1980s at the back of a drawer recently and I didn't look like me, even to me. It wasn't just the long brown hair; the shape of my face was different. I look young. But when I look at myself as I am now, I don't look old. I might to others, but I don't to me. And friends I live beside don't look old either. They look as much themselves as they ever did, although I know this isn't true when I look at photos.

When my friend Ali Clark's husband, Axel, died in 2001, one of the first of our contemporaries to go, his children put up a board with photos going back through his life. I was looking at them with Ali the day after the funeral. The board had been put back in the room that was still in every way Axel's study. We were remembering events from when their children were little, times down on the South Coast, so much life shared and we were still only just into our fifties. Axel was fifty-eight when he died, a year younger than my mother had been when she died. There was a photo of two skinny youths standing in a doorway that didn't look Australian. They had long thin legs in tiny shorts and hair that fell over their faces. Who are they? I asked Ali. That's Axel and me, she said, and for a moment I wasn't sure I believed her. They were in Rome, not yet married, not yet with children, not yet in the house where we spent so much time: Ali made huge pots of bolognaise or trays of roast chicken legs, big salads; there was always someone to help in the kitchen, chopping and talking and drinking the beers that one of the blokes had been out for. We talked about books and paintings, and the children did their homework. I met Helen Garner at that table. I have a photo of her with one leg up on the bench, one arm resting on her knee, looking across at the camera. Why was I taking a photo? I don't remember cameras being there – or even, now I come to think of it, if it was me who took that photo. Either way it was a moment that now seems of more consequence than the anguish of Ross that had preceded it. Axel had met him in the street one afternoon during our short disaster and asked him how his 'lady wife' was, by which he meant me. Ross repeated this to me with a raise of the brow that I took as scornful, and I blushed as if at an obscenity; remembering it now brings the shadow of shame that I'd wished Axel hadn't. That day after his funeral, I didn't recognise Axel, and I didn't recognise Ali standing in that doorway in Rome – though when I worked it out, I realised that when I first met them they would have been closer to that age than to the age we were standing there in the room lined with Axel's books. The point being, obviously enough, that when we live alongside people we don't see the changes – or we do, how could we not, but we accommodate them and discount them. Ali looks fabulous at the age she is now, and she says the same of me, and then we joke that the only people who think women our age look fabulous are women our age. But actually, she does. She looks fully herself – in her face, her posture, her demeanour: full of lived life, of knowledge, of wisdom, dare I say. Why not? Not everyone is wise in their late sixties, but Ali is.

The thing I found most interesting when I looked up Ross on the internet was to see that the courses he teaches have moved from the Marxism he was teaching when I knew him to – among other things – the concept and politics of memory. 'Memory and its traces'; 'Memory, identity and responsibility'. 'The art of memory', I read under one course description. Walter Benjamin and Proust are among his texts; the only listed writer I haven't read is Bergson. 'What is memory?' I read under another course. 'Why has the rhetoric of memory become inescapable in contemporary politics?' Nothing more personal than that. Still, it makes me wonder. I looked him up on the internet that night because I couldn't sleep. I had been tired for days, it was the end of the year, 2013, December already, and my niece Martha, who'd been living with me here in Sydney for much of the last few years, had just that week returned to England. A high-school drama teacher, she'd been offered a job in Singapore and was making a quick visit home before she started at the new school in January. While I was pleased for her – as we are for the young in our lives when they make a move that takes them forward – I was also sad to see her go. I missed the sound of the front door opening, her soft tread on the stairs. I could have gone to England for Christmas with her and our family, but something had kept me here. No, this was not a Christmas for England. And so there I was that night, in a strange drift, becalmed with no energy, and I didn't realise, though it's happened often enough before, that I was book-broody. I couldn't sleep, it was hot, the cricket was on the radio and I've never liked cricket, so I lay there in the muggy air and as I did I could see words on a page, as fresh as paint, of that night I told Ross I couldn't take it over the line, this misery, into the next decade, and he said, Well that's a pity, because I've just told Elena you deserve a time of monogamy. And there he was, Ross, standing on the matting in the room with the table at the back of the house on the corner, its glass doors closed against the rain. I'd put those doors in with the money that came to me after my mother's death, though there wasn't enough to fix the damp in the floor so the matting, new only the year before, was rotting again, underneath. You couldn't see it from above, it hadn't yet made a hole as it had in the old matting, but it left a slight odour that needed the doors open for more air than we were getting that day with the rain. We went out to dinner to celebrate my birthday. There were other people, I can't remember who, or the restaurant, but I do remember the feeling of breath coming shallowly, and the veil, though not of tears, not then at dinner. Not that it mattered, for it obscured my view out across the table, while everything within was dark and disorienting; frightening. Ross drove me home and we went to bed. We didn't make love – love? – and before dawn he left, or maybe I asked him to go, I don't remember, only that I awoke alone in my bed, alone in the house and forty years old, though because of the time difference with England it would be the early hours of the next morning that would mark the exact time of my arrival to my very young mother in a hospital in London.

You were born within the sound of Bow Bells, my father would say, a joke he enjoyed, which makes you a Cockney, though as a girl raised in Hampshire from the age of two nothing was further from the truth – hence the joke – except perhaps that I was born an Indian, which was what I wished, or am said to have wished, as a very small child.

Thursday's child has far to go, my mother used to say, and far I went, all the way to Papua New Guinea, married at twenty to a handsome young anthropologist. It would be a long time before I returned – returned, that is, not in the sense of getting on a plane, but of learning anew the ground on which I was born.

The weekend after my fortieth birthday there was a party. It was a good house for parties, the house on the corner, and that Saturday the sun shone and the doors and windows were open, people spilled out everywhere. Garry who, until recently, had worked at the same university as me was there; tall and thin with his hair tied back in a band, he brought me a book by Thich Nhat Hanh. I let him admire me, his eyes a balm. Ross was furious. He was flirting with you, he said. *In front of me.* I was pleased, vengeful, though when Garry came into my bed, not that night but soon – far too soon – I wept, lost under the veil that he was powerless against. He said he'd marry me tomorrow, which he can't have meant literally, and didn't help either of us; those tears just kept pouring. The next week his mother rang looking for him and I was curt, inexcusably so. I felt cramped and claimed. All in all not a propitious beginning, and it didn't take long for Garry to realise that marrying me wasn't such a great idea, and that anyway it was a projection of his, and unlike me with Ross, he recognised it quickly enough and returned to contemplating the crash that had come in his life and had to do with a woman who'd left, a small boy he adored, and the sadness that came oozing up through the floorboards of the Zen centre where he lived.

I hadn't thought about any of this for years until the other night when I couldn't sleep. I hadn't thought of writing a memoir, and certainly not one that would begin at this lacerating moment. During the decade of my fifties, I'd developed an abhorrence of the first person: I, I, I, I, the sledgehammer of the controlling policeman, or colonialist, or conductor, if you prefer a more artistic image. But that night when I couldn't sleep, there was the first person, returning in the opening words of a memoir, and a title *Second Half First*, mocking. Would I have the nerve, could I use real names without being cast off forever? Well, in the case of Ross it hardly mattered seeing as we'd spoken not a word in almost thirty years, and though I sometimes wondered what he thought of that long-ago past, which I don't suppose he does, it was rather like wondering if there's life on another planet. But what about Lynne – our friendship restored, a story for later – and Ali, Garry, all the ones I haven't mentioned yet; could I write of them without breaking the bounds of confidence? All I knew was that I didn't like the current tell-all genre of memoir, yet how was I to write of those who've shaped my life without exposing what was not mine to expose? Where did the line fall? To that question I had no answer. For the time being I kept on writing as the words that had started so unexpectedly kept on coming: a pour of a very different kind. I'd think about what it meant later – a strategy that in other areas of life hasn't always been successful, but better than succumbing to the inner critic that used to haunt the house on the corner when Helen Garner came to live there. We'd have to flap and snap the tea towels to drive him out, for there it'd be, always male, this ghastly creature saying, *That's no good. You can't say that, they'll tear you apart*, and the reviews came rushing at us – awful all of them – and I, at least, didn't even know if I had a book. And when we talked of what we were writing, full of anxieties that we'd *gone too far*, or *said too much*, Helen would say, Well, it's not as if someone is going to rush in and snatch it off our desks and publish it right now today. This was way before the internet and the temptations of blogs and Facebook. It was before faxes, and the phone was still on a cord and you had to sit in the chair in the room with the mouldy mat and the opening doors to talk, and anyone else in the house could hear every word unless we tactfully retreated, which mostly we did.

It was some years after the Ross debacle that Helen moved in. The first person to live there with me in those years after forty when I started out towards the me that I am now was Sophie. She was English, like me, and had come here for love. She was in Australia for a decade, and unlike me she went back, and I sometimes think I should have too. That disastrous year of 1986 – which was also disastrous for her – she was living in Canberra, where she'd been for two years on the post-doctoral fellowship she'd taken in order to be with the Australian lover she'd met at University College, London. When the lover, whom we called the Economist, got a smart job with the Australian Government, Sophie came too. After working with housing associations in London, the suburban order of Canberra was a shock for Sophie, and it was partly that which precipitated the end of the relationship. The Economist took up with someone else while Lynne was in Sydney staying with me. Sophie knew Lynne from London, but the first I knew, or saw, of Sophie, was late one afternoon when she knocked on my door. I took in her springy blonde hair, her beautiful eyes, her legs

in white jeans. Hi, she said. I'm Sophie. Is Lynne here?
She wasn't. She'd moved over to Ross's house as James
was about to arrive, and Ross was meant to be in my
house, but wasn't – and at that very moment was probably
in the pub with Lynne or Elena, unless she'd gone back
to Melbourne. The only other time I saw her, she was
pushing a stroller at a conference at my university. Her
husband was beside her. I can't remember a thing about
him, but her back was straight despite the stroller, and
her dress was classy. Ross was sitting with me in a sort of
sunken concrete courtyard, very badly designed and since
built over, and they walked across on the path into the
building at the other end. Ah, there's Elena, Ross said,
and while I glowered and a great heavy boulder of misery
came thumping down on me, he sauntered over, cool as
anything, shook the husband's hand, a demonstration of
how one was meant to behave in these circumstances.

'No,' I said to Sophie that day on the doorstep. 'Lynne
is not here.'

And with that I closed the door. I didn't actually slam
it, but as the story has come to be told, I might as well
have done.

Fortunately, as things turned out, I met Sophie
again that Christmas, the one after my fortieth birthday
when I was left in the house by myself with Garry as an
occasional salve, and not feeling any improved for all the
meditating I was doing with him at the Zen centre, legs
crossed on a hard mat looking at a wall. Follow your
breath, Garry would say. Let the thoughts pass through.

But it wasn't thoughts that were passing through my head; instead long monologues of great and dramatic eloquence addressed to Ross. That Christmas there was a party on the roof of a small apartment block where several friends lived overlooking Bondi from above the cliff walk to the south. It was windy up there looking out over the ocean and though it was pretty with the lights coming on across the water, and the stars, and maybe a moon – I don't recall – I wasn't enjoying it, the wind whipping around, and because it was summer and hot over in Enmore away from the sea breezes, I hadn't brought anything warm. All I could think was that at least in England there are fires, and then I recognised Sophie. I watched her for a while, wondering what to do, whether to go over to her, or go home. Her hair was blowing around, and when she put down her glass to pin it back, the glass blew over.

'Your first Christmas in Sydney,' I said, rescuing the glass. 'What a disaster.'

'Disasters all round,' she said.

And I said, 'You must have thought I was awful slamming the door on you like that.'

She laughed. Sophie laughs a lot, it's one of the many things I like about her, and she doesn't hold grudges.

'You were pretty awful,' she said in a direct, un-English way. 'I didn't know anything about what was going on for you. It sounds even worse than the way I was dumped.' And then she told me the story of the Economist who'd brought her to Canberra and then taken up with a girl with a bow in her hair.

'A bow?' I said. 'Really?'

'Yes, a bow,' she said, making a gesture with her own blowing-around hair to demonstrate the dimensions of the monstrosity. I never met the girl with the bow, and Sophie never met Elena; they became cartoon figures in the talk at the table in the room that was filled with light from the doors that needed to be open if the dank smell wasn't to build up. Dank. It's a good word, I like it. There were girls at school with dank hair; it was the weather and only one hair wash a week. At the house on the corner we had a shower with an open window beside it, at enough of an angle not to be seen from the street, so we could shower with the sun streaming in, or lie in the bath and read looking out into the apricot tree that never had apricots.

I don't remember when Sophie moved in, but when she did everything changed: the air, my mood, the rooms we slept in. Even the lemon tree, after struggling for years in the tub I'd got cheap at a place near the dump, produced a harvest of five juicy lemons.

2

We were into allegory in that house, and metaphor, anything symbolic. If this was fiction, which it isn't, I could call it *The Lemon Tree*. It could be one of those recovery novels. All the ingredients were there: Zen, the house on the corner, Sophie, and the friends who gathered for meals around the table, the herbs I planted in pots and the lemon tree that finally came good. A house in Enmore doesn't have quite the allure of Provence, nor Zen with Garry the appeal of spiritual quest in Bali. But something happened there in those years that was restorative. I moved out of the big bedroom at the front upstairs so Sophie could also use it as a study, and into the smaller room next door. My desk was in the large, downstairs room where the television was and the grate we used for a fire in winter. Most of our time was spent in the room at the back, with the doors and the table – or else in our beds. Maybe it's being English and the cold we grew up with, for we both liked to retreat to bed. Sophie worked in hers. I read, and tinkered in my notebook. As our rooms adjoined each

other and were arranged in such a way that our beds were
head to head with the wall between us, we used to say
there should be a hatch through which to pass the teapot
to save us trundling round when we wanted another cup.
The house was shabby, with patches of peeling paint and
rattling window frames and, as I say, the damp floor in
the room with the doors opening out to the side. A small
kitchen had been tacked on at the back long before there
were council regulations, and so badly built that its walls
bowed. But the house itself was solid and generously
proportioned, and being a corner terrace with the long
side facing north, there was plenty of light. There was an
outside lavatory which meant it didn't matter if someone
was in the upstairs bathroom – which was just as well, as
the small room at the back beside it, which also looked
out onto the non-fruiting apricot tree, became a favoured
transit-stop for people visiting from Melbourne, Adelaide,
London, all over.

When it came to my work, the big downstairs room
suited me well. If I shut the doors no one came in to
bother me; if I left one door open I could see who came
in and out, and join them at the table if I wanted to, or
close the door if I didn't. Writing a book, which at first
I wasn't but eventually I was, can be a good excuse for
pleasing oneself, at least in those sorts of ways.

With Sophie in the house, something loosened in
me. The walls seemed lighter, the ceilings higher, as if
there were more space, and in her company I stretched
into it. Well, she'd say, there must be some advantages

to our situation – and one of them was that without the encumbrance of live-in partners and children, we could get in the car on a whim and drive out of town. We went to places I'd never been, to towns in the bush with nothing but a pub and a row of houses. We went to the beach house on the South Coast, four hours away, and she fell under its spell as I had done on first coming to Australia. It's rocky, that stretch of coast, with hills covered in eucalypts coming down to small coves. Like Wales, Sophie would say, though it wasn't; it is like nowhere but itself, with its great crocodile rock brooding across the sandbar. We'd walk over headlands, across small, shingly coves, to a beach that was long only in the context of that area – unlike Australia's celebrated beaches that extend for miles with nothing behind them but exhausted dunes. It took ten minutes to walk the length of our longest beach, with its small dune where the creek came in and boathouses under the cliff at the far end. Sophie loved the sweep of the tides and made sure she walked in a zone that she taught me to appreciate   between the high tide and the low; that liminal space, betwixt and between, with its own life of crabs and seaweeds and feeding birds.

As we walked, we talked. We talked about the problem of lovers, the problem of men. We'd both been admired, we'd both been loved. We'd walked away from lovers who'd loved us, we'd walked away from situations that had cramped us even as they promised security, fidelity, life going on – a marriage in my case, made too young for sure, not that it's an excuse. We talked our private memories as we walked between the tides. Love and security; independence and freedom of mind. Was that the dilemma? And if it was, was it so bad to want both? A great deal was changing in the lives of girls and women, even our fathers had said so; it was why they made sure we had good educations. Now both were possible, did it have to be so hard, putting them together, marriage and a career, love and independence, was it still a choice – surely not, not in the last decades of the twentieth century? Were we the weird ones, wanting both? Or were we the ones who admitted what others clamped down? These were the questions we asked as we climbed the headland back to the house. We talked as we cooked on the campfire outside; we talked of sisters and we talked of parents – hers together, mine divorced; we talked of our mothers, whose educations were cut short by the Second World War, and who, afterwards, carried the burden of making us all happy – husbands, children – as the world they lived in recovered from news of the Holocaust, and from the bombs that had flattened large swathes of London, where Sophie had lived as a child and we had visited every school holiday. A country girl, not used to such sights, I'd looked from the tops of buses into deep holes half-concealed by hoardings, and at terraces that ended in a house with walls hanging open, more rubble. We grew up with photos on the mantelpiece of relatives killed in the war: young men with hopeful faces and barely a whisker of beard on their chins. My young husband, Nick, being American, had faced the Draft, but the boys we'd grown up with in

England hadn't been threatened by war, and nor had we; no nursing at the front for us; no deciphering codes in a dark room at night as an aunt of mine had done at the age of eighteen. Had we grown up soft as a result; soft and self-indulgent? Or were we forging a new way? And if so, what could it look like?

And we talked in the car back to Sydney, Sophie and I, driving through the eucalypt forests, over bridges then still made of planks, where the estuaries came in before widening into lakes where the oyster farms were. We talked through the long, slow outskirts of Sydney with traffic lights we lost count of, suburbs of houses, acres of them spreading west and north, silencing us. Christina Stead, one of us would say, and sigh, a code of our own for the depressing vision of small pert houses with their garages and blank gardens. I'd given Sophie Stead's *For Love Alone*, a novel I'd read on first coming to Sydney fifteen years earlier. It took me a long time to get the full irony of the title, but Sophie and I understood the character Teresa Hawkins at once. She became a figure in our talk, as real as anyone around the table, with her longings and her bad choice of Jonathan Crow – what a name for a figure chosen more for what he projected, and for what she wanted to see, than for what he was. And we shared Teresa's horror of the suburbs, the houses stretching out along the railway lines, where her cousins and friends, rushing into marriage with their glory boxes and trousseaus, were setting up house with overgrown boys 'gone into long trousers'. Were the bouquets of the wedding day worth it? Not to Teresa Hawkins, not to Christina Stead who'd created her. Not to me, not to Sophie. Driving back from the coast, it was always a relief when at last the city buildings came into view, and we could turn off towards Enmore and the house on the corner – two streets back from the railway, an irony lost on neither of us. Still, it was home, at least for the moment.

A home for waifs and strays, we'd say; who knows where any of us will be in five years' time – or even one – as the table filled and we cooked another meal for those who were broken-hearted, and quite a few who weren't. Bit by bit friends of Ross and the Economist were let back in, though they watched their words, for our eyes could narrow quick as maybe. Sophie started with a therapist, an aunty woman with a reassuring face and an impressive array of Indian cushions. She cheered Sophie up so much that I went too. She used to call Sophie's ex Charlie, which wasn't the right name, and Charlie became the name for everyone's exes, until I rarely spoke Ross's name, displaced as it had been by Charlie, a much better figure to vilify seeing as he didn't actually exist and one was under no obligation to consider another point of view – which even I was prepared (reluctantly) to admit Ross had. The veil didn't vanish but there were days, even weeks, when it lifted, though if Sophie was away and I was left alone to contemplate that dark winter of 1986, I'd have dreams of being cold, as bereft as I ever had. I hadn't begun the task of unpicking the knot that was bound tight around the grievous death of my mother, about which I was barely able to speak, even to Sophie; that lay undisturbed for a few years yet, before I gave up the therapeutic comforts of the Indian cushion room and began an altogether different, psychoanalytic venture in a room in a big house in a suburb I had never been to until I drove through it with Sophie. Several years before I knew the significance of that stone house we'd driven past, noticing its steep roof and its trees rising over the bungalows that crouched around it. We'd contemplated its existence when it would have had sheep and forest around it, the first house in the area, displacing those who'd lived for generations along the Lane Cove River – which was where we were heading.

Sophie was teaching Urban Geography, a subject I barely knew existed. As we drove around Sydney on our way to beaches or markets, or just to explore, I began to understand something of the way we live in our built environment, which I hadn't thought about until then. The houses we live in can form us in ways that have to do with more than food and shelter, though as my father, who'd fought in the Second World War, reminded us over and over, we should never forget to be grateful for that. In London Sophie had worked with housing associations in an era when there was a great deal of unused and mismanaged public housing. She lived in collective houses and worked with squatters' groups, women's refuges, organisations for the homeless, which took over unused houses, restoring them from vandalised states of disrepair. This very political action – it was only public housing that was occupied – was drawing attention to the public need, and wastage, at the same time as working to enable other, more communal ways of living than the default family house that had come to make up most of the housing stock in our towns and cities, and still does.

Gaston Bachelard's *The Poetics of Space*, one of the few books that still has a place beside my desk all these years later, came to me from Sophie. Reading it, I began to think of houses as places of interaction and exchange, of engagement of minds and lives, and it was due to Sophie, and to Bachelard, that I realised the significance, the symbolism, of our house being on a corner. When I came to write about it, which I did, with her, in a book called *Inner Cities*, long out of print – which is a pity as it's really quite good, better than I expected when I looked at it again – I called my contribution 'Living on a Corner'. I meant it as a metaphor for living with a certain ambivalence, caught between the new ways of living that came to those of us who were moving into the inner city, and the old expectations that could confound us as longings, born, we supposed, of the family houses of our 1950s childhoods. Our 'inner cities' were of mind and emotion as much as of bricks and mortar, although the harsh reality – which I'm relieved to see I also wrote about – was that 'our' moving into the suburbs near the centre of the city was pushing out those who'd lived there in the unfashionable decades when even the now smartest of inner suburbs were frowned upon by those with the money and the distance to frown. When I moved into the house on the corner towards the end of 1979, there were no trees in the street that ran along the side; from the window of the bedroom that became mine when Sophie came, I could see the flats at the other end. By the time I left, there were trees the whole way along, as the new class moved in and the old working-class families moved out to the west. A few Greek families survived with their gardens of tomatoes and aubergine growing over the paths, but they're long gone now.

When I drive round that corner, which I do occasionally, I no longer stop to contemplate the renovations to the house that is no longer mine. I stop to remember Dulcie and Vince who lived in the single-storey terrace that abutted our garden at the back, facing the street that ran along the side of the house. They lived in their small house with their four boys while Sophie and I had my two-storey house to ourselves. The boys went to the primary school on the other side of the railway line, and in the afternoons they played cricket in the street. We could hear the ball and the glee of the little one when he sent his brothers hurtling down the street while he made his runs between our back gate and their rubbish bin. Until one afternoon, when a car sped round the corner and killed him. Everyone ran out into the street, an ambulance arrived. Dulcie was keening, and the young driver, clearly in his father's car, too shiny-expensive for our neighbourhood, was asking for water, for coffee, which no one gave him, and sure enough when the police came and he was taken for testing, his blood alcohol was way over the limit. When the case came to court, the QC his father hired got his sentence suspended. He was fined barely more than Vince had been fined when he was caught driving over the limit after Christmas drinks at a pub near the factory where he worked. Vince had been stopped in a random breath test; he hadn't been speeding, and he hadn't killed anyone. Dulcie drew her own conclusion, that money ruled, and moved the family away. At the funeral, which everyone from both streets attended, and the kids from the school, and all Vince's workmates, the priest spoke of God's will. Dulcie, who wasn't a believer, sobbed loud, angry sobs that expressed her contempt. If *she* were in charge, she said over and over, the death of a child would be worth more than this. It wouldn't be allowed, she said, not if she had a say.

I didn't write about this in *Inner Cities*. I don't know why, it seems a strange omission. Perhaps it was too raw, still too close. When I took the book down from its shelf, thinking if I'm writing a memoir I'd better check its date, I found it was published in 1989, the year before *Poppy*, when I'd have sworn – on a bible, in a court, if I'd had to – that it had come after: a postscript before I left the house. So sure was I that for a minute I thought Penguin must have made a mistake, ridiculous even as a thought, doubly so to check it on Google. Which raises another question about memoir: if memory is so unreliable even in this small matter – 1989 or 1991 – what else am I wrong about? Not about the death of that child, though I couldn't tell you which year it happened; I remember it as an incident outside time. The easiest place for me to check would be my diaries, but the ones that survived the cull when I sold the house are in the National Library in Canberra. There's an embargo on them for twenty years after my death, by which time I figure most of the people I wrote about will be dead, or demented or otherwise past caring what I said about our feuds and flirtations. The embargo doesn't apply to me so I could, I suppose, go to the library and read them there. But then I'd be researching myself as if I were a subject of history and not myself, and that is a task in which I have no interest. Besides, being a diarist I don't trust diaries; they depend too much on the moment, the mood, the weather, the person you've just talked to, or argued with, the flora in your gut. No, this is not an autobiography in the sense of an account of my life written as a biography of and by myself. Maybe it's not even a memoir, simply a reflection on the arc of life thirty years after the death that propelled me into collision with the Charlie mirror.

As I write this, at the beginning of January 2014, thirty years ago, in January 1984, my mother had just days to live. I'd arrived in England in time to see her before the drift out of consciousness began. She wasn't interested in the news I had to give her, knowing, I suppose, as I did not, that the end was very near. When the hospice rang looking for me in London a few days later to say I should come as soon as possible, they got Lynne, with whom I was staying. When I got back to her house late that afternoon, she handed me the number. I rang and a kind doctor spoke to me. Would tomorrow do? I asked. If she were my mother, the doctor said, I'd come now. So I abandoned the evening with Lynne. I made some toast, drank a quick cup of tea, packed a small bag, and took the tube to Waterloo to catch the train to the town where my mother lived south-west of London. The stations we passed in the dark were bleak, passengers standing under dim lights with their arms wrapped around themselves, or slapping their sides against the cold. At Farnham it was drizzling and there were no taxis on the street outside the station. I walked the mile to the hospice with my head down and collar up. Poppy was in a softly lit room, lying on her back, propped up, peaceful. She looked as she'd looked when I was a child and had climbed into her bed in the mornings. Her eyes opened, dark, dilated, comprehending, I think, that it was me. I dropped to my knees with tears pouring onto her hand, which I felt tighten, very slightly, in mine. *I'm sorry*, I cried. *I'm so sorry. So very, very sorry.* A nurse brought a cup of strong, milky tea and coaxed me into a chair. Then my youngest sister, who'd been there most of the day, arrived back from a break for something to eat. We sat beside our mother, quiet together, and the hours ticked slowly past and the only words she spoke came in a sigh. *Janey, Janey,* the name of my middle sister, her second daughter, her favourite, I always thought, though how are any of us to know how the love of a mother measures itself. She's on the train, we said. She's on her way. She was coming down from Yorkshire and was in London already, crossing the city from King's Cross to Waterloo for the train south. A friend of Poppy was to pick her up at the station; Jane was pregnant, with a baby due in March, my nephew Tom, the first boy into our family of girls: three girls to Poppy, two already to Jane, whom I called May in the book I wrote a few years later in the house on the corner. When Jane was expecting Amy, and then Martha, Poppy had knitted tiny bonnets in fine white wool, trimmed with lace, although we didn't know the sex in advance then. This time, beside her bed at the hospice, not quite finished, was a helmet for the new baby, knitted in a blue and white nylon-wool mix. It can go straight in the washing machine, she'd told Jane. One of her friends finished it in time for the birth, and there he was, Tom, a huge baby bruised from the delivery, in his boy-blue helmet with earflaps.

On the night Poppy died, Jane arrived at the hospice shortly before midnight. She's here, we said. Janey's here. Poppy opened her eyes and registered – or seemed to register – that it was her second-born kissing her forehead, whispering goodbye, tears falling. The room was very quiet, just that soft light, the curtains drawn across the windows, and beside the bed, chairs for her daughters. Later, after I'd written *Poppy* and Katherine Hattam, who'd become a friend, had read it, she gave me a collage, a painting of those chairs. It hangs near my desk, a reminder – of what? The transformations of art? Poppy dying and the chair I could not stay in, down on my knees beside her?

In the winter of 1987, the year after the Ross disaster, I took a semester off from teaching to write *Poppy* – not that I knew when I started what, exactly, I was going to write. I didn't have a title, though I did have her name – Poppy in place of the Pookie she came to dislike as the girlish name of her marriage, not the name of the woman who'd returned to an interrupted education and had become a working woman. Since her death, I'd had the impulse, the *urge* to write about her. Who was she, this woman I could see only as mother? What was her story? How had she lifted up out of the mire, the despair of an abandoning husband? What had happened to send me so far away, and to turn me so hard against England? For three years I'd had the *idea* of a book, but what with Ross and all, I hadn't got far, or rather I hadn't got anywhere at all, and by the middle of that year when I took leave, it had dawned on me that whatever it was that had drawn me into that destructive love affair was part of the same story that had had me on my knees, both literally and figuratively, as Poppy died. I was, you could say, still on my knees. My head was no longer bowed to the ground; I was stretching again but I hadn't raised myself to my full height. I didn't know what my full height was.

So there I was that winter, in the house alone each day, Sophie off at her university, my desk set up under the window at the front, a pen at the ready, a new notebook, a full bottle of ink. I sat down, the writer at work, and nothing happened. Not a word, not a sentence, not a page. I was a fraud. I retreated to the sofa while it was still winter, then to a chair in the garden once spring arrived, and read. That was when the way I read changed. I'd read to a purpose, or a programme, for so long I'd forgotten what it was to pick up a book and try it, as a child does, until either I was swept up into it, or had put it aside without qualm for another. It was a way of reading I'd once known, but had come to think of as self-indulgent – even frivolous – and by the time I was studying, and then teaching, I suppose it was. Alone in the house on the corner that winter I didn't have a reading list or a programme. I learned to read by instinct, and if I wasn't with a book after thirty pages I stopped, laid it aside, and often enough the time would come when I'd pick it up again and find it alive from the first page. I read a lot in those years, I read a lot now, sometimes in the weirdest patterns, and one way of thinking about who I became in the years after forty could be a history of my reading.

What I needed to do, though I wouldn't have put it this way at the time, was to read my way into, or through, that clouded inner place of dread and futility that could still wake me at dawn before the house came to life, before the garbage collectors rumbled round the corner and the men from the streets on two sides of us got into their cars for the first shift in the factories that were still manufacturing in Marrickville and Sydenham. That bleak hour alone in a bed at forty, the age when we might expect a man to be sleeping alongside us, and the sounds of children in adjacent rooms. That bleak hour before I'd hear Sophie get up, go for a pee, the lavatory flush and her bedroom door close again. Then I'd fall asleep and wake groggy to the smell of coffee, and if I wasn't fast down the stairs the front door would close, her car would start up, and I'd know there was another day alone with that desk.

Another book that came through Sophie, which I read that winter, was Christine de Pizan's *The Book of the City of Ladies*. It opens with her sitting alone in her study one day, idly picking up a book and finding herself jolted to attention by a *lamentation* that all the miseries of marriage (for men) were caused by women. It's a remarkably modern opening for 1405, but then it shifts into the prolix, allegorical style of the era as she sets about creating a 'city' built from the lives of exemplary women. Stone by stone, she demolishes the city of culture and value built over centuries by men who have misjudged the nature of woman and slandered her name. Simone de Beauvoir credits Christine de Pizan with being the first woman 'to take up her pen in defence of her sex'. She took the clerics to task in 'a lively attack' (Beauvoir's words), and joined the long-running literary 'quarrel' over the *The Romance of the Rose*, objecting to its depiction of women as mere seducers, and the vulgarity of language that reduced women to the vessels of debased sexuality. Not surprisingly she was attacked for all the things women who take on structural misogynies get attacked for. 'Snubs and chidings', Virginia Woolf called them centuries later. It was only because Christine de Pizan had had a powerful protector in Isabeau of Bavaria, the wife of Charles VI of France, that she was able to keep writing. She needed to; it was her only source of income after her husband died while on a mission for the French court, leaving her, aged twenty-five, with three children, a mother and a niece to support.

Among the women of de Pizan's city was Novella, the daughter of a fourteenth-century 'solemn law professor' at the University of Bologna, a rare man for his times who 'was not of the opinion that it was bad for women to be educated'. He educated Novella in the law 'to such an advanced state that when he was occupied by some task and not at leisure to present his lectures to his students, he would send her in his place'. She would take his chair and 'a little curtain' would be drawn in front of her so as not to distract her audience of men. It was a story that made its point centuries later at the table in the house on the corner, for while we'd all had university educations and took our own rooms (and incomes) as granted, very few of our mothers had either a degree or a room of their own. We knew the cost in their lives; I was not the only one whose mother had vanished for several years into a psychiatric ward. As to us, we didn't sit behind a curtain, we were out there parading, or so we thought, but in our dealings with the world of men, our university colleagues as well as our lovers, there were times when we could feel ourselves condemned to live behind a curtain of misapprehension – though in our case it was never quite clear if we were concealed by it, or revealed. Veils and curtains. Either way, in those years after Poppy's death, long before I encountered Janet Laurence's veils, Novella's curtain became a metaphor for how we were seen, or felt ourselves to be seen, or – more to the point – not seen, and therefore not understood.

By the time Christine de Pizan was sixty-five and had retired to a convent at Poissy, she had written forty works – including treatises, allegories and poetry. Her daughter was already living at the convent, and when you read about the conditions of convents before the church got to work 'reforming' them into places of poverty, chastity and enclosure, they seem an attractive solution to the problem of retirement. A convent was where women who did not want to marry could go – I'm talking of educated women here, I admit; there was a whole other class of serving nuns – taking with them their furnishings, their books, their clothes. With their own rooms they could entertain visitors – including lovers it's sometimes said but I don't know if that's actually the case, or wishful later thinking. What is for sure is that the medieval convents were where women could, and did, live an intellectual life of writing and study, companionship as well as retreat. Virginia Woolf's radical argument – in 1929 – that everything depends (if you are a woman) on having some money of one's own as well as a room of one's own – which no longer seems radical to those of us in the educated West who can assume both – has antecedents most of us know little about.

As does Sophie's housing association work. Looked at from today, all that collective talk might seem naïve and idealistic, very 1970s, but it, too, was built on a legacy now forgotten. From the early nineteenth century, as housing stock and family patterns changed from old forms of extended, more communal living, there were reformers, many of them women, who saw the isolating implications of the move towards the little boxes Pete

Seeger would sing of in the 1960s. Thanks to Sophie, I can
tell you that in 1848 Jane Sophia Appleton, 'a housewife
in Bangor USA', described the cities she imagined we'd
be inhabiting by 1978. There'd be communal kitchens
and laundries, efficiencies of scale: quiet, ordered, under
the control of the women working in them – and certain
of success. Gone would be 'the absurdity of one hundred
housekeepers, one hundred girls in the process of making
pies for one hundred little ovens'.[2] I suppose you could
say the market has taken over the idea and efficiencies of
the communal kitchen – though not the idea of keeping
them in the control of women; it has also taken over the
housing, making our little boxes ever more desirable, and
increasingly out of reach. Sophie joked that she hoped,
for Jane Sophia's sake, that there was no reincarnation.
But Sophie knew, we both knew, that somewhere between
rooms of our own, communal kitchens and collective
housing, between companionship and the space to be
our own thinking selves, lay the question of how we were
to live.

Given my allegorical frame of mind and state of
avoidance, I gathered up these stories, and more. Jane
Sophia Appleton and Christine de Pizan, Novella behind
her curtain, as well as Teresa Hawkins and her creator
Christina Stead who'd left Sydney for London in 1928 on
her own quest for love, became bricks in the city of women
I built from the comfort of a chair. No stonemasons or
slaves hauling huge slabs of rock across deserts for me;
not even the plumbing Sophie had done back in those

squatting days, though I had spent a few days, that's all, with a paint roller at the Women's Refuge in Glebe when, in 1974, it had opened in two of the many derelict houses that belonged to the church. That winter when I took leave from teaching and was supposed to be writing, I was doing nothing so vigorous – though the way it felt, reading and thinking and walking for miles each day, writing in my head and then eventually in the notebooks that filled with a messy scrawl, I may as well have been running barrows of bricks up a steep ramp. At night, I slept as if I had.

After two decades of reading my way into the Pacific and then into this strange antipodean place in which I seemed to be making a life, I returned to writers of my birth country. This was less the influence of Sophie than of Dorothy Auchterlonie Green, one of the few women of my mother's generation here in Australia to whom I could turn for advice. She had read my PhD thesis on that remarkable generation of Australian women writing between the wars. While my official examiners – historians, not literary scholars like her – wrote glowing reports, all very satisfactory to the ego, Dorothy invited me to visit her in Canberra. I sat with her for an afternoon in a room that looked out over a garden full of birdsong while she went through the thesis heavy on her knee, pointing to slippages of meaning, words carelessly used, pushing me further on the novels I'd written about, and asking tough questions about the way I'd understood (or not) the lives of the women who'd written in those years between the wars – when she was a girl and had read them as part of her growing into her own writing and living. It was an exhilarating, exhausting afternoon in which I felt challenged, a double-edged sensation that didn't allow me the satisfaction of staying with those official reports. By the time Dorothy closed the thesis and took off her glasses, I was feeling distinctly wilted.

'Well, dear girl,' she said, getting up to put on the kettle, 'I think we deserve some tea.'

For a moment I thought she was going to say we deserved a whisky, but tea came, I helped her with the tray and a plate of biscuits. The mood shifted and we talked until the light faded and it was time for me to leave.

At the door she complimented me on the thesis she'd just picked apart and told me there were things there that were worth saying. I must have looked at her blankly.

'Dear girl,' she said again. 'A word of advice. When you rewrite this as a book' – the hefty volume now weighing on my arm – 'don't look over your shoulder.'

That was Dorothy: exacting and enabling, in a neat blouse with a brooch at the neck.

After that she became a mentor and a friend. I visited her in Canberra and she came to the house on the corner, sometimes staying the night in the quickly tidied-up room at the back. The only time I saw a mouse in that house was at breakfast one morning with Dorothy. The mouse appeared from under the stairs and there it was in the doorway. I tried to keep Dorothy's attention on the teapot and the toast, but the mouse took its time, sauntering across the room and into the kitchen. Dorothy of course noticed and watched its progress across the matting. It's always good, she said, to be reminded that we cohabit in our houses.

When I was stuck, reading more than I was writing, I wrote her letters and she wrote long, serious replies. Reading was essential to the work of writing, she said. I shouldn't consider it lost time. I couldn't talk to her as the young talk to me, not of sex, and only cautiously of love, though she knew there'd been an unhappy love affair and that my mother had died. She knew there was a crisis, and though I saw the sympathy in the way she looked at me, her advice and help came through books. You've been here for how many years? she once asked. And in that time you've read novels from the Pacific and from here. What have you read from the place you were born, and where your mother was born? Not much since school, I said. Go back, she said. Go back to the mothers, to the world yours was born into and that you came from. She meant in my reading, not on a plane, but that, too, I needed to do.

3

It was Dorothy who put Vera Brittain's *Testament of Youth* in my hand, sending me back to my grandmother's generation and the war both she and my mother were born in the shadow of – Dorothy in 1915, its dark second year, and Poppy in 1924 after the killing was done. The Great War, it was called, a savage and senseless war which sliced through a generation, killing millions of young men, damaging millions more in myriad, horrible ways, and leaving tens of thousands of young women without men to marry. *Superfluous*, the women were called.

Vera Brittain was nineteen when the war began in 1914. She was due to start at Somerville College, Oxford, that autumn. Her brother Edward was seventeen, a prime age to enlist, which he did with his two best friends from school. For these soft-faced boys – barely yet men – there was no question but to enlist. A fellow student who survived the war later described the mood of 'appalling jingoism' at their school, with the headmaster telling the boys that if a man couldn't serve his country he was better off dead. When Vera went up to Oxford, Edward, Roland and Victor, whom she'd known since they were twelve, went to officers' training camp, full of patriotism, expecting the war to be short and heroic. It was neither. All three would be killed: first Roland at the end of 1915, then Victor in 1917, and last Edward, just months before the armistice. 'The three musketeers', Roland's mother had called them.

Vera and Roland, already sweethearts, became engaged the summer of 1915 while he was in London on leave. She was nursing by then, having given up her place at Somerville, much to the dismay of the formidable College Principal, Miss Emily Penrose. Many a woman could nurse at the front, was Miss Penrose's argument; in the longer run, was it not more important to educate women into positions of power that might make war less likely? We might sigh at her optimism, having lived to see women in positions of power; the problem with Mrs Thatcher, Dorothy Green used to say, wasn't that she was a woman who wanted to be a man, but a woman who wanted to be a General. That was a future Miss Penrose hadn't envisaged. For her generation, the education of women had been hard fought – and was not yet won. In 1914, when Vera Brittain began at Oxford, women could study for a degree and take the exams; it was not until after the war, in 1920, that they were finally allowed full degree status. Vera Brittain understood Miss Penrose's argument – how could she not – but the counter-pull was stronger: a kind of 'accursed' generational duty to 'listen and look' whether she wanted to or not, and share, in so far as she could, the fate of her male contemporaries. She spent the rest of the war nursing. By the time Roland was expected back in England on a second leave at the end of 1915, she was at the 1st London General Hospital 'amid the slums of Camberwell Green' in south-east London, where wounded soldiers were brought from the front in France. It was tough work, with long hours, bleak quarters and a daily fare of ugly, festering wounds. The first dressing Vera Brittain had to attend was a 'gangrenous leg wound, slimy and green and scarlet, with the bone laid bare'. She saw orderlies faint at the sight of less. After months of this, when she heard Roland would be in London for Christmas she treated herself to a new dress – black taffeta 'with scarlet and mauve velvet flowers tucked into the waist' – and 'dashed joyously' to the phone expecting to hear his voice. She learned instead of his death at a Casualty Clearing Station in France. It was early on Christmas morning, 1915. She had just come off night duty.

Two months later Roland's kit was returned to his parents, including the uniform – 'those poor remnants of patriotism' – which he was wearing when his stomach took the impact of a machine gun. 'I wondered,' she wrote, 'and I wonder still, why it was thought necessary to return such relics – the tunic torn back and front by the bullet, a khaki vest dark and stiff with blood, and a pair of blood-stained breeches slit open at the top by someone obviously in a violent hurry.'[3] She was glad neither Edward nor Victor was there to see them.

These days Camberwell Green is no longer an area of slums – my niece Amy lives there, in a Victorian terrace in a street lined with trees and window boxes – but in 1915, after Roland's death, the drab area and the mile and a half walk between the hospital and the nurses' quarters at Denmark Hill became unbearable to Vera Brittain. She volunteered for an overseas posting, including in France as a Voluntary Aid Detachment (VAD) nurse at a front-line hospital near Étaples. It was not an easy option, in some ways rather masochistic, she admits, as if suffering could only be borne with more suffering. At Étaples, within sound of the guns, a third of the men were dying: unstoppable haemorrhages, heads torn open, ruptured intestines spilling out. Those who could make the journey were sent back to England – which is what happened to Victor, the next of the three friends to die. In April 1917, during an attack on Arras, he took a bullet in the head, which blinded him, and another in the arm, rendering it useless. Vera managed to return to England in time to spend a few days with a young man she'd known since she was a girl, yet barely recognised at the hospital where he died that June.

While I was reading *Testament of Youth*, I'd wonder aloud at our table if I – if any of us – would have had the courage, the stamina – psychological as well as physical – to keep on working in those hospitals month after month with little in their rooms for solace but 'a candle stuck in the neck of a bottle, a tiny flame flickering in an ice-cold draught'.[4]

Imagining ourselves into those hospitals – where the
nurses were not allowed to sit down while on the ward –
was not a good method for considering history, but we
did it anyway. We knew the cost of war. We'd grown up
with the names of great-uncles and grandfathers killed in
that first war; sepia photos on the walls. Our fathers had
fought in the next war, and those of us born in England as
it ended had seen the bomb damage, and could remember
rationing: eggs counted out singly, a small dab of butter,
a scoop of sugar. We were not yet out of primary school
when we saw the images from the concentration camps;
we'd held our breath through the Cuban Missile Crisis,
old enough to understand the threat. When I read Vera
Brittain's account of being 'pitch-forked' into a ward for
German wounded as soon as she arrived at the hospital
camp, within sound of the guns, I thought of my father,
who had been in Burma at the end of the next war, pushing
the Japanese back one dugout at a time. One of the few
war stories he told was of the day they found a young
enemy soldier, a boy still in his teens, crouched among the
corpses, weeping with the humiliation of not having been
able to take his own life. Like Vera Brittain holding the
hand of dying German soldiers, my father had done what
he could to comfort the boy even as he took him prisoner.

I read Vera Brittain with personal, and very English,
eyes, acutely aware that when she and her close friend, the
writer Winifred Holtby, had toured the defeated regions
of Germany in the autumn of 1924, it was within weeks
of my mother's birth. I was aware, too, that they were

witnessing the humiliation – 'the long reaping in sorrow of that which was sown in pride'[5] – that would grow to become the Second World War, soon after the end of which my mother would be pregnant with me; living alone in a small cottage in Shropshire with no electricity, and a pony and trap to take her into town, while my father returned to Burma to 'mop up', an oddly domestic image that had him, in my imagination, standing at the entrance to that dugout with a cloth mop and an old metal bucket.

My city of women was growing: towers and convents, houses of all shapes, wartime hospitals. It was also creeping towards me, gathering memories, snippets of conversations overheard – a great-aunt weeping, something about a train leaving from Waterloo, a telegram. Cold. Bare threads of a life that came before us. *Shush, Ruby, the children.* At the house on the corner friends at our table brought other memories, their own telling anecdotes, more women to walk my city, whole new streets and neighbourhoods. I dreamed of a huge book, a work of art, built brick by brick, of the stories told at the table. An installation, maybe, a table set with many chairs and in each place a book, handmade. I could see it, laid out in the long entrance hall of the Art Gallery of New South Wales. That would lift the obscuring veil. That would change the shape of my life. Dorothy Green was not impressed. It was no challenge, she said, to amass the stories of women who'd stood up to their circumstances, creditable though they may have been. Was it enough? What do you make of your city? What was its point? I didn't mention the table installation, I wasn't that delusional. Our talk was always of books and writing. My theory of reading might have its merits, she said, but not at the cost of deep reading. Don't flit, she said. Don't skitter. Skitter! Me? Flit! My city of women falling on its own edifice! No.

Instead of knuckling down to Dorothy's questions, undaunted – or so I thought – I set about shoring up the city. If depth was the issue, who better to join us at the table than Virginia Woolf. Seated beside her was Lily Briscoe from *To the Lighthouse*. Of all the threads in that complex novel, Lily was the one I drew out first, the artist who is there at the house in Scotland when the novel opens, a guest among the guests at Mrs Ramsay's table. It wasn't until later readings that I took in the significance of Mrs Ramsay, who holds the household together, so essential she is barely noticed by the guests and children who depend on her, the mother through whom Virginia Woolf exorcised the grief and shock that came with her own mother's death when she, Virginia, was still a girl. No, it was Lily Briscoe who was given a place at the table of my imagination, my city of women: Lily Briscoe, independent and alone, who was admired or overlooked depending on the view, an artist struggling to find a way to express in paint the flux of her thoughts. And all the while having to fend off Mr Tansley, another guest, a man alone – quite a different matter – as he muttered at her, 'Women can't write, women can't paint.' Oh how we loved to hate Mr Tansley, the 'most uncharming human being' Lily had ever met, talking too much, angling to be admired – in need of success, and a wife, Mrs Ramsay could see. We, like Lily, who had neither, were not sympathetic. Yes, we all knew Mr Tansleys. Show me a great novel by a woman that measures up to *War and Peace*, I was challenged more than once by more than one man. *Middlemarch.* Really? Is that what you think? Yes, as a matter of fact, it is. Why did I enter the argument on those terms? Novels aren't horses in a race. Would you ask me to rank *War and Peace* against *Madame Bovary*? *Ulysses*? The curious thing was that Lily Briscoe knew, even as Mr Tansley said the things he said, that it wasn't true to him 'but for some reason helpful to him'. In which case, why did 'her whole being bow, like corn under a wind, and erect itself again from this abasement only with a great and rather powerful effort?'[6] Ridiculous really, all the more so fifty years later when we felt ourselves bow, and then bristle, struggling to get the argument shifted onto stronger ground.

To the Lighthouse is, and remains, a bright star in my constellation of reading, a novel that surprises me anew with each next reading. I first read it in that house, then went to the library for the diaries and the letters from that year Virginia Woolf was writing it. It is centrally placed as the fifth of her nine novels, and in it she transforms the dark, disabling shock that came with her mother's death, when she was just thirteen, and the death soon after of her half-sister, Stella. Virginia Woolf began it in the summer of 1925, not long after the war that changed everything, she said, even, or especially, about the way a woman might write. She wrote '22 pages straight off in less than a fortnight'[7] before juddering to a halt, ill again with the emotional weight of a death that had obsessed her for decades – both an absence and a halting interruption. She returned to the manuscript early in 1926 and had finished a draft by September. She was forty-four years old.

When she started *To the Lighthouse*, she'd drawn a diagram of its shape, an H on its side, 'two blocks joined by a corridor' through which the time passes – in nineteen brief pages – between the Victorian era of her parents and the transformed, uncertain world in which she wrote. She wanted to make something as 'formed and controlled' as a building, an analogy I pointed out to Dorothy, who, of course, knew Woolf better than I did. 'Words are more impalpable than bricks', she quoted back at me.[8] Was it the bricks, she asked, the corridor drawn like an H on its side, that captures the passing of time, the rupture of war and the death of Mrs Ramsay felt even in the furniture? Or was it the fluidity of Virginia Woolf's words, the rise and fall of her language above, around, beneath those building blocks? Both, of course, though at the time I preferred the solidity, the clear shapes of a building. It was years before I could appreciate *The Waves*; all that fluidity. I wanted form. I wanted shape.

To the Lighthouse was published on Thursday, 5 May 1927, the date of Woolf's mother's death thirty-two years before. I liked that – dates for the marking of time, the history of a woman's life, the making of a book. It gave some sort of shape to life, though of course marking your own life by the ages of those who've gone before can bring you up against some difficult moments. For me, it was fifty-nine that loomed as dangerous, a borderline beyond which I could not see; fifty-nine, the age my mother died, and also Virginia Woolf. It wasn't until I was almost that age, shadowing the last months of Poppy's life, returning to Woolf's diaries, that I worked out that they had died at *exactly* the same age: not just at fifty-nine, which I'd long known, but at fifty-nine years, two months and three days.[9] Exactly the same age. The twentieth of December 2005 would be a potent day for me when I reached that age. I had a party in the garden of the man I had been with for a decade by then, a chapter we have not yet reached.

The book that jolted me out of my city of women – book, installation, fantasy – wasn't *To the Lighthouse*, but a biography that took the life of a woman who belonged in my city and treated it in a way that made me furious. Victoria Glendinning's *Rebecca West: A Life* was published in 1987, and I read it soon after. The 'rebellious Rebecca West', Vera Brittain called her. Unlike Vera Brittain, who hadn't so much as held Roland's hand by the start of the First World War, Rebecca West, at twenty, was pregnant from an affair, newly begun, with the much older, married and already famous writer, H. G. Wells. He'd wooed her with his considerable mind, and made no secret of his marriage, which satisfied him in many ways, he told her – as many a man has told his mistress – but not sexually. Although it's hard to like Wells on reading of this decade-long liaison, it was not a crude seduction. He was Rebecca

West's first lover – 'one of the most interesting men I have ever met' – and he, it seems, loved her in a real, if selfish, English, masculine kind of a way. He took her seriously as a writer, and gave her enough intellectually for her to think – at least for a while – that with him she could have both independence and love. Instead, she found herself trapped in a 'divided life'. With the birth of their son – whom Wells was slow to acknowledge and only reluctantly put in his will – Rebecca West was consigned to the country, out of danger and out of sight. She hated it – the exile from London, the sight of German planes coming in over the coast; the quiet beauty of the countryside became 'an affront' to be endured. Even so, the affair lasted all through the war, and on into the 1920s, when she could return to London and live more openly. The child was older, and she was writing, but still she suffered the humiliations and inequities of the divided life that H. G. (as she called him) expected her to deal with 'harmoniously'; when she objected or complained – which she did – the fault was due to failings in her, not to the situation; they were certainly not due to him. The consequence, you won't be surprised to hear, was that Wells took a new mistress.

And yet, despite it all, Rebecca West managed to make headway into journalism and the literary culture of London. In 1918 she published *The Return of the Soldier*, a short novel for which she earned a remarkable £1000 for the serial rights, and which went into a second printing within a month. I stopped the biography at that point to

read the novel. It's an account of a shell-shocked officer
returning to England with amnesia. He has no memory
of having married, is repulsed by the wife who has run
his large country house in his absence, and longs for the
working-class girl whom, for the sake of propriety, he'd
stepped away from fifteen years before. With its reference
to Freud's 'return of the repressed', it's less an anti-war
story than a way of peeling under the surface of class,
convention and marriage; an enactment of the unconscious
that loves where it will, a plea for forms of love and ways of
living that are not accepted as 'normal'. The 'cure' for this
amnesia is the 'talk' – orchestrated by a psychoanalytically-
minded doctor – which brings him back to the present by
restoring to memory the child, now dead, he'd had with
his wife. Here he is on the last page of the novel, returning
to the house after the encounter with the doctor: 'He was
looking up under his brows at the over-arching house as
though it were a hated place to which, against all his hopes,
business had forced him to return . . . He wore a dreadful
decent smile . . . He walked not loose limbed like a boy,
as he had that afternoon, but with the soldier's hard tread
upon the heel.'[10] He was returned to a social norm he had
been able to reject only in the extremis of amnesia. What's
more, cured of his shell shock, he could be sent back to
'that flooded trench in Flanders'. Whether he returns to
the front or not, whether he's killed or not, we don't know.
The novel ends with his wife's satisfaction: 'He's cured!'

Edward Brittain, who'd recovered from a first round
of wounds in the hospital at Camberwell while Vera was

nursing there, was returned to the front to be killed five months before the war ended. It was a bitter loss for his sister, made worse by the revelation years later, after *Testament of Youth* had been published, that he'd learned, just days before, that he was being investigated for a homosexual relationship with a fellow officer – some letters had been intercepted – and was facing a court martial. The circumstances of his death, by a bullet in the head, had always been vague until fifteen years after the war had ended, when Vera Brittain was given these details and had to face the possibility that her brother might have run ahead, inviting the enemy fire, or even have shot himself in the head. Or was it, as with hundreds of thousands of others, simply the horror of war? She would never know. She would live forever with the knowledge that her brother had not been able to confide in her, such was the shame and the stigma of homosexuality in 1918.

The cure of society, I took Rebecca West to be saying in *The Return of the Soldier*, is no cure. There was no cure, no hope for Edward Brittain, and none for the soldier of West's novel. There was certainly no hope for her and Wells, who separated in 1923. Victoria Glendinning, for reasons I couldn't fathom then and still can't now, saw *The Return of the Soldier* as a story about 'salvation through unselfish love', by which I think she meant the suffering one bears for a child. Was she applauding the cure? Surely not. It might have been a sacrifice, but not because of the child – who was dead – but because of the terms on which having a child happened in that society at that time. Salvation it was not, unless, of course, you consider being restored to the acceptance of society – which in this case meant a large house and the prestige of position – a form of salvation.

In some ways I was grateful to this account of the affair with H. G. Wells, which I first read of in *Rebecca West: A Life*. From it, speaking entirely selfishly and from the norms of the society I inhabited, I learned two very personal things. The first – from the story of her struggle to get money out of H. G. to help provide for their son, who'd grow up to hate her anyway – was a profound sense of relief that I hadn't got pregnant with Ross. The second was that when it came to infidelity, maybe lies were worse than honesty. H. G.'s were still rebounding on Rebecca West fifty years later when, for instance, her account of his next (and overlapping) affair as brief and slight, given in the confidence that Wells had told her the truth, was publicly contradicted by his biographer. In an article she wrote in 1925 called 'I Regard Marriage with Fear and Horror', Rebecca West proclaimed that the conjugal life was useful only for 'riveting the fact of paternity in the male mind'.[11] This distaste for marriage, according to Glendinning, was also not true. Bruised by the humiliation that was seen as hers rather than his, West had hoped for a 'conspicuous' marriage to Lord Beaverbrook, who, in 1923, was paying her court, but he, we are told, proved impotent with her. What was Victoria Glendinning doing, catching her out? Was that the role of biographer? *Rebecca West*, the book, did nothing to soften me towards England and Englishness. I loathed the biographical distance that assumed a very English form of superiority, another layer of unquestioned norms, in this case another layer again of humiliation to a woman who'd lived messily, not perfectly – which of us does? – but with courage. Okay, so Rebecca West said one thing in one place, another in another; is there not more that can be said about this than proof of the contradiction between public and private in her attitude to love and marriage? (She did later marry, for the most part happily.)

When Vera Brittain returned to Oxford after the war, she switched from English to history, in order, she said, to understand 'how the whole calamity had happened' and how it had been possible that her generation through 'our own ignorance and others' ingenuity' were 'used, hypnotised and slaughtered'. She wrote *Testament of Youth*, she said, because she felt that it was only by attempting 'to write history in terms of personal life that I could rescue something that might be of value, some element of truth and hope and usefulness from the smashing up of my own youth'.[12] Yes. Rather than catching a woman out, couldn't there be a way of writing her life that honoured – rather than excused – the inconsistencies, the confusions, that – as I knew from my own wavering, crisscrossing desires – were still integral to the struggle to live with both love and independence of mind in a world that did not easily accord this combination to a woman? Wasn't the 'social cure' part of the problem?

Rebecca West deserved better, was my thought, and it was a thought that had implications. If I were to succeed with *Poppy*, which I was on the brink of, it would have to be written from an entirely different angle of vision. It was a *what the fuck* moment. I was forty, with no child, no husband, no mother, living in a house with Sophie, already eating lentils, already bruised enough by the Ross debacle, and – looked at from the point of view of the England I'd left – by the very fact of living here. Orstralia, friends of my father would say, Oh dear. Or, once, from a man at a party: How frightfully jolly. I was never going to please them, no chance. I didn't even know if I'd please anyone here. What the fuck, I said, slamming down *Rebecca West* on the table, going out the back door and marching up the hill to Ali's house. Maybe Dorothy was right. I could tell a lifetime's worth of anecdotes and still not understand what had happened to me, to Poppy, to our small family and the generation I was part of, born to 1950s mothers, our lives turned by feminism, the Pill, university educations, rooms and incomes of our own.

With so much given to us, why the unhappiness, why that dark hour before dawn? With Virginia Woolf's conditions for independence in place, why this mess in our relationships with men? It made no sense, and yet, for many of us, it was a dominant reality.

Ambivalence, uncertainty; the experience of life between the lines of the tide: that was the story, not the certainty of bricks. Life is like the weather, an acupuncturist I visited in New York years later told me, a Mr Lee. You can't expect it otherwise. You must live with it, chi for any weather.

At the moment I opened the door to Ali's house and called out to her, I felt strong, clear, ready for any weather. She was writing poetry then, part of her struggle from the other side, married with children and a household, welcoming, bountiful – and full of needs. Poetry was her way of keeping balance, moments of solitude in the search for something not yet known. She's a psychotherapist now; there were years of training to come after that day we sat in a wedge of sun and talked of the determination we could feel in ourselves, a strange impulse we didn't understand. Today she'd say writers and psychotherapists have in common that they do what they do in order to discover 'what they don't know about themselves'; an urge, a process, she suspects, in which 'the element of unconsciousness in their undertaking is somehow crucial to it'.[13] And that's how it was for me, that day: raw, uncomprehended, necessary. It wasn't a solution, but it was a spur, a challenge that changed the shape of my days at the desk in the large downstairs room at the house on the corner.

By a strange coincidence, the first time I spoke at a writers' festival, I was on a panel with Victoria Glendinning. It was about biography. I had published *Exiles at Home*, rewritten from the thesis Dorothy had pulled apart; it was there in the bookshop, but *Poppy*, though written, was not yet on the stands. This, despite my low opinion of *Rebecca West*, left me feeling at a disadvantage in the company of not only one, but two famous English biographers. The other was Andrew Motion, who spoke of his book *The Lamberts*, which had faced him with the question of which members of this talented family to include, or not. I met him again years later and liked him; but that day I was awed by his confident Englishness. Fortunately Brian Matthews was also on the panel. He'd just published *Louisa*, his biography of Henry Lawson's mother – which turned the conventions of biography by writing of the mother rather than the famous son. Victoria Glendinning's contribution to the panel was suave and polished; the audience loved her. I rose to the occasion if not with English panache then at least with conviction, saying something to the effect that here in Australia we were thinking about what biography might mean if we took as our subjects those who are not usually considered 'worthy' of 'A Life' – and if, as a result of this choice, we let our own story as biographer onto the page, what would that tell us about the way a life became a narrative? How extraordinary, Victoria Glendinning said. We're not thinking about that in England.

Sophie laughed when I told her this story – an excellent example of what she called the *English* English. They think they are Greenwich Mean Time, she said. Like men. There was something to be said, we agreed, for living on the periphery, even if we periphery-dwellers were the only ones who knew it.

4

Don't get the idea that our household disavowed men. On the contrary, men were frequent and welcomed visitors, even temporary inhabitants. Garry was often there, as he and I slid into something that was more than a friendship, less than a love affair, and certainly not a marriage. He was funny and clever and had good stories. Sophie liked him, and he fitted around that table more easily than some of the women who came, driving their cars from miles away, from Canberra, or the Victorian border towns, with enormous dogs, and some with girlfriends who drank whisky by the bottle, and argued that the mere fact of being female was always a greater point of disadvantage than class, or education, or race, or disability; a ridiculous position that neither Sophie nor I came anywhere near to agreeing with – nor did Ali, or most of the others who were regulars at that table. Having painted those walls in the women's refuge back in the 1970s, and having lived and studied in Papua New Guinea, I was impatient with the whole noisy business, but it wasn't until my cat,

Hackney, was chased under the house by one of the dogs that I managed to put a stop to it. For an entire weekend, the dog sat growling by the fallen-in grate through which Hackney had escaped into the dark underbelly of the house, and nothing would keep the dog away, or persuade the woman who'd brought it to tie it up. After that I banned dogs, which dealt with that, but not with poor Hackney, who came out a nervous wreck and must have got something under there, for not long afterwards, she had to be put down, suffering some chronic, unfixable disease. I held her while the vet prepared the needle, a more monstrous task than I could have imagined; no easy death this, as she struggled and fought. Before the needle went in she bit me, or scratched, or both, a deep gash in that soft fold of skin between the thumb and finger. Wash it, the vet said, pointing me to a sink. His assistant passed the bottle of disinfectant soap. I scrubbed, the water ran rusty red from the blood and by the time I returned to the table Hackney was dead.

Who says we wait for karma? That was where I got, or probably got, the toxoplasmosis that attacked my eyes a few years later, when I sold the house on the corner and bought a flat on the hill behind Bondi – the worst possible move in financial terms, downsizing exactly as the property market began its boom, but I didn't think in those terms then. None of us believed in unregulated capitalism, or could imagine that its inequities and the money-makers would triumph as they have; hadn't the battle of extreme inequality been won, and the lesson learned, through the two World Wars and a Depression? Hadn't a new way been born of social democracy? Even as I child I knew what the Beveridge Report was, which had ushered in the Welfare State; we all did, the new order we celebrated with the Festival of Britain. Such hopefulness. Such naïveté. There we were in the late 1980s, the money tide already beginning to rise around our ankles, exactly as I gave up a tenured position at the University of Technology to embark on a life of writing. An individualist choice, nothing communal about it at all, which is why, I suppose, it felt necessary, even essential, to eliminate the mortgage I had which, with no guarantee of income, seemed enormous, though a fraction of an average mortgage today.

So I moved into a small flat and almost immediately regretted it, not because of the financial error but because I missed the house on the corner and everything about it – though Sophie had left by then, and so had Helen who'd moved in after her. In that house there had always been room for others, and there was room for parties, which there wasn't at the flat, and while it might sound trivial – what's a party when all's washed up and done? – actually it wasn't. The gathering of people together, the flow in and out of that house, was rich and enriching. We got good at cooking up bowls of chickpea salad, and we bought beans and olives and tomatoes from the market, loaves from the new bakeries, rye and sourdough, slabs of unsalted butter. You can, or could then, throw a party on very little and everyone brought grog (as it was

called) and our standards weren't high. The talk was of
art and books, of politics and ideas, of news and gossip
as people visited who were newly arrived in Sydney from
England, or were visiting from Melbourne, or returning
from travelling through Asia. Love affairs began at
those parties, flirtations and friendships, all kinds of
collaboration. I still meet people who remember coming
to that house, brought by someone who knew someone
who knew one of us. I met Hilary McPhee that way when
she was in Sydney, visiting Helen. McPhee Gribble, the
independent publishing house she and Di Gribble had
started, was still in its prime, not yet defeated by interest
rates of 17 per cent. Helen's *Monkey Grip* had been one
of their first books, and *Poppy* would be one of the last
before the imprint went to Penguin, in a move Hilary
described as like having your head cut off and waking in
the morning to find yourself still alive.

She told this story at a wake for McPhee Gribble,
another party in another house. So powerful was the
image of a head coming off that she thought she must
have been hallucinating when she heard on the radio, or
thought she'd heard, a taxi-driver in Adelaide say exactly
that had happened to him at the end of the war, in Malaya.
He was lined up to be executed with other prisoners-of-
war, but the Japanese soldier who wielded the sword was
either tired, or inept, or merciful. He was injured – badly,
of course – but critical arteries weren't cut. He fell in the
trench and played dead until some Malay villagers came
and rescued him. We laughed; such imaginings! Then

the writer Jessica Anderson raised her voice to say that she had heard this story on the radio too.

They were good parties, the parties we had at the house on the corner, even if I had to get out the broom late in the evening and start sweeping the kitchen before the last of the men, still drinking, propped against the sink, would leave. Sophie said it was a passive-aggressive English way of doing things and I'd be better off telling them to leave. So after that I'd get out the broom and say that if they didn't leave soon I'd start sweeping – and when they didn't, I did, until eventually they did. Oh, they'd say, we're enjoying ourselves. We like this house. Why don't you girls have another drink and talk to us? Because we're going to bed, I'd say, still with the broom, no invitation this, as they shuffled out the gate to the street at the side.

Yes, there were men in that house, and those we liked returned, calling out as they opened the gate. Some came with tools and did chores for us. The pergola in the garden went up that way – three blokes, a ladder, a saw and a drill – and all I did was brew up large pots of tea and butter more slabs of bread. The men seemed to enjoy themselves sawing and hammering – activities in which I had no interest – and when it was finished they drank beer with Sophie while I planted the grapevine that gave us shade in the summer and produced small, rather sour grapes. Another man, someone's boyfriend, unblocked the drain under the sink where the washing machine I'd bought with the money that came after Poppy's death had been badly installed. Poppy was right, a washing machine could transform a woman's life even if you had the use of a laundromat as I had – except in Papua New Guinea, where I'd had to boil up the copper as Poppy had when we were children, and put everything through a mangle. All these years later I can still remember the pattern of sun coming through the door of the dark laundry at the back of the house where we lived when Poppy came out of hospital and I was sent away to school. The light was dappled from the tree outside, a memory of summer, a canopy of trees, and the fields beckoning where I could be alone, or with a book, and not in that dark laundry with my mother's face set firm to the task, and Mrs Hill, who came to help, turning the mangle until she was red and sweating, and Poppy calling to me, Make yourself useful, and the chance of that door closed, and the clouds coming over, and the shadow of trees and leaves disappearing into the worn, uneven tiles as sheet after sheet went through the wringer, two for each bed, and the pillowcases and tea towels. On and on it went, and when at last it was done and the sheets were on the lines, propped up with poles cut from the woods, the best of the day was gone and a kind of inertia hung over us all.

Years later, when I'd married and was living way out in the Highlands of PNG, where Nick, my husband, was doing his fieldwork, we were given an old mangle by a mission further up the valley. We set it up outside in the long grass so that while we turned the handle I could see across the airstrip to the lake and the mountains, a view that, when it came to the mangle, never entirely overrode that memory of laundry and longing. Not that we used the mangle often. Mostly we were out in a hamlet a day's walk away and the river would do, our clothes laid out on the rocks with everyone else's, and when it came to sheets, well, they just got browner and browner, until they smelled so bad that as soon as we got back to the house by the airstrip, we'd put them in the copper and boil and poke at them with long sticks until the water bubbled the brown away and they emerged, not white exactly, but pleasingly clean, when they were hitched up under the roof to dry.

The worst thing about living with Sophie – who was otherwise verging on perfect in that regard – was that she was a terrible washer. She'd mix up loads, scoop in too much soap, never separate her whites, so that if I wasn't diligent and something of mine got in with hers, it inevitably came out grey. Though in her case what was so annoying was that she always looked crisp and clean and elegant. I don't know how she did it, given the clothes that were pegged any old how on the line. I was in PNG recently with her and her daughter, who was then thirteen, and Martha, my niece, who was in her thirties, and on the last day in the village Sophie appeared in a white shirt, looking as if she was ready for a fashion shoot. Martha, who is a very good washer, and has a similar capacity with clothes and rarely looks less than her best but was distinctly dishevelled that day, was so astonished she took a photo to prove it. Men, not surprisingly, fell for Sophie, not just because of her clothes, or even her very blue eyes; it was the spirit of her that drew so many to her, as if she had life to spare, and that took some managing when it came to the men who'd drink it in, all of it, given the chance.

Men. Oh, they were difficult years, so many of us wounded – them as much as us. But while we had each other and our conversations, our table, the men, many of them it seemed, needed a woman, one particular woman or another, to listen to them, sympathise. It's much harder for us, they'd say, with you women wanting to be independent. Look at this house, they'd say; what role was left for them? We wanted it both ways, they'd say, and maybe we did. But hadn't men always had both, lives of work and travel, independent movement, other affairs of the heart, and certainly the body? And didn't all that depend on the domestic and emotional support, the *servitude*, of women? Do you want mothers all your lives? Not a sophisticated line of thought, I admit, and it didn't always go down well, an indication of our defensiveness as well as of theirs, perhaps. There were also men, a few, with whom we could talk, and even if they were stuck on Greenwich Mean Time, even if it became argument, or worse, the conversation could go two ways – as long as we weren't sleeping with them – and be instructive. But when we slept with them, and even if we didn't, we were full of wild feeling, perverse responses, wanting and not wanting, testing them, challenging, finding ourselves repulsed – by one meaning of the word, or the other. We were insulted, we found them repulsive; we found them laughable; we found them enraging. There were also men we found endearing, and interesting, and sometimes we could take them as lovers and enjoy them, even if we kept them at bay, protecting our wounded selves; yet when they touched some deep region of our hearts, and when we were the most satisfied, it was then, often enough, that we'd want more. No easy pattern this, words inadequate to express the shifting moods and feelings that came with the dilemma of knowing the value – the essential value – of those rooms of our own, and yet being ambushed, despite everything, by the dream of the shared bedroom, or mourning for the baby's cot. From this distance I can feel sorry for the men who encountered us, but remembering back to that time I see myself standing there in the room with the table as someone recounted the next maddening encounter, hands on my hips, saying, What is the matter with them?

I still sometimes wonder what goes on in the minds of men (some men), which might be why I like Philip Roth as a writer. I hated him back in those days in the house on the corner, still outraged by *Portnoy's Complaint* and at the mere title of books I didn't read, *The Breast* or *The Professor of Desire*, which is a pity as I might have learned something useful, both about writing and about the minds of men. I read him now on the sorrow of old men who realise they'll never again know the breast of a young woman. I have friends who laugh when I say I'm moved by this. Sob, they say. Poor dears. And it's true, there's little need for sympathy when the professor can no longer enact his desires. But still, there's something, maybe not sympathy, that I feel, though to some extent it is, but mostly it's curiosity about the vulnerability that lies within these strange beings, in some ways like us and in others so profoundly different.

No one has given shape to the paradoxical vulnerability of men more eloquently than the artist Louise Bourgeois with her great sculptured penis, *Fillette*. Robert Mapplethorpe took a wonderful photograph of her in her monkey coat, holding it under her arm.[14] *Fillette*, small girl: a latex and plaster penis, 59.9 x 19.5 cm. I saw it with Obelia, Nick's daughter, early in 2008 at the Tate Modern, when we were in London for Amy's wedding – my niece, Obelia's friend – a woman of the next generation marrying at thirty-two, knowing what she was doing – if not entirely, marriage being as it is, but knowing a great deal more than her grandmother or her aunt had done when they married at twenty. That day at Tate Modern, Obelia and I stood in front of *Fillette*. It was hung by a hook through the shaft; we had to look up to see it, with nothing to obscure the testicles, and between them soft feminine folds that could be labia. A tender, vulnerable being, *Fillette*. Of course, Louise Bourgeois said. Was she not married to a man? Did she not have three sons?[15]

I was living in the house on the corner when I first discovered Louise Bourgeois. She'd been there all the time, of course – the Mapplethorpe photo was taken in 1968 – but it was a discovery for many of us when the catalogue of her 1982 retrospective at the Museum of Modern Art in New York reached Sydney. The work that struck me then, in the mid-1980s when so much in my life was awry, was not *Fillette*, but the tall, thin sculptured *Personages*, made of wood – shaved and rubbed rather than carved – until she could afford to cast some in bronze. If I were an artist – a fantasy I still sometimes have – I'd make personages just like hers, I'd say, and I'd move them around, as she did, so they faced each other in different combinations: lovers, parents, friends, enemies – categories that were not fixed as she realigned them first this way, and then that. Oh, to be able to give shape to feelings and confusions – would that not be better than words with their relentless march onwards, one by one? I'd imagine my large downstairs workroom stripped of its chairs, its desk and tables, its shelves of books. Even then I doubt that it'd have accommodated those tall thin beings, let alone the table for the Art Gallery of New South Wales with a handmade book for each woman of my city. Ridiculous imaginings for someone who couldn't even draw, though maybe imagining what we are not can be a part of finding who we are. Maybe.

Louise Bourgeois was born in Paris in 1911, and in September 1938, a year before the start of the Second World War, she married the American art historian Robert Goldwater and moved with him to New York. It was there, after the war, after the birth of her sons, that she began work on her *Personages*, which she assembled on the roof of the apartment where they lived in Manhattan, the city spread out around her, giving shape and pattern to her life: her exile, her maternity, her irritation – and loathing, often enough – of the masculine certainties of the artists she encountered through her well-connected husband. Ambivalence. Rage. Determination. Later she'd say that the *Personages*, tall and unbending, were the work of someone 'scared stiff'. Of what? Of the need to understand, as Ali might say, what was not yet known? The unconscious pressure that had to be released before she could work in shapes and materials more pliable? So you can see why I responded to those works, even before I tell you that Robert Goldwater, who would became the first director of the Museum of Primitive Art in New York, published a key book called *Primitivism and Modern Painting*, one of the first books I read on Oceanic art.[16] And there in *Personages* were echoes of the art I'd seen on my one trip near the Sepik with Nick. We saw carvings, house poles, carved canoe prows and paddles in the villages and on the rivers, but it wasn't until we were taken into a shed near Maprik – I think by a mission, though my memory is hazy – that I saw their majesty. When the door opened, light flooded in, illuminating carvings alight with the spirit of the world outside that shed: some were indeed tall and thin, others elaborately carved, some boat-like, some as large as canoes. All I could afford – for to buy was why we were taken there – was a small clay pot carved like a drinking vessel with four faces moulded into the sides of the bowl, one for each quarter of the sky. It is on my desk, a small chip in its pedestal, otherwise complete: a holder, these last forty years, for my pens and pencils.

Given the confusions, it was something of an achievement that Garry and I tottered on for as long as we did, almost a decade; a patchy decade, but still, that's ten years. Though he'd recovered, and retreated, from the wish to marry me as fast as he'd tripped into it, there remained something, some small something – comfort, friendship, a compatibility of mind (despite Zen), a certain tenderness – that gave us a basis for a continuing connection. To the extent that we were friends who were also lovers it was a good enough arrangement. It could also set off longings, in me if not in him – not always, but sometimes – that were hard to comprehend, so at odds were they with the actuality – which in a lot of ways suited me well. If I was working, or away on a road trip with Sophie, if I paid him no attention for days, weeks even, he let me be, he didn't seem to mind, and I think he didn't. I was the one who could be demanding, wanting some sort of certainty when there was none. When I pressed for assurances – of what? Of enduring love? A pact against death? The sense of the security I needed to balance (and enjoy?) the independence I took? – he was evasive and I became anxious and he stubborn and we wouldn't see each other for a while, and life could feel precarious. Then he'd arrive at the house and we'd welcome him in to join us at the table.

I rarely see Garry these days but when I do we are pleased and greet each other happily. Last time I saw him was pure happenstance. I'd been across the Blue Mountains staying at a house a friend then had in a valley running back into the mountains from the inland side. I was there with Robyn Davidson. Jo, our friend, an artist, had painted portraits of us both: an interesting experience, I found, being looked at as an older woman by a younger woman. It was as intense a gaze as any I've experienced, and very different from the gaze of men. It was a scrutiny that began uncomfortably – vanity is not easily banished and I could remember the dismay with which I had regarded my mother at fifty, her boxy hips, the drop of her cheeks – but I found I could tolerate it, and far from feeling Jo's victim, her object, as sometimes the subjects of portraits complain, I felt a kind of kinship, as if I had become part of the making of the portrait, which of course I hadn't. She signed the drawing that preceded the painting 'Jo Bertini by Drusilla Modjeska', in part a private joke, but also to say something about the way we look, that convoluted scrutiny between the perceiver and the perceived, which tells us something about ourselves as well as about the painting, the image, the picture that, in the case of portraiture, emerges between them.

That winter week at Jo's house over the mountains, Robyn and I overlapped with her briefly and then stayed on when she went back to Sydney. It was glorious up there: foothills, mountains behind, a river curving around the hill on which the house was built. We had roaring fires and read a lot, talked and slept. We didn't wash – there was scarce water and no need – so by the third or fourth day we smelled of wood smoke and sweat. Then a storm rolled in, rain pounding down all day and all night, twenty-four hours solid. The morning it stopped, Robyn woke early, walked down to the river and came back to report that it was rising, and dark clouds were coming in from the mountains. Our car was parked on the far side of the river. On the way in, Jo had driven us across in her truck. She wouldn't get across now, Robyn said. So we packed up, tidied the house, swept the floors, made sure the fire was out and any food secured in tins against the bush rats. At the river we stripped to our waists and waded through the cold, fast-running water, bags and books carried above our heads. We kept our shoes on against the rocks and logs – we'd never have made it barefoot – and when we were on the other bank, dried after a fashion, and dressed again, I put my slippers on, which were all I had other than the soaked runners dripping in the boot. The slippers were so old and familiar they were held together with sellotape, a solution to their collapse that wasn't helped when my not entirely dry feet went into them. We looked a sight, Robyn and me, rugs tied around our waists for warmth; you can see where this story is going . . . And sure enough when we stumbled hungry into a café in the mountain town of Blackheath, there was Garry, silhouetted against the window talking to a group of young women with children in strollers. I squinted, not thinking, There's Garry; more, That man

looks like Garry, when he said, Yes it's me, and came over
and joined us. Actually my chagrin wasn't so bad; it's not
as if he hadn't seen me looking pretty awful, and his laugh
at the sight we made was kind, enjoying the expression
on the faces of the young women he was talking to when
they realised he knew these two bag lady apparitions who
had walked in, despite the rain, in slippers.

Afterwards, in the car as Robyn and I drove down the
mountains and through the suburbs of Sydney that now
follow the railway line all the way to their base, I told her
about the day Garry and I were cut off by the tide. We were
down the coast, alone at the house on the bay with the
rock. It was glorious autumnal weather, the water wasn't
yet too cold to swim, and after a few days of lazing, we
felt adventurous and set out around the rocks beneath the
headland with the lighthouse. It was a fine day, as I say,
clear to the horizon, when we walked round the bay and
climbed to the next cove, using a steep, well-worn path.
Instead of stopping there, as we usually did, or going back
to check the tides – it wasn't as if we didn't know how
large the headland was, or how steep – we decided, just
like that, on impulse, to see if we could get the whole way
round. Two hours later and still nowhere near the point,
we were in a small cove with a narrow shingle beach, wet
from a wave that'd caught us on the rocky cliff we'd just
clambered round. We sat on the shingle to dry, pleased
with ourselves, not noticing that the tide was coming in
until we had to jump out of the way, and saw that waves
were breaking against the cliff we'd come from, and also

against the one ahead. White foam against black rock in either direction. Behind us, what was left of the shingle ended against a sandstone cliff, not sheer or overhanging like the black cliffs, but steep, very, with some dark rock poking through, a few hardy wisps of trees hanging on. It was a long way up, but it was our only option: the shingly beach was fast vanishing, there'd be no shelter unless we climbed up above the tide line, which, now that we looked, we could see quite clearly. There was nothing to stand on there, and the prospect of clinging on all day until the tide turned again was less promising than the prospect of climbing. We should be able to make it, Garry said, though I was doubtful, and he started to climb in a slightly zigzag way, reaching from protrusion of rock to spindly tree, finding the next foothold as I followed behind, until suddenly it was too steep; there was nothing to hold onto, and the top wasn't close. Chunks of crumbling sandstone were coming loose and tumbling down. I can't, I said, as if there were a choice. You can, he said, climbing on, balancing himself and turning back to tell me where to put my foot, where I could safely hold on, testing the strength of a small, bent tree that was growing out of the cliff not far from the top. I got there. I don't know how, but I did. He hauled himself up the last few feet to the grass at the top, lay on his stomach, and with one hand on another of those spindly trees, reached down an arm strong as rope. One last haul, and I was beside him, as alive as the grass we lay on, the trees above. The sky. A tremble started in my legs, a shaking, shuddering tremble that spread to my arms, my chest, everywhere, as I looked back down to the rocks, the little beach that had vanished and the water where we could well both be lying, dead and broken. No one would have known, it was back before mobile phones, and who would think we'd be stupid enough to have done what we did.

Lying there on the ground, alive and shaking, we wrapped our arms around each other, and when our legs returned to a state that would hold us upright, we walked slowly through the gnarled banksia trees to the lighthouse, which I always visit even if it is a modern lighthouse with no window or walkway, no keeper, nothing of character or romance, nothing like Virginia Woolf's lighthouse: just a white smooth tower marking a line in the bush. We walked around it in superstitious thanksgiving, then back to the house, where we made huge toasted sandwiches and spent the rest of the day recovering on a blanket under the trees until the sun went over the hills behind and the cold crept in. A fire, fish on the grill, a bottle of wine. Was that not enough? In memory it is replete. So why, after something like that, did I want Garry to say that yes, he'd love me forever and make sure I never fell, and I needn't give up anything, not my independence, not even Ben who arrived one of those years and whom I'm not yet ready to talk about. I could be just as I was *and* safe. Double standards? Yes. But double standards work in strange ways; for Garry, with all that Zen, no commitment beyond the moment worked just fine; but for me, while it could, it didn't always. It was, of course, when we enjoyed each other most that I wanted the words he wouldn't give. As if the words could turn into a certificate I could hold in my hand, absolve me from my own infelicities, or an artwork I could walk around, or a fine pen that would know my thoughts even before they arrived on the page.

'Bound. Free. Good. Bad. Yes. No. Capitalism. Socialism. Sex. Love . . .' This is Anna in Doris Lessing's *The Golden Notebook*, a free woman, like her friend Molly, in the London of my childhood, though not the London we saw on school-holiday visits to the Law Courts in the Strand with our father, or a pantomime with his mother, our grandmother. These were 'free women' of our mothers' generation, whose education hadn't been disrupted and cut short, who worked and wrote and earned through those years of the 1950s, who lived without husbands, though not without lovers; very different lives from those of our married mothers – though no less difficult, no less split; free and bound in different ways. When Doris Lessing wrote the introduction to the paperback edition in 1971, she likened it – the introduction – to 'writing a letter to post into the distant past: I am so sure that everything we now take for granted is going to be utterly swept away in the next decade'.[17] Well, she got that wrong, we all did, we optimistic feminists with our housing associations and politics of liberation. We'd underestimated the power of ambivalence, the *volcano unconscious*, Louise Bourgeois called it, meaning the ways we are formed, deep down in our psyches, at our mother's breast, in this uneasy world we inhabit. What Doris Lessing does get right – in the novel, not the introduction – is the baffling nature of it all. *The Golden Notebook* is not just a portrait of a historical moment, though it's that, but a plumbline through all the contradictions and dilemmas. *Bound. Free. Good. Bad. Yes. No. Sex. Love.*

Argumentative and contested though our relationships with men could be, sometimes wounding, sometimes tender, in that house we were free, as free as I've ever been. Complicatedly free, but free. Free to move; free to enjoy our lovers. But most of all, there was a freedom of mind that was new to me: a sense of my own voice as a writer, and the potential of writing, as I began to understand how to work the pliability of words. Yes, we wrote them one by one, an exacting art, but change the image to a thread rather than a road, and then words bend and weave, sentences and paragraphs gathering in stories, digressing and doubling back, making a pattern that may not be able to be apprehended as an embodied work to walk around, but can reveal its shape in the mind of a reader, a compatriot, a stranger. I knew that from my reading, of course: and I'd long known it in theory. The challenge was to work it on the page – and that was not so easy.

When Sophie went back to London, only briefly as it turned out, Helen – who'd been visiting from Melbourne staying in our small spare room at the back – moved into her room. The life of the house took on a new shape with Helen there during the day, writing upstairs while I was writing downstairs. I was well into *Poppy* by then. I'd bought a golf-ball electric typewriter, which had pride of place on a separate table in my workroom. Not only were pages building up, but *chapters* and *sections*. Hilary would stay when she was in Sydney, and she'd read the pages I showed her, the start of another long friendship as well as a collaboration that made *Poppy* possible. Yes, something was definitely happening. I don't remember how it started or how I got through the impasse of that first winter of 1987. Bernard in *The Waves* says, 'Some people go to priests, others to poetry, I to my friends.' It's a line that is often attributed to Virginia Woolf in lists of wise sayings, when it was her character who said it, and he was a writer, which makes it doubly unreliable as coming from her (or indeed from him). It is a thought, like a wave, like language that rises and falls, catches us and lets us go, which I copied out and pinned above the piano in the room where I worked. Helen and I had lunch each day, and in that house a conversation began that has continued on to this day, with interruptions and hiatuses, but still now, though with less intensity, we can drop back into the talk that started all those years ago. Not the same conversation but a continuation. Much of it about writers and writing. She was reading writers I'd never heard of, like Ingeborg Bachmann and Céline. Murray Bail – whom Helen was soon to marry, not that it eliminated ambivalence, just gave it another hue – said that if I was writing in the first person, which I was, I should at least read Thomas Bernhard. So I did, sort of, though really it was Virginia Woolf I was interested in, the 'I', the 'eye' she sent out to do duty for her, a creature called 'I' which was both her and not her, a screen that allowed her a certain privacy even as it gave her words their force. I read most of the books that came from Murray, European for the most part, and those I didn't Garry would read, returning them when he went to Murray's flat to watch the cricket with him. I'd grumble to Helen when I fell behind, the pile tottering beside my bed, or to Garry, but never to Murray, with his thick dark hair, the real deal of a writer with all those books on the table. Not that Helen wasn't a real writer, but in that house she was also one of us, part of our city, our world, where there was nothing we didn't speak of.

Even at the time Helen would say, as Sophie had said, we'd look back and see that they were good years in that house with the doors open and music playing and people coming in, and meals around the table. I could still wake early from a dream that had taken me back to the abyss, but there were also days, more as time passed, when I'd wake with the light coming through the expensive slatted wooden blinds I bought on a whim I couldn't afford given the amount of leave I was taking in order to write, and I'd realise that, yes, I was happy. Or if not happy, at least not unhappy. Though the veil fluttered close enough for me not to forget, there were days when I'd find myself out in the garden with the pergola and the ochre paving stones Poppy had helped me lay on her one visit to that house, stretching from too long at the desk while the kettle was on, looking at my pots and at the astonishing sight of those lemons, and at least for that moment I'd know I was alive – wonderfully, marvellously alive.

5

Another person who came to the house during those years was Hazel Rowley, and although she and I lived in the same city only for a few years, another conversation began that continued, albeit intermittently, until her sudden, shocking death in 2011. Like me, Hazel was born in London, but unlike me, she had come to Australia as a child when her family emigrated. She was restless for Europe: not England, but France. When I first met her she'd recently returned from Paris where she'd been researching her doctorate on 'Simone de Beauvoir and Existential Autobiography'. This made her the perfect interlocutor when I turned to *The Second Sex* to learn more about Christine de Pizan, only to find a short, rather abrupt paragraph. Pizan might have taken up her pen in defence of women, but the 'quarrel' she joined, Beauvoir wrote, was but a 'secondary phenomenon reflecting social attitudes, not changing them'. A damning end to the paragraph. I've never known if it was this that made *The Second Sex* so hard for me to read, a personal prejudice, or whether it was the legacy of failure with it in Papua New Guinea, where I'd tried it at the age of twenty-three, hardly the best place for it, way out in the Highlands where Nick was collecting genealogies and I spent hours reading in the shade of a small thatched house. I was overwhelmed by the excess of information that goes into her argument – and actually, I still am – most of it dispiriting. So, I asked Hazel, what does it take to change the secondary phenomena of social attitudes? Did Beauvoir? Could writers? Could we? Had Simone de Beauvoir found her way out from under the weight of male certainty that – as she'd gone to such trouble to show – had been with us in the Judaeo-Christian West for centuries, or was she, too, as the radical feminists would say, caught up in exactly the 'male' thinking that makes us the second sex? If she couldn't escape the weight of history, who could, I'd grumble to Hazel? But she was on Beauvoir's side. Hazel's view was that it was *seeing* it that mattered, *showing* it to us, and anyway Beauvoir had achieved a lot.

Hazel had interviewed her in Paris at the end of 1976, and it'd been a bruising experience. Looking back, it was easy to see how bad a time it had been for Beauvoir, with Sartre suffering his long, miserable decline into death. (He died in 1980.) The women's movement was in early bloom, she was besieged by feminists of our generation wanting her wisdom, her imprimatur, and her time. Among them was Hazel, who arrived at her apartment in Rue Schoelcher well prepared and bright with anticipation. 'Beauvoir changed my life,' Hazel wrote many years later, 'and I worshipped her. I asked burning questions about her relationship with Sartre – about truth-telling, jealousy, third parties, and double standards for men and women. Beauvoir insisted there had been no jealousy between them, and as for double standards, she thought relationships between the sexes easier for women than for men because, given women's secondary status, men tended to feel guilty when they left them.' That doesn't happen now, and it didn't happen in our era; the price of claiming independence, I suppose. Beauvoir gave Hazel her attention for a short afternoon, then bustled her out, having answered, Hazel felt, 'as if by rote, without the slightest reflection or hesitation'. Hazel could see, and it saddened her, that '[Beauvoir] herself could not disentangle the reality of her life from the myth'.[18]

Poor Hazel, it'd been a rough afternoon, as had my morning with Christina Stead, whom I'd interviewed in 1980. Mine ended a bit better if for no other reason than that Christina Stead was not pressed for time as Beauvoir had been – quite the opposite; the sorrow of Stead's last years was a great loneliness when she returned to Australia after decades away. I interviewed her in Canberra, at University House where she was living. Her room was bleak, with institutional furniture and not much other than books and a bottle of vermouth to mark it as hers. When I packed up my notes and turned off the cumbersome tape recorder, to my surprise she invited me to lunch in the bistro downstairs. It was a bright, wintry day, and after the dim light of her room the gardens were dazzling: fresh air, silvery leaves, carp lazing in the pools. Over a bottle of wine something real happened between us; fleeting, but real. During the interview in its formal stage she had railed – as Beauvoir had not – about all the young women turning up to pump her for something – what exactly did we think she could give us? – when we could be writing our own books. Why does anyone want to know about the life of a writer? she asked in just about every interview from those last lonely years back in Australia, and before she died in March 1983, in a small hospital just up the road from where I live now, a piece of information I find oddly uncomfortable, I don't know why. At the interview, I'd ploughed gallantly on, and she scowled, her face a dangerous red. When I asked about first being published, she found the question ridiculous. It was irrelevant, she insisted, nothing to do with writing at all. It wouldn't have mattered a jot if all her books had ended up in a trunk under her bed. *Really?* Really. I didn't believe her, but I was hardly going to say so, and I was far too – what, polite? girlish? cowed? – to challenge her. I went on down the list and it wasn't much better. Hence my surprise when she suggested lunch. Wine? After that, definitely.

So, she said with a big, open smile, now it's your turn. What was I doing here when I was clearly English? (I always sound more English when I'm nervous.) What had brought me here? So I told her about Nick, and a marriage made too young, and being the wrong shape for England, or that's how it'd seemed growing up, and the liberation of discovering a place like Papua New Guinea, and coming here to Australia, alone, confused, not knowing

what to do, whether to stay, to accept the offer of a place
at ANU, here in Canberra where we were eating lunch,
or limp back to England. What decided you? she asked.
For Love Alone, I said, and I told her of the bleak days,
alone in Sydney at the beginning of 1972, when I'd found
her novel in a second-hand shop in George Street. I was
staying in a cheap place up behind Central Station, near
where Teresa Hawkins worked in the office of a factory,
saving for her fare to London. I told her how I lay on my
bed and read, how I walked for days, following Teresa's
footsteps out to Watsons Bay, to the university, to the
Quay. If Teresa could make the journey in that direction,
I could make it in this direction. It was she – you, I said,
into that ferocious gaze – who gave me the courage to stay.
Her rheumy old eyes glistened with tears, and she leaned
across the table, her hand on mine, and said, That's the
best thing anyone can say to a writer. To move someone,
that is what matters. Otherwise, she said, one's books
might as well stay in the trunk under the bed. I grinned at
her, and there was nothing shame-faced in her response:
a laugh, more wine in our glasses. There's nothing more
irritating than interview questions, she said again. Why
didn't we just read the novels; that's where the life is. Yes,
it is, Hazel and I agreed, especially in her case – but the
point of interest for us, the fascination we shared, was for
the 'unpruned, tangled past', as Hazel would later call it,
and its pruned re-emergence in the masks of fiction or
memoir, and the inevitable slippages into, or out from
under, the mythologies a writer creates for herself, or are

created around her. For us, the life and the work were not so easily disentangled. In fact, it was the tangle we liked – and that we lived. It would be the foundation of the four major biographical works Hazel would go on to write, starting with *Christina Stead*, which was published in 1993, three years after *Poppy*. And for me, too, it was a starting point, albeit contradictory, as I set about untangling my mother's life, and its tangle with my own.

It was with Hazel more than anyone else that I talked about the written life, the biographical life. Sartre called it the *biographical illusion*; for him and Beauvoir a central tenet of their philosophy was that 'a lived life can resemble a recounted life'. Could it? What would it mean to live life as if it were recounted, or with the recounting always in mind? Wouldn't that be as bad as an all-observing, judging god? I was sceptical, thinking sequentially that the recounted life came *after* – but I didn't then understand the fundamental premise of existentialism: the challenge to create meaning from the meaninglessness of existence. If there is no God – the secular starting point – then it is for us – for 'man', and woman too – to find truth in the face of uncertainty, or worse, and create meaning in our own lives. 'Man is responsible for what he is,' Sartre famously wrote. 'We are alone, without excuses.' That is why moral conduct matters. Otherwise it's nihilism, as Nietzsche warned, or the rule of might, as in the occupation of Paris Sartre and Beauvoir lived through, or – in our case in the twenty-first century – the reign of unbridled capital and the flourishing of religious fundamentalisms: debased certainties in a world of uncertainty.

For Beauvoir, the challenge of creating moral meaning in her own life meant truth-telling, responsibility-taking, a life lived to an intellectual and ethical standard – which made some sense of the biographical illusion. It wasn't that we should, or could, live a recounted life, but we could – and should? – live with an awareness of how we would answer, not at the gates of heaven, but to history, to the world we leave, and to biography. Or fiction – which is where the conversation joined with my, and our, conversation with Helen Garner. Would not the three of us agree, as Hazel wrote in her prologue to *Christina Stead*, that 'turning life into story is one of humanity's enduring pleasures'? She read to us from Stead's 1936 novel *The Beauties and Furies* long before she quoted this in print: 'The true portrait of a person should be built up as a painter builds it, with hints from everyone, brush strokes, thousands of little touches.'[19] This could have been Lily Briscoe in *To the Lighthouse*, trying to find the structure for her painting to hold together the many brush strokes.

Fifty years later, it could be Helen Garner finding the right form to hold together the small moments, the flicker of eros, as she'd put it, those tiny moments of connection, or disconnection, that can turn a life, a friendship, a love affair. She'd published *The Children's Bach*, a near perfect novella, it's been said, in 1984, the year after Christina Stead – and also Rebecca West – died, the year Poppy died, two years before Beauvoir joined Sartre in Montparnasse Cemetery. If I mark everything by death, it's because during those years I did, and now, looking back, I can see that those years in the house on the corner spanned a decade in which the generations shifted forward, a decade in which the mothers died, the literary mothers and, in my case, an actual mother as well. If I were writing as a historian and not as myself, a participant, I'd say that those three books – *The Children's Bach*, *Poppy* and *Christina Stead* – published within a decade of each other, marked a shift about more than just us. But this is a memoir not a history, and at the time I'm not at all sure we understood the significance of what we were doing as women, as writers, as part of a generation that was reframing the way we write the lives of women. It was not a perspective that we had then, or could have; we might think of Virginia Woolf in history, but not of ourselves, our own biographical illusion; we were living day by day, as one does in life not fiction, and the conversations at the table were as likely to be about our encounters with men – not just lovers, but the world of men that we saw all around us – as about literature – more probably, given the turbulence of our own lives of love, a sphere in which we were not doing so well at forging a new path.

Why was it, Sophie asked only this year, that our generation of feminists – clever, able women who had never known war or hunger and had had all the benefits of a university education – made such a hash of it with men (and women too, often enough)? It's a question we'd also asked in the house on the corner. Although Helen was about to embark on a third marriage, it remained to be seen, when she left the house on the corner to live with Murray, how two writers would live, and work, alongside each other. For Hazel and me, the messiness of it was more obvious as we negotiated our uneasy love affairs from the not entirely easy bastion of our own rooms. Hazel was another one who was tall and elegant, but despite her casual flair with clothes, she was very different from Sophie: different angles, different colouring. Men were drawn to her but they were also alarmed by her, not a good combination for an equal relationship. Men can like the idea of a prestigious or celebrated woman – it reflects well on them – but the reality can leave them feeling secondary. Helen knew it. Hazel knew it. Sophie knew it. So, in a muddled, contradictory way, did I, though it'd be a few years yet before I'd be attracting attention for anything I'd written. One of the reasons we, or at least I, loved Lily Briscoe was that she could, and did, 'feel violently two opposite things at the same time', such were the complexity of things. Merely watching a young couple in love – well, supposedly; they thought they were and everyone else did too – she experienced that rush of feeling at its beauty, its excitement, even while thinking it the 'stupidest, the most barbaric of human passions', that can turn a young man 'with a profile like a gem . . . into a bully with a crowbar'.

Yet, she said to herself, from the dawn of time odes have been sung to love; wreaths heaped and roses; and if you asked nine people out of ten they would say they wanted nothing but this; while the women, judging from her own experience, would all the time be feeling, This is not what we want; there is nothing more tedious, puerile, and inhumane than love; yet it is also beautiful and necessary. Well then, well then? she asked, as if in an argument like this one threw one's own little bolt which fell short obviously and left the others to carry it on.[20]

Lily Briscoe would have done better at our table than where she was, at Mrs Ramsay's pre-war table, at least in terms of this conversation. We threw down our bolts and caught them and ran, and while we never solved the conundrum, the ambivalences were bracing; sparks flew around the room, the light poured through the doors; a bowl of flowers on the table, bought by Helen as she walked down King Street on her way from Murray's flat to her desk upstairs at the house on the corner.

But the question remained, and so did the quandary. Was it our fate as the second sex? Was it the legacy of our 1950s mothers, and their unhappinesses? Was it some self-defeating aspect of the female psyche? Were we, as Beauvoir said of women, impeding our own independence? Was Christina Stead right in *For Love Alone* that without a man, even (or perhaps especially) a clever, able woman like Teresa Hawkins will fear the loneliness of being forever alone, yet once she secures a man, she'll fear that this is all she'll ever have, and freedom will never have seemed so sweet? 'When you get what you want, you don't want it,' Marilyn Monroe sang in one of the first films I watched, aged eighteen, at a smoke-filled fleapit in Oxford, holding hands with Nick as we sleepwalked our way towards marriage. Or was it, as Sophie would say, that we lived in houses designed for a family of the pared-down, nuclear variety that had become the norm when most of Sydney's housing stock was built? Sophie put the break-up of her Charlie relationship down, at least in part, to the move from collective living in north London, 'with an Asian shop on the corner reeking of halal meat, discarded vegetable baskets in the street' to a house in Captain Cook Crescent, Canberra, 'one of the most planned, homogeneous cities in the world'. It was hard to meet people, to escape, to dream, 'to build a life of one's own' she wrote in *Inner Cities*. 'I felt I had become the suburban wife. My centre slipped away.'[21] Even in inner Sydney, the house on the corner and every house in the street, and the house Sophie moved into at Bondi, and every house in that street, were designed for a standard-shaped family: lounge, dining and kitchen, two beds or three, a bathroom upstairs if you were doing well. The small and singular flat into which I moved to on the hill behind Bondi wasn't much better, for it too existed in a sea of suburban houses, each with its own lawn and barbecue.

Would our lives have been different in the great cities of Europe? Sartre and Beauvoir lived in hotel rooms and studio apartments in the same or nearby buildings; how much was that part of their story, never forced into the strictures of houses like ours? Beauvoir eventually tired of the hotel rooms and the colour of the walls which, unlike in our houses, could not (or not easily) be changed. She bought her first apartment in 1955 with the money from the Prix Goncourt, which she won for *The Mandarins.* It was in the cream-coloured building in Rue Schoelcher, opposite Montparnasse Cemetery, where Hazel interviewed her in 1976. I wish I'd had the sense to ask Hazel what it looked like inside: what colour the walls, how easy the chairs? And the desk I've seen in photos, had it been tidied for the occasion? How did the light fall? It is not easy to tell from the photograph in *Tête-à-Tête*. When Beauvoir stood up, were the photos of her men on the shelf above her desk at eye level? Did she see them every time she stood, or were they high enough, outside the arc of light from the lamp, for her to live around them without feeling their gaze?

Hazel came back from Paris to finish her thesis in Sydney, and it was sometime in the early 1980s that I met her, and our conversation began. It was only ever a temporary return, and by the time she was writing *Christina Stead* she had moved to Melbourne, where the housing stock was no better than here in Sydney. She was teaching at Deakin University, which meant driving to Geelong most days, which meant speeding fines, which meant installing a gadget in the car that beeped nastily when she overshot. Oh how she hated it. I drove with her on visits to Melbourne and she'd swear when it beeped, and switch it off, then back on, swear and sigh, and laugh (sort of) and ask when she was ever going to get out of the place. She hated Deakin's ugly buildings and she hated the system of research points that rewarded a scholarly article in an academic journal over a biography, even one as acclaimed as hers. The irony was that while *Christina Stead* didn't do much to get her ahead here, academically speaking, it enabled her move to a fellowship at Harvard's W. E. B. Du Bois Research Institute, where she began her work on the African-American writer Richard Wright. It was the first step in her move to the States. She never came back for more than a visit. It wasn't simply that she disliked Australia; there were people she liked, even loved here, and some of them were at Deakin. When I said I'd found Australia a place of freedom after growing up in England, she was astonished. For her, the reverse was true. She'd been snatched from the hazy nostalgia of a childhood she remembered as free, for strictures that deeply offended her. She was hauled up before the headmistress of her Adelaide primary school for not wearing gloves. Gloves! At nine years old! Not good for any but the most respectable of childhood spirits, and damning for Hazel. Her spirit was profoundly cosmopolitan. Mine's not. I travel, move around, more than I like – it's the condition of our age for people like us – but ever since I left the country of my birth where I never felt the right shape – and also suffered indignities to do with gloves and the world's ugliest school berets – I've been seeking somewhere I could fit, somewhere I could call *home*, if only a house on the corner across the railway line at the back end of Newtown, with its cafés and bookshops on the long street down to the university. I still dream of that house, and when I do it is as full of absences as it is of presence, for the household we created there was always reshaping itself by the gaps left at the table when people moved, reshaped themselves in other houses, other cities, other countries.

Writing this, I can hear the elegiac tone to my words. Hazel died in New York in 2011, of a series of cerebral haemorrhages as a result of an infection she didn't know she had, or not until too late. She fell on the floor of the apartment where she was living alone in the midst of a great city. Another one dead at fifty-nine. How long she lay there before she was found, I don't know, or for how much of that time she was conscious. For those of us who heard the news after she was found and taken to hospital, it was shocking in its suddenness; for her my fear is that it was slow. It's only now, thinking back to the last time I saw Hazel, that I've finally read *Tête-à-Tête*, her book about Beauvoir and Sartre. It came out in 2006 when my mind and my days had become re-entangled with Papua New Guinea. I'd recently returned there after an absence of thirty years, and my life was arcing that way. Beauvoir seemed impossibly distant, not exactly irrelevant, but right then, after decades of writing (and reading) about the lives of women, I was frankly not that interested. I was interested in Hazel, of course, but not, then, in Beauvoir, let alone Sartre. Being in New York, Hazel was geographically distant, but she remained not only a friend, someone I cared about, but a figure who inhabited my internal landscape. She came to Sydney for the writers' festival when *Tête-à-Tête* came out. Read it later, she said when we had dinner at the hotel where she was staying. We could see down the harbour and over the lights of the city. There was a gaudiness to the room where we ate food that looked more than it was. Even so, she said, she was glad to be here, in Sydney, more than she expected; it was a kind of homecoming, but it wasn't home. Was anywhere? It certainly wasn't where she wanted to live. That was New York. She talked about the pleasures of the libraries in New York, and I amused her with the vicissitudes of research when it came to PNG. It was only in the most oblique way that we spoke of writing about race, which seems, in retrospect, now that Hazel is dead, another missed opportunity. I suppose we thought there'd be years ahead in which to talk; that night nothing was urgent, and so we slipped back into the then essential talk, which now seems peripheral, about our lives with men. Both of us thought that something might have been resolving; we each had a new man, we each thought that maybe this time the cross-currents of love and independence could flow more harmoniously. But no story ends happily ever after and Hazel's last love affair didn't – which was why she was in an apartment alone in Manhattan when that infection hit her brilliant brain.

Reading *Tête-à-Tête* this year, I can hear Hazel on every page. I hear her voice, her clarity, her sorrow. It's there she has answered the questions that were unanswered that afternoon in November 1976 when she had interviewed Beauvoir, and found her preoccupied with the decline of the man she had indeed loved since she was a student, and with whom she'd had a 'pact' that their love would remain lifelong, 'primary' and 'essential', but that it would not limit their freedom, including for other loves, other 'contingent' love affairs. Instead of sexual fidelity, there would be 'transparency' between them, an absolute honesty. It was clear from the start what this pact might look like from Sartre's point of view: it had been lived before by many a man, if not with such existential clarity. It was the Greenwich Mean Time problem writ large in Paris. But what did contingent love and freedom look like to Beauvoir? Would she have the same independence to love in this way? If anyone knew that society viewed the infidelities of women very differently from those of men, it was the author of *The Second Sex*. 'The tragedy for women,' Beauvoir wrote, 'is that we lose desirability before we lose desire.' She was thirty-three when – during the war, as if there wasn't enough to be anxious about – Sartre tired of her sexually and began a major new affair. In the spirit of transparency, she wrote to him that it was 'especially in the mornings on waking that it causes me a little anguish'.[22] There's a photo of her in *Tête-à-Tête* from 1950 during her affair with Nelson Algren. She was then forty-two. Taken from the door of a bathroom, we see her back view, naked, pinning up her hair after a bath. She is *gorgeous*: tall, firm back, an elegant waist, rounded bottom and sturdy, beautiful legs. And Sartre tired of her at *thirty-three*! Algren

didn't tire of her; he would have married her, but she had
a pact to consider. He didn't tire of her, but he tired,
eventually, of the pact. Men, on the whole, do not tolerate
a secondary position. So, yes, there were double standards,
and no, three did not always fit. But for the most part she
didn't let on how much it could hurt. Sartre 'hated tears',
and having once experienced jealousy during his twenties
had made a 'decision' not to feel it again, arranging his life
to ensure that he wouldn't. Louise Bourgeois' opinion was
that he managed to keep the 'protective, friendly, modest
mother' he'd had as a child in Beauvoir.

Reading *Tête-à-Tête*, I see, with Hazel's eyes and her
judiciously placed exclamation marks, how well Sartre
protected himself against not only his own jealousies,
but the jealous tears of lovers as he moved from one
vulnerable young woman to another. Part of his strategy
of protection was to keep his lovers largely ignorant of
each other. He lied to them, but not to Beauvoir, with
the consequence that she, the great champion of truth-
telling, became complicit in 'situations' (Sartre's word)
that required, for him, a 'temporary moral code', a
philosophical out he devised in order not to compromise
the fundamental challenge of truth. She may have gained
some small comfort from knowing what was going on,
but what did the tearful and demanding young women
know of their lover's 'essential' and 'primary' pact with
her? In order to pacify a tearful woman Sartre would
make last-minute cancellations to arrangements with
Beauvoir, including when they were booked to travel

together, sometimes for several weeks. She'd have made her arrangements with Algren to suit Sartre, and when Sartre changed his with her to suit his state of moral contingency, Algren wasn't filling the gap. It was never an option that Sartre might bend his arrangements to fit in with her other loves. He did not, or could not, as my friend Ali Clark would say, 'surrender the authoritative stance of the ego', a move forced on Beauvoir, maybe, but necessary in the writer, and woman, she became. And yet the pact mattered to her – the intellectual fidelity, even, or perhaps especially, as 'life sinks its teeth into my neck'.[23] She lived the biographical illusion in both senses. She took up the existential challenge; she was the one, not Sartre, who understood the emotional cost of his slogan that 'man was condemned to be free.' And she lived up to the principle of responsibility with an acute eye to history, writing volumes of memoir, and refracting the more ambivalent aspects of her life onto her novels.

'We are continually revising our memories and hopes,' Hazel wrote in her introduction to *Christina Stead*, 'rationalising disappointments, modifying the way we present ourselves to ourselves and others. Everything we do has a hidden aspect.'[24] We have to continually revise, or we couldn't live, and we couldn't write. To do both, Beauvoir needed the biographical illusion in the other sense: the pact by which intellectual fidelity could trump the pain and grief of sexual loss. Did it act as a certificate in her hand? Did it mitigate the shame even a woman who has lived freely can still feel as her lovers lose desire for her and move to another, and another, ever-younger woman, never to return in that way to her, though purporting to love and respect her mind and her intellect all the more for the connection long gone?

These are the thoughts of now, not then, thoughts I can't have with Hazel. I could have them with Helen but she is in Melbourne, too far for a drink in a quiet bar – which is exactly what I'd like right now, at the end of a day as well as a chapter. I'd ask her if she remembers the image from Nietzsche – it must have come from Murray – about our lives being like boats swimming in the sea, and that while we know that one day our boat will capsize, it's the faithful 'good old boats' of our friends – he says 'neighbours' – that keep us afloat through calm seas and good winds, a steady hand stretched to us in the storms and tempests we might wish we could protect each other from, and cannot. Or am I being nostalgic, remembering the house on the corner in these terms? A house, after all, that is long gone for all that it is vivid in memory – the phone on its table, the doors open to the sun – gone, the lemon tree in its large tub, long gone, twenty years sold, more. Helen is in Melbourne, Sophie is in London, Hazel is dead. Absence and presence shadow each other, the paradox of memoir, of words creating the illusion, the biographical illusion, of a house lived in now by who knows who, but once by us, in our forties, writing our books and keeping our boats from capsizing.

Making Shapes Square Up

6

There's a pub on the river outside Oxford, on a bend, near a bridge, close to a weir and a cutting. My father lived across the river and in winter when the trees were bare, he could see the lights of the pub from the window by his bed. Nearly a hundred years ago, when the devastation of the First World War was almost over, his parents, my grandparents, spent their honeymoon at that pub, five miles from the town where they both lived. Ted, my grandfather, had not seen active service, disqualified by weak eyes that were inadequate to the challenge of a gun yet without his thick, round glasses could see every pore on the greatly loved face of my grandmother, Gertie, every tiny fluff of hair on her lip, every crease on her as yet unlined skin. Ted and Gertie were married on the last day of August 1918, and it was at the pub across the river from the house where he died that my father was conceived.

The rooms at the pub can still be let; £39 a night it cost me when I could no longer endure the tension in the house as he died. The bed was uncomfortable, the window small, but from it I could see across to his house, the river flowing, a dark channel between us. I saw when he switched off the light by the bed and the small light for the night nurse came on. I only stayed there one night – it upset him too much to see me exiled so close, and I didn't like it either; not long after that friends in London lent me their cottage in a nearby village.

My father took a long time dying. It was a hard, laborious death. Western medicine can keep the body going against the odds: surgery, radiation, the full panoply of the pharmaceutical industry – he had it all. But it was more than this, and more than a determination to live. It was, it seemed to me, the watching daughter, a matter of a soul bewildered by the mystery of its ending, and more, perhaps, by the nature of its living.

My father's name was Patrick William Medd, a lawyer born of a line of lawyers and clergymen who left Yorkshire at the end of the seventeenth century and moved south to settle around Oxford. He was a man who would have been more comfortable had he been born in the nineteenth century, or even late in the eighteenth, like a distant relative on Gertie's side, the reforming lawyer Samuel Romilly. Gertie's mother's family had been Huguenot refugees, and somewhere in this line was Romilly, the son of a jeweller in London's Soho, a man almost entirely self-educated, who used a small inheritance to sit for the Bar, and from there became a Whig member of Parliament. As Solicitor-General, he introduced bills to reduce the number of offences punishable by death, of which there were over two hundred on the statute books, including for misdeeds as minor as pickpocketing, stealing from a shop or from a bleaching ground to the value of five shillings. Most of the bills Romilly put before the House failed to become law, though in 1814 he did succeed in abolishing the barbaric practice of hanging, drawing and quartering. He died in 1818 before the abolition of the slave trade in 1833 and the Great Reform Act of 1832, for which he had worked and argued throughout his public life.[25] It wasn't until Patrick was a young barrister after the Second World War that the death penalty was finally abolished; as Secretary to the Inns of Court Conservative and Unionist Society – which Patrick joined in the early 1950s after leaving the Labour Party, finding it 'too socialist' – he played a small but effective part in a process of reform set in train by Romilly. Poppy remained proud of Patrick for that, even after they divorced and she moved way to the left of him. What she never forgave was the way he *buried himself* in researching Romilly's biography while she was struggling and needed his help in the months before she was taken to hospital with a 'nervous breakdown'. She saw that book as an escape, so that he wasn't really present even when she returned, and it was: escape and survival both.

By the time my father had finished *Romilly*, I had left school and was doing a secretarial course – much to his dismay, having paid for an education that would prepare me 'for the professions'. As a kind of atonement, I suppose, I typed a good slab of the manuscript and I've read the book, which Poppy never did, so I know the story

well and how important Romilly's Whig rectitude was to
Patrick, who believed in a society of decent individuals,
and although his liberalism – in a twentieth-century
sense – gave consideration to the claims of daughters, it
was a society of decent men that he judged himself by. As if
to test him, fate had arranged not only to bring him to life
in the wrong century, but to throw him into the society
of women. Born into a family of sisters, and bringing into
the world a family of daughters, he was a man who lived
among women and yet kept himself distant and distinct.
Kind when he was with us, solicitous for our education,
proud of our achievements, attentive when we made our
requests, he was nonetheless, in his own consideration as
well as ours, another order of being. We all had insides –
Girls' insides, he'd say, can be very worrying – but until
the day he was diagnosed with a cancer that had spread
from his bowel to his liver, there was never the slightest
suggestion that insides were anything that need concern
him. Every day he caught the train up to London. As far
back as I remember he daily left us for the Temple, that
lawyers' enclave between Aldwych and the Embankment,
where he had his chambers and was a bencher of the
Middle Temple. My earliest memories of the great edifice
of the law were the fluttering gowns that appeared like
bats along the huge stone hallways of the Law Courts.
'An admirable manly atmosphere,' Virginia Woolf said.[26]
We'd be taken there, holding our mother's skirts for
safety, as part of the ritual school-holiday visit to London.
From beneath his wig, those frizzled scrolls of wiry hair,

would emerge our father, and although he'd gather us up for a treat at a restaurant along the Strand, something of that wig and gown, so recently shed, would remain with him, a kind of palimpsest, so that instead of insides – those leaky recesses of our bodies – he seemed to have a reinforced exterior. So much so that as a child it always rather shocked me to see him come out of the lavatory, or to notice a smear of blood on his face after he'd shaved. Of course I knew, but knowing is a many-layered business. And presumably he too knew that supporting the life he led in the courts and in chambers was a body with the frailties that flesh entailed. It was, after all, his body not his mind that had produced the daughters whose mewling and crying had filled his house for so many years. Yet with the diagnosis of his last disease came news of his insides that he found difficult to acknowledge.

'Absolutely nothing to worry about,' he said when I rang on a crackly line from Sydney. 'Why don't you put off coming over until I'm better?'

'I was going to come while you're in hospital,' I said.

'I don't want you troubled with that,' he said. 'And besides, if you come later, we could go on an expedition.'

An expedition. Did he really think we'd be going on any more expeditions? But I abided, as I always had, by his decision, and booked my ticket for several months ahead when it'd be summer, and we did indeed go on an expedition. I drove him north to Yorkshire where my sister Jane lives, and after a few days there with her family, the three of us drove on north to the town of Westerdale, which our family had left back in the seventeenth century. The graveyard of the church is full of Medd tombstones, quite strange to see with a name as unusual as ours recorded in Yorkshire stone. Patrick had a map and after a sandwich at the pub in a village where everyone had noses like ours, we walked along the River Esk and up onto the Dales to find the house where the family began. Patrick managed the walk well considering the operation he'd had a few months before; it was a fine June day and we stopped several times beside the Esk, a small, tumbling river with grassy banks and overhanging trees, until we left it for the final climb up to the place marked Esklets on the map. We'd expected a village, or at least a hamlet, but no, nothing but the bare Cleveland Hills stretched into the distance. All that was left of our ancestral home was a chimney and the outline of crumbling walls, nettles growing from the long grass. We wondered at the modesty of our origins, walls that would have enclosed but a few small rooms, and in the slight laugh of that wonder, certainly for Patrick, and maybe also for Jane and me, there was an element of pride in a family who'd made their way by their brains – though I also had the thought, the image, of a young girl arriving at that bleak place to marry a Medd son.

I have a photograph of my father and my sister from that trip, taken a few days later when we were in Northumberland and had crossed the causeway to Lindisfarne. A dry, salty wind was blowing in from the North Sea, and in the walled garden that Gertrude Jekyll had carved out of the bare slope of the island, Patrick is holding his Panama hat; his face is thin, his cheekbones pronounced, but in every other respect – his dress so careful and his specs polished clean – it would be quite possible to miss the illness of which he would die the next year. In the months after he had recovered from the operation that removed a large chunk of his bowel, he rarely referred to it, and when he did his comments were oblique. When I asked him what the surgeon had done, he talked about 'rerouting his plumbing'. When he was taken over by pain or nausea, he'd apologise – I really am most terribly sorry – and absent himself. We'd creep past his door to see how he was, but he'd shoo us away until he was well enough to join us. It's important not to give in to this, he'd say. In that first phase of his illness, before he was confined to the narrow walls of one room, the life of the house was curiously partitioned as if we were living two lives simultaneously: a public life undisturbed by illness or death, and a private layer that, rather like the lavatory, was never referred to and, had it not been for the bottles of pills on the kitchen table, might well not have existed. Betsy, Patrick's second wife, the friend of Poppy whom he'd left her for, was by nature and predisposition more comfortable with the surface of things, and unlike Patrick, who seemed not to notice, became flustered at any sign of movement from the depths. In this she was supported by neighbours, doctors, even the local vicar. No one wished to speak of death. Look on the bright side, the neighbours said. We find it kinder to be optimistic, the GP said. He's in good hands, the vicar said. I really just called round to see if I could take some cuttings from the garden for the fete.

Patrick, I had always thought, was one of those men whose face and mask had grown into one. There was no sense of a double life, of something struggling to get out. In his decent society of decent individuals he had been well-regarded, respected, even loved – if such a word can be used – by the men, the lawyers among whom he had worked. At the end of each day he came back to the family as if to the ground from which he grew, and he was no more conscious of this than a daisy is conscious of the earth into which it pushes its roots. If, when we visited, there were tensions among his women – his girls, as he called us, wife and daughters alike – he left us to it, as he did more literal manifestations of our leaky insides, and retreated to the garden where he tended the lawns and the vegetables, wide flowerbeds, the sunny nooks and shady corners where trays could be brought, deckchairs opened, books read. We, in our turn, spared him the details of the disputes that occurred in the kitchen between the wife he had taken in midlife and the daughters of his earlier wife. We, his daughters, found our ways around it mainly by avoidance, dashing down for the day, a couple of nights at the most, and by taking him off somewhere – a house, a gallery, a long walk. Until it came time for him to die. Then the masks of Englishness slipped and skewed, and our faces could not endure the weight. With Patrick it wasn't that the mask he wore failed him – on the contrary, it could be said to have sustained him – more that it left him unprotected against other forces, other voices, which had, until that moment, been barely visible to him. Not so much the tears in the kitchen, the slamming doors, the running feet, though these did impinge on him as they had not before. But, if he wanted Jane to come down from Yorkshire, as he did, with her children, and Betsy would not accommodate their vegetarian meals – Your daughters are so *difficult*, Patrick – how was he to manage this if he could no longer drive to Sainsbury's or take them out for lunch in Oxford? And when, on our return from the expedition north, the proofs of *The Orchard* were waiting for me and the courier was booked to collect them the next day, he couldn't escape the loud voices on the stairs when Betsy wanted help with the washing, and I, in Patrick's study with the proofs, refused.

'They're your father's sheets,' she shouted up from the kitchen.

'He's your husband,' I shouted back.

'I thought you were a feminist.'

'I am,' I said.

'Then you shouldn't expect me always to be doing the sheets.'

'He supports you,' I shouted, 'I support myself, and right now I have proofs to correct.'

'Well, that's your choice,' she said.

'It's my *work*.'

In his bedroom beside the study, Patrick heard every word. Can I help, he offered, which of course he couldn't, either with the proofs or the sheets, which were indeed a problem, to be washed every day. The deadly cells massing in his bowel and burrowing into the rich flesh of his liver were a powerful challenge to those masculine regiments of knowing, those compendia of knowledge, those legal certainties by which he had understood so much of his life. It was all very well for the doctors and the neighbours to jolly along on the surface – and on the surface Patrick responded as he always had, with courtesy and an element of wit – but it didn't alter the reality that pressed on him. Death by bowel malfunction is a putrid affair. Would it have been less shocking to us before the lavatory was invented with the brilliantly conceived S-bend sealing out the smell and sight of waste matter we barely need glance at? When there were cesspits beside roads and open drains under windows would we have been so shocked by the emptying of a foul-smelling pot?

Late one afternoon towards the end, after a particularly bad day, when his bowel had leaked a shiny grey-green liquid until the doctor had come and injected him with something to dry it up, after a day of washing sheets and wiping his scrawny legs and haunches where the flesh hung in folds, he asked me to read to him. Betsy had gone to stay with one of her children for two nights, the front door had banged shut, and Amy, Jane's eldest, who was on a break from Manchester University, and I were alone with him. Suddenly the house was very silent, as if at last there was room for us in it, but by the time it came we had lost the capacity to move. The morning nurse had left; Patrick was propped on his pillows in his bed beside the window, where on the sill was his radio, tuned always to Radio 4, and his books, including the essays of Montaigne that are now on my desk. On the table on the other side of the bed were a glass and a jug of water, tissues, the accoutrements of the sickbed, a telephone and a lamp he could angle to his book, or away towards the watercolour of his parents' garden on the wall behind the bed. Amy and I sat still and quiet on low chairs beside him.

'Will you read to me?' he asked.

'What would you like us to read?'

'Tennyson,' he said. So I went to the shelf in his study next door and returned with the blue leather-bound book from which he had read to us as children. I opened it to the lilting verses of 'The Lady of Shalott' – *Willows whiten, aspens quiver, / Little breezes dusk and shiver* – lines I've always associated, quite wrongly, with the river that runs outside the window where we sat.

'No,' he said, his eyes closed and his voice so quiet that we had to strain to hear him. '"Ulysses",' he said. 'Read me "Ulysses".'

I faltered; for to me *Ulysses* means Joyce, that's the automatic association, a leap which, in that room, I couldn't encompass. But my clever niece took the book from my hands and turned to the poem. So completely had I switched my allegiance from the poetry of the nineteenth century on which we were brought up, I hadn't even known of Tennyson's 'Ulysses' until Amy handed me the book, and I read it to Patrick that afternoon. It is a poem in the voice of an old king dying.

It little profits that an idle king, / By this still hearth, among these barren crags . . . A strange poem that moved me greatly, not so much when I read it as when Amy read it again and took in the awful struggle of the king who must lay aside his kingly prides. What is the secret that lies behind those robes, under that orb and sceptre, beneath that crown? *Much have I seen and known; cities of men / And manners, climates, councils, governments, / Myself not least . . . Yet all experience is an arch wherethro' / Gleams that untravell'd world, whose margin fades . . .* As we read that autumn afternoon, the sky outside the window was darkening. Across the river we could see the lights come on in the pub. There were tables on the grass outside, a kind of patio built beside the river, where torn and tatty umbrellas turned in the wind. There was a silver line of tears along Amy's lashes. *Death closes all: but something ere the end, / Some work of noble note, may yet be done.*

At last, she said when we went down to the kitchen and stood together in a silent embrace. At last it's been said. For upstairs in that darkening room when we sat still and quiet together, my father, her grandfather, had watched us closely. When we began to read I'd assumed it would lull him to sleep as once 'The Lady of Shalott' had lulled me, but when we closed the book and laid it on the table beside him, his eyes were cleared of the morphine haze.

'I shall miss you,' he said. I don't think he meant my absence in Australia, or Jane's in Yorkshire. 'All of you,' he said. Then, very quietly – did we hear him right? – 'Sometimes I think I missed you all.'

That poem was the first gesture by my father that truly acknowledged what was happening – I don't count the times he took me through his will, a practical exercise – and I didn't respond well. Reluctant as I am to admit it, I could not remove those ancient masks, some of which it seems are born with us as we claw our way into air, an inheritance that, even as we snuffle in our cribs, conceals our original face. *What was your face*, a Zen koan asks, *before your parents were born?* My response was not to say that I would miss him and maybe always had; instead, as the tide of grief rose in me, I found an excuse – the classic, English excuse – for leaving the room. It's time for tea, I said.

On the table in the hall downstairs were all the family wedding photos. As Betsy had six children and there are three of us, the hall table rattled with photos. At the end near the door onto the stairs, in pride of place, was mine, the eldest of the nine and the first to marry. There I was, twenty years old, dressed in white, smiling anxiously into the camera as I stepped from the church (Norman, flinted) on the arm of my sweet-faced and equally young husband. When I considered Amy launching into her life at university and the turbulence of a first love, I thought it should be forbidden, marrying that young. Not that it was a disaster for me marrying at twenty – far from it, it took me to Papua New Guinea – but as a long union it was quite inappropriate, and why at that age should it be anything else? One is not yet formed, one's layers are thin, there is an absence; even one's secrets are slight. Every time I passed that photo, every time I walked in or out of my father's house, I received that image of my younger self with flowers in her hair as a rebuke. I never moved it, I never asked for it to be taken away, but every time I passed it I flinched. Upstairs in Patrick's study was another photo of me. It was taken at the beach house on that rocky stretch of coast south of Sydney early in the year I turned forty. It was taken at a moment of change, on the cusp of a decade of great complexity. In the privacy of the room only my father inhabited was a photograph of me as I was, and though he knew little of the context or significance of that moment, in it I smiled at him from a life that, for better or worse, was mine. Yet publicly the only photo of me was taken in the fairytale moment of the wedding day. It was a split I'd spoken of often, a split I'd wept over in the safety of a room in a stone house in an obscure suburb of Sydney some half-hour from the house on the corner, where I began the journey of an analytic psychotherapy. For several years I had driven there three times a week and spoken to the man who, from his chair across the room, would come to know me in my split and fractured reality, and in the curious process of being known, I would come to know something of myself, though, in the nature of knowing, that doesn't always make the fractures less fractured; it rearranges them into another pattern, another shape, that's all, and maybe that is enough.

Not long before I began this therapy, Patrick made his only visit to Australia. He and Betsy came for a month in the Australian autumn of 1988, while Jane and her husband Nigel were living in Sydney on a two-year work stint. Amy and Martha were at primary school, and Tom, their little brother of the blue knitted helmet, began at kindergarten. For most of Patrick and Betsy's visit we were all together, on expeditions, which Patrick took great interest in, though I could rarely name the plants he noticed or give him the details of the constitution he enquired about, while Betsy complained that the place was without culture. It was not easy, the split in me was raw, with Poppy dead, the absence of a husband, which in the presence of my father I felt acutely, all ambivalence gone, and Garry refusing to play the role – Just for a few weeks, I'd say. *Please.* Later, in the room in the stone house, I'd return to that visit again and again, and to the paradox of my sense of inadequacy, the inadequacy of the life I had shown my father, although the life I didn't have – 'the disguise of marriage', Virginia Woolf calls it – was not the life I wanted to live. Fortunately there were Jane's children: at times of unspoken stress, they'd run around, they'd lean on their grandfather, ask for stories, or lead him off to look at something they'd made, or found, and the moment, whatever it was, that might have produced tears, passed.

One evening when Patrick and Betsy were with me at the house on the corner, they went up to bed early. We'd eaten alone, just the three of us – Helen must have been at Murray's – and they were tired. I pottered around in my workroom downstairs, but with my father in the house I couldn't contemplate my desk or anything on it. So I sat at the piano, an upright against the wall, and practised the two-page Haydn sonata I was learning. I'd rented the piano after Poppy died and had gone back to lessons, but music is not in my hands and all I could do was pick out the notes. That I could make my way through this learning piece was a personal triumph, no more; that Patrick was impressed and came downstairs is a comment more on his lack of musicality than my capabilities. But there he was in his dressing-gown. He walked round the room looking at the photos on the mantelpiece – a mix of family and friends, England and Australia, PNG. What a life you've had, he said. He admired my golf-ball typewriter and the pile of pages – of *Poppy* – about which I said very little. He took Patrick White's *Voss* from the shelf, opened it and, still holding it, looked at the pictures on the wall, posters mostly and a few collages by an artist friend. He stopped in front of a large poster from the Fine Arts print workshop at Sydney University: *You are on Aboriginal land*.

'I think I'd find it hard,' he said, 'living on land that hadn't been the land of my ancestors.'

'Sometimes I wonder if I should take that down,' I said, standing beside him. 'Some days it seems hypocritical having it up there. Other days I like it, a reminder.'

Then we sat together, just Patrick and me, and talked of Voss's trek into the desert interior, of the poet Kath Walker, the first Aboriginal woman to be published and who had just that year taken the name Oodgeroo Noonuccal. He liked that, practised the sound of it. A strange country, he said. Not so strange when you learn how to see it, I said. I told him about reading Christina Stead when I first came here and meeting her years later when she returned to Sydney, and about the writers of her generation whom I'd met while I was researching *Exiles at Home*. I told him about visiting Eleanor Dark – I took *The Timeless Land* off the shelf and put it on the table. Her husband was a gardener, like you, I said. She told me off once, when she asked me what I was doing here, in Australia. I'd said something flippant; I was young at the time, and I guess I didn't know. This is a place to take seriously, she'd said. Too many people come here and live only on the surface. It does them no good, she said, and it does us no good. Patrick opened *The Timeless Land*. Ah, he said, what we were talking about yesterday. We'd walked up onto South Head where we could look out to the ocean and turn to see all the way down the harbour. Whenever I'm up here, I'd said, I always imagine the first ships sailing through the Heads. Patrick saw at once the view from the ships, and I reminded him there'd have been people standing up here. They'd all be gone by now, Betsy said. Patrick put his hand on her shoulder. Everything about their lives was about to change, he said. Not *everything*, Amy, aged twelve, insisted: she'd done a school project. All the way back to the car she listed the things that would remain: the rocks, the sky, their babies, their songs, their stories, their religious beliefs, the fish they caught, the way they walked through the bush. The settlers got lost, she said, they couldn't tell where anything was.

'She'll soon be old enough for this,' Patrick said, still looking at the book.

We'd always talked well of books, Patrick and I, and we did that night, a kind of code that brought us as close as we could come to talk of feeling or emotion. There was something comforting about my father in his dressing-gown in my workroom in Sydney, and also disturbing, a collision of worlds that had for twenty years or so kept themselves apart – or rather that I had kept apart. That evening the tears welled in my eyes but they didn't fall until the next year, when I'd tell the man in the stone house who took the chair across from mine of that visit, able to say to him as I could not to my father that somehow I needed to bridge this deep split in me, or least give it another shape.

As evening fell that day we read the poem 'Ulysses', Amy and I were downstairs cooking supper when the phone rang. I picked it up in the kitchen, and at the same moment Patrick picked it up beside his bed upstairs. Hello, we all said. Hello! Hello! Hello! I knew at once that it was Ben, but Ben, ashamed, was slow to identify himself. As a consequence Patrick took a while to realise that the call was for me, and round we went until at last he put the receiver down. All Ben could say was that it had shocked him to hear my father's voice, and in that short call in the kitchen I had never felt such distance from him. What did he expect? That my life ceased to exist when I was away from him? I waited until the night nurse came, and when Amy went downstairs to watch a film on television, I ran a bath and, pleading tiredness, shut the door of the room where I was sleeping and took a Valium.

The next evening, after I'd taken Amy to the station for her train back to Manchester, after his carers had been to wash and change Patrick, after I'd made lunch for his sister, my aunt, who'd driven over to see him, and walked along the river with her while he had his nap, after I'd waved her goodbye and watched the news, I took the tray for supper upstairs: soup and a little steamed fish, invalid fare. There was a fire in the grate, and with Betsy away I poured a glass of red for him as well as for me.

'Who was that who rang last night?' he asked.

'That was Ben,' I said.

'Who's Ben?'

'A friend,' I said, and as the words left my mouth, or is it our hearts they leave, before I realised what they would be, I added, 'a man I have loved.' Past tense. And to my astonishment, I told him of this other fracture in my life, loving a man who matched me in so many ways, yet was married and had small children.

'Very hard for a man with young children to leave,' Patrick said.

'Is that why you waited?'

'I sometimes wonder if that was right,' he said.

'Leaving,' I asked, 'or leaving when you did?'

'At the end of your life it's hard to know.'

Which did he mean? I didn't press.

'Tell me about Ben,' he said. 'What does he do?'

'He restores furniture. Antiques. He imports things, he buys for museums – you know, proper furniture.'

Patrick wanted to know how he'd come by this trade, and how, from my university life, I'd come to know him. I told him that one of the things I had liked about Australia and my university education there was the mix of people I knew, the children of immigrants who'd come from Southern Europe after the war, and the children of Jewish refugees whose parents had escaped Europe before the war, or had come on the ships that brought them after. I told him the story of Ben's father leaving Hungary in 1939, just in time before the borders closed, the rest of his family left behind, and most of them killed.

'How old are his children?'

'Young,' I said. 'The eldest is ten.'

'So you're his escape.'

'Or safety valve,' I said. 'I sometimes think I keep that marriage going.'

'Maybe,' Patrick said, 'but you must know what it means to a man in that situation.'

Did Ben's marriage have to be unhappy to justify our affair? And anyway, was it? And if it was, would it not be the worst of reasons? These were not questions for Patrick, not then, not ever.

'Was it like that for you?' I asked. 'The sense of compromise?'

He didn't answer, but I could see it in him.

'And you?' he asked. 'How is it for you?'

'Sometimes it's been hard and I've felt closed out. But other times it suits me well,' I said, and finally, for the first time, I talked to my father about the love and independence conundrum, the pull two ways, rather like the tug between England and Australia, here and there, one part of myself against another. And I talked to him about feminism – had I ever used the word in his presence? – and what a relationship between a man and a woman might look like if the woman was, truly, independent.

'You should write about it,' he said.

'What!' I said. 'You'd have me write all that in public?'

'No, no,' my father said. 'It could be a novel. I've often wondered why you don't write novels. You told such good stories when you were little.'

'And got into trouble for them, for exaggerating. . .'

'You always insisted they were real.'

'They were,' I said. 'To me, they were real. Stories only work if you believe them.'

'I can see that now,' he said, 'but at the time, you know, when the school would complain that you'd told a story about a helicopter taking you up so high you could see all of England all at once. . .'

'I don't remember that,' I said.

'There was quite a fuss. You were very little, six or seven. The trouble was that other children wanted to go up too. You said the helicopter lived behind a hedge, and only you knew where it was.'

'Oh dear,' I said, the shame of childhood sweeping over me, but my father was smiling. '*Poppy* was almost a novel,' he said.

'Would you have preferred it if it was?'

'Well, it makes it easier,' he said, 'to know it's all fiction, than to be left wondering.'

'Were you? Left wondering, I mean.'

'You called me Richard. It made me wonder what kind of man I'd be if I'd been called Richard.'

He took my hand. 'You can write,' he said. 'You always could, it was there in your letters, even from school.'

That evening with my father, I pondered whether I'd have written if I'd stayed in England, and if I had, what would I have written? Did it take the split to let me write as I did? What would there have been in its absence? If I'd stayed, would I have married a solicitor and lived in the suburbs that stretched along the railway lines out from London, a portly husband and a brace of daughters in tartan dresses? And if I had, would I have written? Would I even have had the idea? Or, without writing, would I have followed in Poppy's footsteps, straight into the psychiatric hospital? That evening it was with my father that I wept, as I hadn't, with him, since childhood. I heard the night nurse come in downstairs. And still I wept. I dropped my head onto the bed beside him, I could feel the warm pulse of his chest against the crown of my head, I could feel the scratchy caress of his fingers in my hair. I could hear his voice exactly as it had been all those years ago when it was I who lay in bed and leaned into the gentle pressure of him as he sat on the edge of my mattress to read the stories of Dr Doolittle, and Rikki-Tikki-Tavi.

The next morning there was an air of relief in the house. Rather than this unaccustomed display of emotion wearing him down – as the night nurse who'd come clucking into the room had predicted – Patrick was better than he'd been for days. When I pulled my chair up to his bed the next morning he told me he'd been thinking about his mother, Gertie, my grandmother – not that he'd been thinking anything in particular, more that she'd come to him in a sweep of images: kissing him goodnight when he was a boy, smelling of freesias; waving him off on the school train, holding down her hat in the rush of air along the platform; hurrying along the corridor from the kitchen as he opened the door to visit her; sitting at her desk all afternoon writing in a small notebook.

'What do you suppose she wrote?' he said. 'I haven't really thought about it until now. It must have been a diary. I wonder if anyone kept it.'

'Would the aunts know?' I asked.

'Have you ever had the feeling,' he said, 'of knowing someone without really knowing them at all?'

'Often,' I said.

'What a race we are,' he said, and I didn't have the wit to ask him what he meant by race. Us humans? Us English?

In a small box in the bottom drawer of Patrick's desk – which is now mine, here in the house near a park on the edge of Sydney's inner harbour where I am living twenty years after the events leading up to his death in October 1995 – are his letters to Gertie. She kept them all, tied into bundles with old-fashioned black ribbon. Jane and I found them after he died. The first are from prep school where he was sent to board at the age of seven. In a jerky hand he wrote: 'Darling Mummy, Last week I had a poisoned hand. I am real very homesick. Please come and get me at once.' 'Darling Mummy, I've still got a pain. I am 4 st 8 and 4 ft 9ins high. PS Send a long letter soon.' The tearful letters didn't last long; by the following summer: 'Cricket was spiffing, we're doing awfully well and Jones made a jolly good showing.' His only complaints were about the custard. It was 'a lark' even when his glasses were flushed down the lavatory. There aren't many letters from his next school, Uppingham, where he went at twelve – the school, incidentally, from which Edward Brittain and his fellow musketeers enlisted for the First World War. Preserved in the box were odd pieces of memorabilia: concert programmes, a hand-drawn map from a cadet's exercise, a note in Patrick's hand instructing that 'In future people who do prep in hall will, on the conclusion of prep, leave hall immediately. They will not, as sometimes previously, loiter in hall much to Raeburn's and the senior clear-ups inconvenience.' This matches the photo of him as a prefect, arms crossed, face stern, the boy performing the man. Did he not write his mother more than the few letters that remain? Is this what it takes, the making of the Englishman away from his mother from the age of seven? Writing of mothers and politics in 2014, Jacqueline Rose comments – in the context of a British Cabinet dominated by those from public schools: 'The one who most proudly proclaims the idea of iron-clad self-sufficiency must surely have the echo of the baby in the nursery hovering in the back of his or her – mostly his – head.'[27]

Patrick's letters from the war still address Gertie as 'Darling Mummy', but gone was any trace of vulnerability. 'There's absolutely no reason to worry at all,' he wrote from Burma. 'Our command knows what it's doing, and we're seeing some splendid countryside.' The letters are here with me in Sydney, still in Gertie's box that once held octavo-sized 'Alabaster note paper, triple thick', because when we found them I thought I'd write about the making of an Englishman. 'I wake up every morning and give thanks I was born an Englishman,' he once said. But as it is, I have barely looked at them. While Martha was living here we got them out, but it was too ghostly to read more than a random few. We put them back in the box and closed the drawer.

'I wish I'd been with Gertie when she died,' Patrick said that morning after the night of my tears, when his mother had come to him.

'Where were you?' I asked.

'In court. My clerk sent in a message.' And then, as if there was only a certain distance he could go, as if he was afraid of burdening me, he said, 'Quite enough of that.' He looked at the clock. 'Betsy will be back soon. Are you really going to London?'

'The cottage will be free next week,' I said. 'I'll come down then and spend each day with you.'

'You won't stay here?'

I shook my head. No more.

7

From the damp air over the river to the noise of London streets, from the desolation of an approaching death to life rushing on – a drive that didn't take much more than an hour – my life consisted of splits and divisions. Back and forth; up and down; past and present; here and there. Where? During the eighteen months of Patrick's illness, I returned to England three times; for the third I arrived in summer, hot blazing days with pale Londoners stretched out in the parks, and stayed until the trees lost their leaves and he died in the middle of October. In London I stayed in Stoke Newington with Virginia, an Australian friend who worked for a Shadow Minister in the soon-to-be-elected Blair government. In the aftermath of Thatcher there was a sense of possibility and renewal, and arguments that went to and fro between the hopes that New Labour – which would be swept into power in May 1997 – would restore the welfare state, and with it the idea of a common good, and the fear that the break with the collectivist past of old Labour signalled a further triumph to the market, and greater inequality. The answer might be clear now, but it wasn't then, or not entirely. At night at the houses of friends, there'd be noisy meals and talk that, too, would bat back and forth; which way were we going? What could be achieved by working with the government-in-waiting? Could the welfare state and the market be harmonised? What would be lost by trying? What should be given up, and in what name? I'd take it all in, split upon split, and it'd seem at once urgent and oddly distant – not because it didn't matter, or even because part of me was still in that house by the river. It was as if I was in someone else's memories, the person I might have been, but wasn't. While I'd got to know a lot of people in London after twenty years of travelling between, it wasn't the world in which I had a voice. In Australia, after *Poppy* and *The Orchard*, I did have a voice, of sorts; I knew the way into, and around, the talk that went to and fro in Sydney, or Melbourne. In London there was a part of me that felt out of place, and I'd look around at these people I liked and considered friends, many of them through Lynne – with whom friendship had been restored – and wondered if I'd have found my way to them if I hadn't gone to Australia. And if I had, would I have had a voice then? I didn't know. There wasn't an easy answer to any of it, the big and the small, here in London or there in the house by the river where only *The Times* and the *Daily Mail* were delivered.

One evening at a pub in Hackney I was almost tempted into forgetting by the attentions of a man in

the group in which I stood with a glass in my hand. He'd
been arguing with an old communist (in both senses of
the word, a man of the 1950s in his sixties) who wasn't
budging in his distrust of Blair, and eventually the
younger man gave up and moved over to me. I'd met
him a few times and during the argument he'd raised
his glass to me, and smiled a smile that broke through
my sombre mood. Ah yes, he was attentive, that man,
and his attentions snapped me into the present. He was
good-looking in a lanky, leftist kind of way; I knew the
type well. I also knew the danger signs; he might not
be so keen on a free market, but free love, well that was
another matter. I'd been vaguely tempted by him before,
and that night I wavered; what better way of resolving
the splits, the divisions, what better form of forgetting
than the forgetting of the body? But I'd learned enough
to know that form of escape is rarely an escape – or
perhaps it was just that I was old enough to know that
a night of forgetting could magnify every split come the
morning. So I got in the car with Virginia and drove
home with her, to the house in Stoke Newington and
my small room at the back overlooking the cemetery.
In the morning, when she left for another long day at
Westminster, I read the *Guardian* at the kitchen table
and listened to Radio 4, gathering strength for the drive
back to the house on the river. The cottage I'd been
lent in a nearby village, five miles away, was comfortable,
warm as the chill of autumn began, and I was grateful.
I was lonely there, as I was not in London, but lonely,

I discovered, was a small price to be away from the barely concealed enmity that filled the house.

In September, a month before the end, Betsy wanted Patrick put in a home. One of her sons came over to 'talk sense' to Jane and me. We were in the kitchen, the door open to the hall and the stairs.

'No,' my sister said, her voice resolute. 'After all he's done for you, no. He stays here.'

'It's not fair on Mum,' the son said.

'Not fair? There are nurses.'

'They're expensive.'

'For goodness sake. So's a home.'

'Not necessarily,' the son said.

'It's not as if it's for long,' I said. 'He's dying.'

'That's a terrible thing to say,' Betsy said.

'Why? He knows it, we all know it, and he wants to die at home.'

'The doctors say we should look on the bright side.'

Really! Hadn't she watched Monty Python? What is it with the English?

'You move him,' Jane said, 'and you'll have to move us first.'

'You're so *extreme*,' the son said.

Compared with the bad thoughts that kept me awake at night, and the sound of the night nurse helping him to the lavatory and the groans I could hear from my bed, the loneliness of the cottage was insignificant. The friend whose cottage it was would ring from London. I'd talk to her, and prowl among the books on the shelves, a comforting mix of England and Australia. In the morning while the nurses were washing Patrick and changing his sheets, I'd go for long walks through the village and into the countryside. Beech trees. There's something about beech trees. Childhood, I suppose. Then I'd drive over to the house by the river, and take his lunch up while Betsy went to have her hair done, or shut herself into the sitting room with the midday movie.

'Thank you,' he'd say, and I'd sit beside him, reading while he dozed. Death was close, drawing him into a dream zone that was not quite sleep, but not awake either.

'Where are Tom and the little Indian boy?' he asked one afternoon as he emerged from this zone. By Tom he meant his grandson, of course, who was eleven by then. As to the little Indian boy, I have no idea, but there he was, as much a part of the dream as Tom.

'When were they here?' I asked.

'They're loading the car for my journey,' he said, and then he looked at me with a small, slight laugh. 'I think I must have been dreaming,' he said.

Another afternoon he woke from a dream about Poppy. He was looking for her in a cathedral but she had gone. 'Maybe there was another door,' he said, 'and I missed her.'

He put out his hand to me, bony knuckles, veins standing out from the loose, empty skin.

'You're wearing her pearls,' he said.

Yes, I was, even with jeans. I wore them every day.

'Take care of them,' he said. 'They're seed pearls.'

'I know,' I said, and told him about the time the string had broken while I was waiting to cross a busy street in downtown Sydney. I'd been wearing them since Poppy had given them to me not long before she died; I hadn't thought to take them to a jeweller and until that moment hadn't understood the value of a necklace strung on silk with a tiny knot between each pearl. There the necklace lay on the edge of the pavement, a frayed break but otherwise intact, with one end dipping into the gutter as the lights changed and people pushed past to cross. I picked it up and saw how threadbare the silk had become, and as I tested it, it broke again. A single pearl dropped. I stooped down and couldn't find it. When I took the necklace to the jeweller, he could tell me exactly how many pearls I'd lost. Five, all from the back where the silk rots first – all that Sydney sweat, I suppose – and where the pearls are the tiniest.

'She was wearing them when I met her,' Patrick said, his hand still stretched towards me.

I took the necklace off and handed it to him. He held it up close, lifted his glasses, his myopic eyes acting as a magnifying glass to the small pearls.

'What was she like?' I asked, though I knew the answer he'd give.

'She was the prettiest girl I'd ever seen. She had on the loveliest dress.'

'I know, you've always said so.'

It was a story, smoothed down into the shape of stone. It was early in the war, January 1940, when they met at a dance in Shropshire on the borderlands of Wales. Her father, my grandfather, whose temperament was over-imaginative and somewhat paranoid, had evacuated his wife and daughters from London before the Germans (whom he was certain were about to invade) had a chance to get them. Poppy was fifteen, taken out of a school to which she wouldn't return. Patrick was twenty, had enlisted and was at an officers' training camp nearby. They met at a dance in a hotel called the Craven Arms. Her mother, my grandmother Toto, watched as they danced that first night in the shortest of courtships before he was sent on service, first to East Africa and then to Burma; theirs was a romance of letters and poems, with one leave back in the middle. We all knew the story of the dance, and Patrick in his uniform, a soldier ready for war, having to *muster all his courage* to ask her to dance. And did she? we asked as children, holding our breath as if she might still say no, and we'd never be born. But she did, and they danced one dance, and then another, until late in the evening they were dancing only with each other. That was the story: Poppy and her dress and her pearls.

It wasn't until much later that I understood that the war, for her, wasn't only the prelude to us children; it also meant that while Patrick was in the line of the guns, she, as a woman in an unoccupied Allied country, had a whiff of freedom and felt herself, briefly, part of a larger polity. As soon as she turned sixteen in November 1940, she enlisted in the FANYs (the First Aid Nursing Yeomanry), a branch of the British army; to her father's annoyance she could only be contacted via an address in Whitehall.

She was stationed in an undisclosed house in the country where Polish servicemen were being prepared to be dropped back into their occupied homeland with radio transmitters and forged papers. Nothing the men wore or carried could show any sign of coming from England – except, of course, the heavy radio transmitters, which seemed rather a major exception when we heard the story as children. But that was the point, Poppy would say, they were *spies* – though at sixteen the work of decoding the messages transmitted at night to a quiet room in the house terrified her. Knowing that the smallest mistake could result in a man's death, she asked to be taken off the decoding. Instead she sewed clothes with Polish thread and went for long walks through the English countryside with the men who were in the uniform of their vanquished air force until it was time to don their disguise. There were photos of her in her uniform, and the Polish men in theirs, on a lawn with trees spreading into the distance. It wasn't until I asked her at the end of her life that she talked about hearing the men's stories of families and friends and sweethearts, whose fate they had no way of knowing. The peace of the fields and woods where they walked, and the war the men were to return to, became very vivid for Poppy, a contrast that seemed cruel and arbitrary. It was from these Polish servicemen – not her parents, nor her school, nor the man she'd marry – that Poppy learned her first political lessons; arbitrary, yes, the accident of birth, but nothing, no fate, no destiny, was just one thing. Our most personal lives are also formed

by the contingencies of history and power and politics.
I don't think I realised the significance of this until now,
not even when I was writing *Poppy*; I was more interested
then in the nervous breakdown that had taken her away
from us and begun my exile in a school a long train-ride
away. Me, me, me; the perils of memoir.

Patrick's sister, Betty – who was the same age as Poppy,
born in 1924 – was also a FANY. Though just as young,
she proved an expert decoder and was moved to Grendon
Hall in Buckinghamshire, not far from Bletchley Park.
Forty women, Betty among the youngest of them,
worked as decoders at the high-security transmitting and
receiving station there. The implications of a mistake
didn't deter Patrick's sister; with a steadier disposition,
she became one of the most proficient of that small
cohort. On a recent visit to England, many years after
both Patrick and Poppy were dead, I took this aunt, then
in her late eighties, out for an early dinner in the town
where she lives near London. When we arrived at the
restaurant, we were the only diners and the Italian waiter
paid us extravagant attention. On a hunch, I asked her the
question I never asked Poppy.

'Did she fall for any of them?' I asked.

'Oh,' my aunt said, turning a little pink. 'Oh, no,
I wouldn't think so.'

But when I pressed, she said, 'Well, there may have
been one. Just a little.'

'What was he like?'

'Oh, he was terribly handsome. They used to run races

in the garden, and he'd let Poppy win and then carry her back to the house. I never told Patrick.'

Over a second glass of wine that sent her even pinker, I heard for the first time that she was in Germany four days after the Armistice, part of a Special Operations Executive contingent stationed in Cologne. From there she drove east to the Displaced Persons camps, where many of the agents she'd tracked from Grendon Hall were trapped with no papers. The task was to find and identify them. The Official Secrets Act casts a long shadow, and even the charming Italian waiter couldn't get more from her than that, or how many they rescued, but he did coax her into describing the bomb damage that had flattened Cologne, the acres of rubble surrounding what was left of the building in which they were billeted. It was a ghost town, she said, until at night the flickers of light from lamps and fires revealed the city's population living beneath the ruins.

'Did the one Poppy liked survive?' I asked.

'I don't think so.' She shook her head, and I saw the shadow pass over her.

'And you? Did you fall for anyone?'

'We were very young,' she said, and the shutters came down.

It was time to take her home.

Poppy's friend Gillian, whose sister had been a FANY, told the story of the dog Poppy managed to keep with her, despite a stern sergeant and a litter of puppies, right through the war. The big shaggy dog was there in the cottage in Shropshire where Poppy and my father lived when they were first married and I was a baby. There was no electricity, and only a pony and trap to get into town. Poppy, at twenty-two years old, embraced this as further liberation from her father. She'd rather a remote cottage and the slow clop into town with me in a basket beside her than all the cars in London, Gillian said.

Patrick never said much about Poppy's time as a FANY, again the Official Secrets Act perhaps, or a lingering reluctance to speak of the war that had kept them apart; besides, I think he was jealous of those photos. Handsome chaps, he'd said when we'd looked at them on a visit to Jane. But when I sat beside him at the end, he'd return to that Shropshire cottage, and how Poppy would sing in the kitchen and how pretty she was; he'd turn the pearl necklace between his fingers and small snatches of memory would come to him: the carrots they grew, an apple tree, meeting Gertie and Ted at the station with the pony and trap. When I pushed the story forward to the dark years of her 'nervous breakdown' and the doctor at the hospital, he handed the necklace back to me. His eyelids became heavy and he slipped into another dream zone, until Betsy came bustling in at the end of her movie.

Martha has the pearls now, and she too wears them often. I gave them to her when she was engaged to be married. When she broke off the engagement in an act of great courage given that the date had been set and the venue booked, she offered to give them back. I refused. It wasn't a reward for 'achieving marriage', as her great-aunt had put it in her letter of congratulation. The necklace was a gift from me to her, and through me a gift from her grandmother Poppy, who would have been right behind her in this refusal of a marriage she came to realise would be a mistake. By then I'd learned that those tiny pearls grow naturally in freshwater mussels or saltwater oysters when a grain of sand gets into their soft interior and the creature encases it in a smooth substance that hardens into pearl. It's a protection against an irritant, a remaking of a grain of sand into an object of beauty. Seed pearls, coming into being as they do by chance and processes of nature, need a lot of work to prepare them for use in jewellery, and they are often imperfect, without the uniformity of larger cultured pearls. This imperfection pleases me, and it pleases Martha.

It was in the summer of 2005 that Martha didn't marry. It was also the summer of the London tube bombings. Amy was working as a producer for the London bureau of Tokyo Broadcasting System TV (she is fluent in Japanese) and on 7 July she spent much of the day and most of the night with a camera crew outside Edgware Road tube station, not knowing until late in the evening that Martha's close friend Laura was thought to have been on the train that had been bombed; she was, though it took days before she could be identified. Of all the people in London, that Laura should be in the same carriage as that bomber. The shock of it. And Sophie, my Sophie (who had a daughter at primary school by then), was on a bus in

front of the bus with the bomb that went off in Tavistock
Square. Why? Why Laura? Why that summer? What if it'd
been Sophie? The harsh answer is why should it not? Why
should it not be any of us? It was a tough reminder – that
we in the safe West can forget – that private life and public
history are always contingent, as Poppy had learned in the
war. Were you born in England, or in Poland? We forget
this, and it is a dangerous forgetting. Not because we
might get blown up, which we might, but because we live
in the same world as the bombers, as the angry young men
and women who strap on the explosives that will kill them
as well as us. We are part of a world – just a part, but not
apart, though we'd like to deny it – that produces their
hardened hearts, as well as those we love, who are doing
nothing more exceptional than catching the tube or the
bus on their way to work on a regular London morning.

That summer we went as a family to Italy. Jane had
found a villa near Padua, and had booked it as an after-
wedding holiday. It had changed its mood by the time
we were there, Martha with us, pale and quiet, lying in
the garden, face down, breathing into the grass. We lived
around her, one of us sitting quietly beside her, taking her
food, coaxing her to eat when she didn't want to join us.
When she did come to the table under the awning (buffalo
mozzarella, fat soft tomatoes), it was Tom she wanted
beside her; a quiet brotherly presence that didn't require
words when there were none. I knew what it was to be
brought so low that the ground is the only place for you:
the smell of grass, the sounds of the sky that you can't yet

turn to face. I knew that it was better for her to be there with us around her than to suffer it alone, but I saw my sister's sorrow watching a daughter no longer the child she could pick up and kiss better. I felt it too, and it surprised me, this fierce insistence, the instinct that says, Why her, why not us, we're older, we should take the bullet.

Three years later, when Amy's first baby was born, another English summer to welcome this first child of a new generation, the man Martha was then living with woke one morning with a blurry eye. A blurry eye, that's all, though it wasn't, and a few weeks later the eye was removed along with the melanoma growing across its retina. You couldn't write it in a novel, I thought, when the phone rang in Sydney with this news; an editor would say it was too much, too coincidental, piling all that onto the same character. But Martha is not a character and life can, and does, deliver blow after blow to the same person, even if she is a middle-class English girl who's never had a parking fine. Martha had a lot to square up to, and she did. She began her own journey in a quiet room with the woman who took the therapist's chair opposite her. And as she did, she wore the pearls that had come from her grandmother. She was barely six when Poppy died, yet she remembers her, snatches of memory, a presence that lived in her through those dark times. When she was ready, Martha strapped on her boots and came here, to Sydney, to stay with me. Back and forth, she flew, needing another view of the sky, other ground to practise her tread upon, until she came for a year, giving up her job at a tough school on the outskirts of Leeds, where for eight years, through all that grief, she'd taught drama to students, some of whom had never been outside the county, or to a theatre. *Not for the likes of us, Miss.* For Martha, Poppy's granddaughter, the challenge was not only to show them that a theatre like the West Yorkshire Playhouse was theirs to enter, but that they could *make* theatre, give voice to the drama of their own lives.

One of the books I sent to Martha was Maggie MacKellar's *When It Rains*, a memoir of two deaths that came dizzyingly close together: first her husband and then her mother. It was published exactly as Martha's relationship with the man with the melanoma ended; I sent it because it takes us deep into grief and lets us return; no misery memoir this, no easy salvation, no saving romance. (That came later.) And I sent it because I knew Maggie and I could say to Martha, Here is a young woman only a few years older than you who was also knocked to the ground, and as well as the testimony of her book, I'm here to tell you that I watched her regain her footing. It was tough, but she did it, and you will too. I had worked with Maggie on her earlier book, *Core of My Heart, My Country*, about women settlers on the frontier in Canada and Australia. I'd first met her within months of her husband's death that left her with a baby son and a small daughter. Less than two years later, when *Core of My Heart* was published in 2004, Maggie's mother was dying; at the launch she was wearing an elegant turban to conceal the effect of chemotherapy. In the midst of the chatter and clink, she and I had a brief conversation in which she asked me to look out for the side of Maggie that she always knew could write. There was a clarified quality to her, as if there was no time for the extraneous or the unnecessary. I liked her, I liked her directness, and in that short exchange before she was swept back into the crowd, I felt as if I were looking also at Poppy, or that she was looking at the part of me that carries the traces of Poppy.

Reading Maggie's first tentative drafts of *When It Rains*, watching her find the confidence to write it boldly, made me think not only of Martha, but of my younger self. Books don't *solve* grief, or erase it, but they can, and do, give shape and language to experience that at the time leaves us inchoate, literally without words. For the writer and for the reader. So of course I sent Martha that book. She read it at once, and then turned back to the first page, read it again, and when she finished it the second time, she rang me in the middle of her night when she couldn't sleep but I was awake in Sydney's daylight. The first time she flew out in a state of grief, we drove to Orange to see Maggie on the family farm where she'd moved after her mother's death. That week, as I watched these two young women walk across the paddocks, Maggie's children on their ponies ahead of them, talking, talking as they strode the dry ground, I knew that Martha would come through – as Maggie had, as I had, as Poppy had. I've watched them in the years since, as Martha's tread has firmed, and their friendship; through them, with them, I have learned the pleasure of living long enough to see the movement of change as the generations shift forward.

Where would we have been, Martha and Maggie and me, fifty years ago, or a hundred, when a stumble, a fall, could force a woman further into the margins – no room of her own, no voice to be heard – with extreme consequences. Emily Dickinson had a niece called Martha, who recalled visiting her aunt in her corner bedroom in the house at Amherst. 'She made as if to lock the door with an imaginary key, turned and said, "Matty: here's freedom."'[28]

Another piece of information that Patrick's sister Betty was reticent about was the story of their aunt, Gertie's sister Muriel, who went into an asylum in Manchester before the First World War and never came out. Presumably it was Cheadle Royal Hospital, which was then called the Manchester Royal Lunatic Asylum. I knew about this great-aunt in a vague and shadowy way from stories of Gertie taking Patrick and his sisters to Manchester when they were young, and them waiting while she visited Muriel in a tall, imposing building: a minor mention in a minor story that was about the annual train-ride there, the biscuits they ate, and playing among the trees outside. There was a sort of bleakness to these stories, Manchester. When I was in England last year, at a part-family gathering at this aunt's house, Martha and I were looking at old photos, and there in one – just one – was a square-faced girl, Muriel, standing beside the young Gertie. What happened? we asked. It was her nerves,

Betty said. Nerves? How can a young woman go into an asylum for the whole of the rest of her life from *nerves*? She'd died there, sometime in the 1950s, Betty said. What happened? Do you know? My aged aunt went vague again, another closing down, a stoic refusal she'd used all her life. Things not to be talked of.

Virginia Woolf was admitted to psychiatric hospitals several times, first in 1895, after her mother died, next in 1904, after her father died, then another three times, until she filled her pockets with stones and sank into the river rather than face it again. The 'rest cure' she was subjected to required the opposite of talk. No books, no conversation, no stimulation. Rest in the context of a rest cure meant no activity beyond careful walks: no reading, no stimulation, certainly no writing. 'You can't conceive how I want intelligent conversation,' Woolf wrote to her sister, Vanessa Bell, in 1910. 'Rest' was to be supplemented by sedative drugs – chloral, bromide, digitalis, veronal – and rich food, including half a pint of milk *every two hours*. 'I have never spent such a wretched 8 months in my life,' she wrote during an earlier incarceration. 'Really, a doctor is worse than a husband.' Her biographer Hermione Lee has 'no doubt' that the development of Woolf's political position, 'her intellectual resistance to tyranny and conventionality, derived to a great extent from her experiences as a woman patient'.[29]

Similarly, when I think of the work Poppy went on to do after Patrick left her, I have little doubt that this also came, at least in part, from her experience as a woman patient in the 1950s. A generation after Woolf, Poppy was taken to hospital in 1959, the start of a long absence from us, her children, to cure her of the 'nervous breakdown' that had reduced her to inconsolable weeping. She was treated with insulin and ECT. It did nothing to restore her, as the doctor had assured Patrick, to 'the lovely wife and mother she's always been'. The social cure failed. There was no one to whom she could talk of the confusion of feeling, the burden of being, and not being, that happy and contented wife and mother. She returned home – if home is the word for it – wounded, unhappy, with the words she hadn't been able to say, the reckoning she hadn't been able to make, pushed down into her, bowing her with age though she was still in her thirties, until something would rise up in her, a burst of words and energy, a torrent of tears, an incomprehensible language to those of us who stood back, aghast. An open-mouthed gasp. It was not until after Patrick left, when she was forty-four, that she found the psychoanalyst in a house in South London where she went several times a week, and the words could begin to be said.

When she started that move towards an unanticipated freedom, she had only fifteen years to live, not much time to turn that accumulation of sand into a pearl – but she did. In the short time left to her, she went back to study, passed her 'A' levels, and enrolled in a social work degree at Southampton University. As Patrick grew more conservative, Poppy grew more radical. He continued to read *The Times*; she read the *Guardian*. The work she

chose was as a probation officer, 'at the coalface' of the
court system, she'd say. Understanding the limitations of
a system that did little more than monitor those recently
out of jail, who slouched into her office once a week, or
month, she made her case for an alternative and took on
the authorities until she got the resources – meagre but
enough – to open one of England's first day centres for
young offenders. Most of them were men, overgrown boys
who'd had none of the education or possibilities she'd
made sure her daughters got; she knew that punishing
these young men, monitoring them, would solve nothing
if there was no reparation for the absences, the lack, the
inequalities that had brought them to jail in the first place.

She'd seen the law at work, watching her husband and
his lawyer friends who came to the house, listened to their
talk of trials and the points of law on which they turned,
congratulating each other as if in a debating contest. And
the man in the dock? she'd ask. Did he think it was such a
good point? The men would shuffle and fall silent, holding
out their plates for another serving of the dinner she had
made for them – and so did we, her watching daughters.
Fifty years after Mrs Ramsay presided at the table in *To the
Lighthouse*, serving the boeuf en daube, there was Poppy
doing the same. 'The whole effort of merging and flowing
and creating rested on her. Again she felt, as a fact without
hostility' – this is Mrs Ramsay, not Poppy – 'the sterility
of men, for if she did not do it nobody would do it, and
so giving herself a little shake that one gives a watch that
had stopped, the old familiar pulse began beating, as the

watch began ticking – one, two, three, one two three. . .'[30]
Poppy would sigh and glower. The watch had stopped,
but still she was there at the table, and afterwards at the
sink, washing up, tears on her face. Nothing was going to
get that watch ticking, and in the end Patrick knew it and
left for a wife all too happy, or so it seemed, at least for a
while, to preside at his table.

Poppy began her work with the day centre as Margaret
Thatcher came to power. She loathed Thatcher. No such
thing as Society? Does she not remember the war, the
coming through together? Where would we be if there
were no society? We'd have riots on the streets and
overflowing jails; didn't Martin Luther King say that riots
were the voice of the unheard? I wish I'd been able to tell
Poppy what Dorothy Green had said about Mrs Thatcher
wanting to be a General – she'd have liked it, but she was
dead by then. She had recognised the conservative shift as
the break it was, while my friends in London still thought
it could be resisted, that Society would prevail.

It was a strange experience researching *Poppy* in those
years after her death, catching the train from Waterloo to
Farnham, as I had the night she died, or to Guildford,
carrying a tape recorder to interview the people who'd
worked with her at the probation centres named after
her. Everyone spoke of her with respect: her vision of the
possible, her dogged persistence. 'Your mum used to put
flowers on the table,' one of her boys said, one who'd
broken the cycle of jail, had a job and his own motorbike,
licensed and everything. 'She was like that, and at first we

thought, this will be a pushover, but she weren't. Some of the lads laughed at the flowers, but you wouldn't laugh at her.' 'She changed the way we worked,' a colleague in a woolly jumper said, showing me the statistics, good enough that they'd managed to keep the funding, even with the cuts. Did I find it hard, discovering this side of my mother, this man asked me, seeing as I lived in Australia, which to him, then, meant conservative, provincial. I bet you had no idea, he said with a grin. We have a Labor government, I said, as if that was an answer that made Australia other than it was, and me along with it.

My bag filled up with tapes of interviews, my notebooks with observations and thoughts as I walked back to the station for the train to London, back to Waterloo.

Back and forth, up and down. Past and present. Maternal and paternal. Inner and outer. Society and the individual self.

Making shapes square up. For a long time I had these words – from Virginia Woolf, slightly adapted – pinned above my desk. They were there as I wrote *Poppy*, and I didn't take them down until I moved from that house on the corner. They come from Woolf's diary in 1928 when she was reflecting on the writing of *To the Lighthouse*. It was there that she had returned to the shock, the wound, of her mother's death, and it was there, in the writing of that novel, she wrote, that 'I . . . got down to my depths and made shapes square up.'

8

The house where I went for therapy was the only one of its kind on that street. Set back from the road, I always thought of it as English, or perhaps Scottish, with its steep slate roof. It would once have stood there alone, surrounded by sheep as the forests were cut; without the bungalows that stretch around it in every direction, it would have been a short ride to the Lane Cove River where the Eora still camped, what was left of them after the diseases that had arrived with the settlers. Would the inhabitants of that house have pitied them, or feared them, eyes seeing where they could not see? Or would they not even have noticed them as they waited at the river for the boat to Sydney Town? This is the past I gave the house that I drove to three times a week, parking round the corner, walking back to the house with its own shade of trees, its short driveway, gardens that had been adapted to the needs of working psychiatrists. Two of them: husband and wife. They had two daughters. Beyond that, I knew almost nothing of the thin, quiet man who opened the door to his room punctually for each session and closed it behind me. The room was at the front of the house, large, a little gloomy despite the windows, spare dark furniture and a fireplace I never saw used. I thought of him as well as the house as English, though I knew he was not. In a sense it didn't matter what he was, which is not to be disparaging, for that is what an analytic psychiatrist is trained for. Unlike the mirror of Ross, which was entirely about wanting and not having and striving to have – the looking glass of desire – here, the projections, the fractures, the desires, the angers, the griefs, the ambivalences and contradictory versions were heard by someone who could not be damaged by them. Unjudged, they were received and considered, reflected on, and not so much offered back in a new form as reconfigured in the air around us in that room. It was a strangely cerebral experience, full of feeling, yet consisting entirely of words and tears, and on the days I didn't drive there, I went to the pool and remembered I had limbs and muscles, length after length, kicking off from the wall at each end. At weekends we'd go to the beach, whoever was in the house, whoever was staying, whoever wanted to come. Waves, a towel in the sun, fish and chips on the grass. And the next week I'd drive the half-hour to the stone house and that austere room I came to like. He once put his hand on my head, just briefly, a moment of comfort when the toxoplasmosis had attacked my eyes, the retinas had bled dark swirls, and I asked, Must I give this up

too, the gift of sight? Was this, too, being asked of me?
My tears were operatic, and his hand returned me to the
room, to the now, to my still-seeing eyes. It was the only
moment of touch between an initial handshake at the
first session and the end of the last session three years
later when he held open his arms and smiled as I'd never
seen him smile, and hugged me. It was the embrace of a
father. *A* father, not *my* father.

I'd known right off that he was the analyst for me, in
the very first session, after trying two others, both women,
neither of whom came anywhere near Doris Lessing's
Mother Sugar in *The Golden Notebook*, that 'vigorous old
woman' with her 'efficient blouse and skirt, her white hair
dragged back into a hasty knot'. This time I knew, and
was consequently offended that he insisted we still had
six trial meetings. There will be times when we won't like
each other, he said. We must know that we start from a
strong base. I never didn't like him. How much I liked
him varied, as did his age, or how I registered it: over
those years he became younger, closer in age to me than
to my father. My view of him changed, and I suppose that
is an indication of how therapy changes us, and how we
view those around us. There were times when I bored
him, times when his lids became heavy, and even as I saw
them droop I'd keep talking, a torrent of words, words,
words as if to remake the world, my world, in language,
and banish uncertainty. 'This danger coming from inside,'
Louise Bourgeois wrote, 'that only this continual flow of
words could push aside.'[31] Then the words would stop,

and in their place an inchoate swelling, a field of feeling, unexpressed, raw. I once read an essay called 'A History of My Tears'; I remember nothing about it but the title, and now can't find it, but it seemed to me the perfect description of what took place in that room, the streams running under the house, streams of tears, mine and all the others who went there, each stream with its own history making its way down to the Lane Cover River to join that other, greater history of tears that lies beneath the shiny surface of this city. And all the time the house sat there, solid beneath its high, sloping roof, dry on its hill in a suburb with no whiff of river through the houses pressed around it. Whatever it was that happened there was profound. Analytic psychotherapy is rather like writing a book and can take the same kind of time. Day by day, week by week, nothing much seems to be happening – you might think you are writing one book, one sort of book, and find yourself writing another; you follow one river and find it runs dry; you turn your attention and there rises another, a damp patch of earth, and beneath it a spring. Sudden images, a rush of pleasure, or understanding, and then the days return, one after another, and your attention is turned to just this paragraph, just this session. The end is a distant prospect rarely contemplated from the daily mulch – and yet cumulatively there it is. In the case of a book there's a manuscript, piles of typed pages. Psychotherapy is not like that, obviously; there is no manuscript, not even a certificate. There is language and metaphor. There is the rest of your life.

Towards the end of Barack Obama's *Dreams from My Father*, his Kenyan half-sister Auma tells him that she sometimes has 'this dream that I will build a beautiful house on our grandfather's land. A big house where we can all stay and bring our families, you see. We could plant fruit trees like our grandfather, and our children would really know the land . . . and learn our ways from the old people. It would belong to them.'[32] And then she sighs and says she'll never build it. It doesn't matter that the young Obama says, 'We can do all that.' She knows it can't be built. This dream isn't about a house – if it were, it might be easier; it's about the father who not only provides that house, but *is* the house. It's the dream of the good father, that figure, both real and symbolic, who stands for the embodiment of memory and connection, the steady centre from which we step into the future. As it is, Auma's the one to send money when someone needs it, and to fix things when they break. 'Why do we have to take care of everyone?' she asks. 'Everything is upside-down, crazy.'

We don't need to be in Kenya, or abandoned as a child, to recognise the dream of the good father, or to ask where it's gone, or to know the cost of living in the upside-down world where, too often, there is no father.

I did have a good father. He did have a house where we could all go. He did send money when we needed it. The problem was that in hope of a new and lovely wife, he'd married a woman who had six children of her own and did not want the benefits of this saving marriage diluted by three interloping cubs. Poppy said that when Betsy's first husband left her alone with the children and not enough money to keep the electricity on, she tried out every husband in the area, including Patrick. Poppy is probably not the most reliable witness – there were stories about books thrown out of windows, clothes dumped on doorsteps – but actually this I do believe if for no other reason than that when Patrick was dying and things in the house were particularly bad, I stomped down to Betsy's daughter, who lived in the same village, and said that something had to give, it was intolerable, and maybe this daughter could get through to her. The daughter agreed that it was hard, but beyond that was not sympathetic. You have to understand, she said, that she realises she's probably too old to find another husband. Another husband! And this one not yet dead!

When Patrick left Poppy for a woman she'd thought was a friend, she was stricken with fury, an impotent vengeance that lasted a year, or maybe more, before she, too, found the room in which she could deposit the history of her tears and begin the work of finding or re-finding life. I missed most of that maternal rage, being elsewhere – Patrick waited until I'd married and left England – but not its echoes, the reverberations that arrived in letters which, with the efficiency of a colonial postal service, reached me even in a remote district of the Highlands of Papua New Guinea. In the drawer in which, after Patrick's death, we found his letters to Gertie, there was also a cache of

letters from me to him, most of them written in the house
by the airstrip at Lake Kopiago. I didn't read them until
recently. They are typed on a typewriter I recognise with
a strange pang, most of them two pages, single spaced,
written to catch the weekly plane that brought in supplies
and exchanged the bag of mail. The government station at
Lake Kopiago, I told my father, 'is in a high valley, a couple
of miles across with beautiful mountains rising up on either
side and a kidney shaped lake at the far side. We are staying
in a house built out of bush material for the princely sum
of 180 dollars by an ANU student called Lyle who is
working with some people a five day walk away called the
Hewa.' A letter from Nick catalogues the population as
'4 kiaps, 8 missionaries, 3 anthropologists, 1 land rover,
4 motorbikes, 1 tractor, 2 stereophonic tape-recorders,
3000 Duna, and an estimated 1000 Hewa (visible now and
again when not running from the police – nevertheless the
Hewa have a real sense of decency and they always insist
that Lyle wear a shirt whenever he visits them)'.

I describe patrols we took, the bush house a day's walk
from the station, where we lived for weeks at a time, and
the sound of whooping and yodelling when a travelling
geographer and his patrol came into the valley, through
the gardens and up the last hill towards us. I lamented the
parties we knew we were missing in Port Moresby when a
conference at the university brought people in from across
Australia and beyond. I described the parties of the year
before, when we'd been among people 'leaping through the
house and garden dancing to early Beatles (we're not very

up to date in Moresby)'. But for the most part I portrayed myself as content with the life of the anthropologist's wife. 'Last week dawned blue and beautiful,' I wrote in April 1970, 'and everyone immediately said, Ah, Time good. We must go over the mountains to gather wily karoka. Right, we said, we'll come too. I don't know how we managed it, but we did. It was quite an achievement and now we can look up at those mountains looming greyly above us and say we've been over the top of you.' I remember it, the hardest of the hard walks we made in those mountains, up beyond the line of agriculture and gardens, beyond the hunting grounds, to the peak of a mountain – which Nick reminded me recently was called Halepula, meaning banana skin – and over into a high, crater-like valley of moss and 'perfectly shaped' lakes. 'I arrived,' I told Patrick, 'in what I suppose would be medically termed "a state of exhaustion". We were in moss forest and I'd never seen the like of it before yet I didn't notice it at all until I woke up the next morning. We'd been walking through it for over an hour! Nick said I walked along logs and over things that normally I would have at least commented on, if not detoured. I can't remember anything about arriving at the shelter, finding it collapsed, building another, etc. I just lay on the moss with a tarp over me. I vaguely remember Nick holding me up to drink boullion and the sting of the antiseptic he put on my cuts and sores; but it all happened as if I didn't exist. Anyway I recovered with remarkable alacrity (as always, hoho!) and made the journey down without a hitch.'

Oh, for youth! It'd be good to wake again with that particular form of vigour, though beyond that carefree spirit of adventure, I meet my young self of those letters with a kind of dismay, so distant does she seem not only from the me I am now, but from the me I remember having been. After a 'dismal' week of rain, I describe a sunset we watched from the steps of the house on the government station. 'The air was warm and the lake was a shiny silver and smoke was coming from the little houses beneath us and roosters were cockadoodadooing and children singing . . . We feel a bit like God, surveying everything from our perch up here.' God, I suppose, should be taken as a metaphor. Even so, it has to be said that the colonial order is lived in the letters as the natural order of things, for all that I set us 'long haired, left wing, anti-racialist' research people against the 'conservative and mostly boring' officials of the 'system' that brought our mail and ensured our safety and sent a plane for me when I was bleeding from a miscarriage that the maternity welfare nurse at the mission could do nothing to staunch. There's a brief mention of that, which surprised me almost as much as God, the tepid Anglican version in whom I couldn't believe, even as a child. We never told our mortal father when something went seriously wrong: abortions, miscarriages, a rape, these were not for him to know. I wrote of it after I'd returned from the town of Mount Hagen – a one-hour flight away in a small plane – and said nothing of the kiap on the radio phone, or the long wait for the plane to arrive, or blood trickling down to my sandals, or the pilot finding a blanket for me to wrap myself in when we arrived in Hagen and then driving me to the hospital. Whenever we were on the station after that I'd go down to the strip to see him when he brought in the mail, which meant that some months later the kiap and I were the last people to speak to him when the clouds had massed as they can in the afternoons and he took off late for his return to Hagen, entered the wrong valley and crashed into a cliff.

In another letter, from Moresby this time, I tell Patrick a long story about driving to a beach out of town with another couple, friends, young like us. It was late afternoon, the worst of the heat over, a swim, a walk along the beach, round the headland, a rucksack with the food we'd brought to cook over a fire on the beach, a flagon of wine, a camera, our clothes, all left in the shade of a windbreak we'd built to mark out the spot. Gone, of course, on our return an hour later. What were we doing, assuming we could set up on a beach as if it were ours? Did we not know, of course we knew, there was a settlement nearby of people from the Gulf of Papua, which was way to the west; people who had only the smallest toehold of rights to camp on that land, no room for gardens, slim pickings for jobs in town, walking the road where cars, including ours, blew dust around them. And what did we do when we saw that our belongings were gone? We drove to the nearest village and found the pastor, and while three of us sat on the porch of his house, given food and water by his wife, Nick drove the pastor to the settlement, where he took the matter in hand. The food had been eaten, but the rest came back – camera, clothes, everything. And there I was congratulating us in my letter to Patrick for not calling the police, all the while saying nothing, not a whisper, of my betraying heart and the glances of the other man on that picnic, the one who was not Nick, the husband of the woman we both called a friend.

Harder to read than the absences in these letters were those in which I was also responding to the drama of Patrick and Poppy's separation, being acted out through an argument about where my youngest sister should go to school. Poppy said later she wanted Patrick to pay in school fees if nothing else. She wanted my sister to stay at her very expensive boarding school. Patrick was suggesting an arrangement at another school, or crammer, where she could do two years in one. What I didn't know until much later was that, though not yet married to Betsy, Patrick was paying the school fees of her youngest son. Would it have made a difference had I known that? In the letters I aligned myself with Patrick against Poppy – even sending love to Betsy, whom I'd known since childhood, though, in the English way, sending love does not actually mean love. My antagonism to Poppy, my lack of compassion for her position, strike me now as shocking. Was I warding off the evil possibility? Was I, as we said in the consciousness-raising groups I discovered after the demise of my own short marriage, that male-identified? Or was it simply the arrogance of a young woman in the full bloom of her sexuality who knew she had it over pretty much any male; a casual power that accepted the kindnesses of a husband and relayed them to a father without a whisper or a glimpse of her betraying heart, the subterranean move she had already begun away from marriage towards the flicker of some other kind of desire, an eddy of different air in a familiar room. I had tumbled, I suppose, into the dilemma Christina Stead gives to Teresa in *For Love Alone* when she crosses the world for love, and finds it – though not in the shape of the man in whom she expected to find it – and promptly feels the world closing around her, *life* stretching ahead with nothing but this. What if we live to be sixty-four, I'd said on our honeymoon. Poor, kind Nick. Still, and still, it was a real question. What if we did live all those years, our whole lives? Was that what we'd signed up for? I apologised to him many years later, after Patrick had died and I no longer made my weekly visits to the house above the Lane Cove River, many too many years later, as if it took all that time to square up to what I had done, what I'd brought on him, and on myself. Squaring up didn't mean the union between us would have been any more viable had I behaved better. These days it'd be a first relationship without the weight of marriage; as that it was good. And the connection that has remained through his daughter, Obelia, has been wholly good.

Kind husband, good father. Why was there a problem? Poppy said the problem was more to do with my unresolved anger with her than with the father with whom I'd aligned myself since childhood. Among the photos she gave me as we sorted through the albums in the months before she died was one of Patrick leaning on a fence and me standing on a stool beside him, my arms crossed and leaning, just as he was. Blow it up, she said, and put it on the wall. I didn't, though I still might. Poppy's family was Welsh. They were classier than the Medds, had once had money, wore stylish clothes and drank cocktails from long-stemmed glasses. Her father, my grandfather, came to rely on Patrick, this once-unwelcome son-in-law from a clever but plain family – which was not what he'd had in mind for his beautiful daughter. But when things in that family spun into disarray of one sort or another, it was to Patrick, man of letters and the law, that he turned. Rather than the quiet surface offered by the Medds – Betty once told me that when she confided in Patrick about troubles in her marriage, he told her that in these situations he found a long walk helpful – in Poppy's family there were dramas and scenes, flying bottles and midnight phone calls. I hated it, and when we went on holidays to Wales in the halcyon years before my breasts grew and Poppy went into the hospital, I am said to have declared I wanted to drain every drop of Welsh blood from my body. Yes, I was the child of the father. Clever girls often are; the daughters of educated men, we once were called.

Vanessa Bell remembers an incident when, as children, Virginia asked her to choose a parent. 'Such a question seemed to me rather terrible . . . However, being asked, one had to reply and I found I had little doubt as to my answer. "Mother," I said, and she went on to explain why she, on the whole, preferred Father.'[33] For Virginia Woolf the father was a clear line in the wash of feeling, rather like the line through Lily Briscoe's painting 'there, in the centre', and she could never decide if he was a good father or not; his rectitude, his self-obsession, his emotional distance, his ambition with its vulnerable underside of failure are all there in *To the Lighthouse* – which she had initially, and briefly, thought of calling *The Old Man*. 'Virginia wrote and rewrote her father all her life,' her biographer Hermione Lee writes. 'She was in love with him, she was furious with him, she was like him, she never stopped arguing with him, and when she finally read Freud in 1939 she recognised exactly what he meant by "ambivalence".'[34]

It shouldn't have shocked me to encounter the dark shadow of those long-ago letters siding with the paternal, order against the demanding, enveloping maternal. It shouldn't have surprised me, reading them this year for this book – because the slow uncovering of anger battened down since childhood, buried beneath the silt of grief and remorse, had been a discovery of that room in the stone house. When anger showed itself, it was with Poppy, not with Patrick. I wasn't even angry with Ross. It might have been better if I had been. I wept over him, no doubt, and railed as I hadn't even with Sophie, as if I knew that once I started I'd have to face what it meant, falling in love – if that's what it was – with a man who could not have been other than dangerous to the grief-stricken, wounded creature I was. Why is it that we choose dangerous men? Because they mesmerise us? And why do they mesmerise us at certain times, and at others not at all? Louise Bourgeois thought it has to do with fear: the greater the fear, the more we're mesmerised; like a bird with a snake, we're not afraid, we're *thrilled*; the fear is short-circuited.[35] Our attention, our whole being, is removed from whatever it is we're escaping, or avoiding – so deep down, often enough, so concealed, that we don't know that's what we're doing. It didn't take long in that room for it to become apparent that the loss of Ross, like the choice in the first place, was a screen for the greater loss of Poppy, and that behind the hard fact of her death was the wound of her leaving us for that long stay in the hospital and my exile to a cold and distant school. Beneath that was the outrage of a five-year-old at having to share her mother with small sisters. Even when I knew there was nothing I could not say in that room, no thought I could not have, the anger I could muster against men came in the form of plots for novels, revenge fantasies I'd never write: men in dark cellars, or in the bright light of public downfall, or me in a sparkling crown: ridiculous plots, I wouldn't even read them if they were on sale in the shops: another screen, another form of protection concealing the shape of the anger goddess, who showed herself not in a presence that swept into the room so I could take a good look, but in a terrifying absence. It was the mother's absence which I felt as anger – and more than the anger of men, it was her anger, and my own, I feared. I don't remember hers directed at me or my sisters, only at Patrick when she demanded that he listen and understand. *Don't you see?* she'd shout, and I'd stand with him, silenced by the raging words spilling over. She was powerful in her fury, powerful in her grief; a force I turned my back against. When the door slammed behind her, I took my book and sat beside my father.

Maybe it was necessary to let all this history flow over the listening mind of a man; maybe I chose that austere room to save a woman from an anger that all the time was an entangled form of love, the great love affair we have with our mother when we look in the mirror and see the reflection, hers and ours. Poppy said my problem with men wasn't that I was ambivalent about husbands, or not only; what I was demanding was a mother, or someone to stand in for her, a fantasy mother, a prop; a wife perhaps. If anyone behaved as if they were Greenwich Mean Time, she said, it was me. Even though it was close to the end of her life and she was very ill, I was furious. Me! Like a man! She said it was a bad analogy anyway as men might think they hold the world steady but, on the contrary, if there is steadiness, it comes from us, not from them. Their posturing and performing was a defence, she said, against the mothers they turn from in order to become men; it's them, not us, she said, who find the one they need to stand in for her, a replacement in another form.

The prettiest girl in all of England, Patrick would say, raising his glass to her, and we children would raise our shoulders and clap. He'd written poems to her, England and Poppy merged together in the small black notebook he carried with him all through the war. Was she to remain that prettiest girl? In the early photos you can see that Poppy was happy with us at her feet, and happy beside Patrick in the garden, secateurs in hand. She loved us, that wasn't in doubt; but motherhood is not the sweet dream a pretty girl might expect; the bearing of children, their dependence and their needs, gives rise to complex emotions that can be exacerbated by the gap that exists between the ideal and the reality. Yes, Poppy loved us, she was a good mother, 'good enough' in the sense of holding us safe in our early years; not perfect, that cruel impossibility, just an 'ordinary mother' in 'the ordinary loving care' of her children. She was also more than a mother, and whatever it was that she could be, she didn't know, and there was no one to help her know, when she was taken to hospital in 1959. Little wonder she had sunk into despair and depression; it's a common story, I've heard it many times of that generation of 1950s mothers which, after a whiff of freedom during the war, was returned to the home and motherhood, as Jacqueline Rose puts it, 'under the harshest obligation to be happy and fulfilled in that role'.[36] 'We'll have her home again in no time, the lovely wife and mother she's always been,' the doctor wrote of the weeping woman, just thirty-five years old, who came into what was called his care. The social cure. It'd be another decade before Poppy found her way not to a 'cure', but to the room in South London that would allow her to find a way of living and return her to the world.

How psychotherapy works, that shedding of tears, that talking cure in a room with a closed door is as mysterious to me as how a book gets written: some small accrual of understanding, maybe, an expanding of a personal repertoire, a plunge into the darkness we harbour inside ourselves. Maybe shedding the history of our tears isn't so much about rewriting, or righting, a narrative that has gone awry, *getting over* obstacles, as about changing the angle of vision, rearranging the shapes, the fragments, into other patterns. Which is why diaries can be so unreliable, and also memoirs, as a source of information about this thing that we call life; the ambivalence of the moment can appear very solid on the page. And why Victoria Glendinning's biography of Rebecca West annoyed me so, catching West out in a contradiction, everything hammered into place, as if there should be one story, one history, one attitude to something as difficult and contradictory as marriage – especially in the case of a young, bruised, talented woman left literally holding the baby. Move the pieces around, change the assumptions, and things look rather different. Like Louise Bourgeois' *Personages*, those tall, separate beings she made on the rooftop of her apartment when she was first in New York, moving them around to look at each other from different angles as she found a way to live in the city spread beneath her.

So was Poppy the vulnerable one as she railed against Patrick? Was he the powerful one when he left? Or was his turned back also born of the vulnerability that exists in the hearts of so many men, that refusal of the dark regions? We might stand beside the father, the line they draw through the wash of paint, but the brush strokes remain – for them, and for us. When it came time for Patrick to die, an erudite Catholic friend of his said that the reason it was so hard for men *who've lived in logos* to die was that death requires that we surrender. Death calls forth the feminine, he'd said, when he came downstairs and found Jane and me desolate in the kitchen. Strength and weakness; thought and feeling; public and private. Do we let the coin spin and watch only the two heads, or do we try for the solid metal in between? To live with ambivalence, to live with uncertainty, is that the challenge, and the achievement? Do we attach ourselves to one pole or the other, inner or outer, solid or fluid, or do we step into the ground between? Even the lighthouse isn't 'simply one thing' in that novel of shapes that change and vary, depending on how they are viewed, and by whom, and when. It's there on its rock, 'stark and straight' with the lighthouse keeper's washing laid out on the rocks to dry, 'hardly to be seen across the bay'; at night it's 'a yellow eye that opened suddenly and softly'. It's the line Lily Briscoe drew in the centre of her painting, and she never even went there; it was the line that gave shape not only to Lily's canvas, but to her ambivalence, her uncertainties. 'So much depends, she thought, upon distance.'[37] Writing *To the Lighthouse* was as close as Virginia Woolf came, Hermione Lee writes, to psychoanalysis. It was there, not with her doctors, or her husband, or her sister Vanessa, that she got down to the depths that had first enveloped her at the age of thirteen, when Julia Stephen died, the mother whose laugh ended in 'little drops', and who many years later would be transformed into Mrs Ramsay. Virginia Woolf was forty-four when she finished the novel, the age Lily Briscoe is at its end. After that, she said, she 'ceased to be obsessed' by her mother. 'I no longer hear her voice; I do not see her.'[38]

Poppy was forty-four when Patrick left her, and I was forty-four when *Poppy* was published in 1990. I'd like to be able to say that afterwards I, too, ceased to be obsessed, or haunted, by my mother. I had got some way down into the depths, and shapes had begun to square up. I could raise my head to the sky and see that it was bountiful; but something remained, I didn't know what, that could wake me at night and return me to that dark moment before dawn. Whatever that something was – I now can name it as buried anger, the subsoil of grief, or the paradox of an exile that started long before Australia was an idea in my mind – took me to the stone house. What I found there wasn't a cure – there is no cure – and if the shapes haven't always squared up in the years since, they have changed and moved, and when they slip back towards their old positions, I know that's what they are doing, and I need not be captive to them. There was no 'closure': the abyss didn't fill, obstacles didn't vanish, subterranean regions could still stir at night. But the dread that had risen in me with Poppy's death and the debacle of Ross abated; it was not gone, not entirely – but even a breast cancer diagnosis didn't return me there. There was dread, of course; a diagnosis of cancer, even an early, treatable cancer (as mine turned out to be), comes with a reminder of mortality. It was not a good time, but there was not that dark and terrible dread as if a summons to be executed. Isn't Freud said to have told a patient that all he could offer was a return to ordinary human unhappiness? Ordinary, human dread. Not normal; *ordinary*.

And also ordinary human happiness. That, too, yes.

Sometime during those years of therapy, between finishing *Poppy* – that act of contrition and reparation – and hearing the news that Patrick was soon to die, I was down at the beach house on the coast with friends. I woke at dawn one morning, and while the house slept I walked to the end of the beach and climbed the steep path that leads over to the next cove, beyond which we'd never ventured after that climb with Garry. I stopped on the highest point of the path, where I could see across the bay and out to sea. The sun was a low orange orb, there was no one on the beach, and I was calm, not thinking anything in particular, when there was a rush of air strong enough to make me hold onto the rock where I sat. It wasn't a wind, the trees on the headland were still, there were no white caps on the ocean; there was a tremendous sense of Poppy, as if she were swirling around me, her spirit and essence. This essence didn't speak, and I saw nothing, no ghost, no apparition. I wasn't stoned, and wasn't in an altered state of mind. Poppy was leaving me, or I was leaving her, a final farewell. I was on my own, and it was okay.

Inner or outer? That stone house, or the hours at my desk? The life of friends, those little boats sailing alongside, keeping us from capsizing, or a life of reading and writing? Or simply the passing of time? I didn't know then, and I don't know now, only that she was leaving, yes, and what remained with me was alive in that air.

9

After Patrick died, I lived for several years with a title in my head: *The Death of a Good Father*. I wrote part of a book to go with it, some of which has found its way in here; the rest has gone out with the recycling. Not because it was no good, or even for reasons of family divisions and splits, though they are a consideration, as is the inheritance we leave the next generation. The years passed and the memory of that time faded, leaving in its place a strong sense of his bewilderment rather than ours; Betsy died and my vengeful thoughts died with her. I lost the urge to add another personal story to the many being written as our generation's fathers died: Blake Morrison, Martin Amis, Graham Swift, Craig Raine: the list goes on. Grief and disappointment. Reparation and revenge. And as I read them, and the next generation of sons, the thought expressed in the title changed from 'The death of *a* good father' to 'The death of *the* good father'.

On the long flight back to Sydney after Patrick's death, I read Philip Roth's *Patrimony: A True Story*, which he wrote after the death of the irascible father, the eternal nag he'd battled with in book after book, writing him out even as he drank him in. In a scene as brilliant as any Roth has written, he finds his visiting father on the verge of tears in the bathroom. He's 'beshat' himself. Roth the son attends to him with the solicitude of a mother, and then he gets down on the floor and scrubs the shit from the cracks between the tiles. He does this without resentment, even without disgust. He does it because it is required of him as a son to a father, as one man to another, and when he puts the bag of stinking laundry in the car, he knows it is right. 'So that was the patrimony,' he writes. 'And not because cleaning it up was symbolic of something else but because it wasn't, because it was nothing more or less than the lived reality that it was.' But, of course, *the* father doesn't die just because you've cleaned up your father's shit. On the night before his father's second MRI, Roth dreams a long, complicated Rothian dream. In it, he is a child standing on a pier with a group of 'unescorted children who may or may not have been waiting to be evacuated'. They are watching for a boat. But the boat that comes is old, a stripped and disabled American warship. The waiting child, the dreamer, expects his father to be on board, among the crew, but as the boat floats towards them, he sees that it is empty, 'dead-silent . . . frightening and eerie: a ghostly hulk'. The mood of this dream, Roth writes, was 'heartbreaking' in exactly the way it had been when FDR died of a cerebral haemorrhage. Roth was twelve then, when an entire nation had been 'stunned and bereft' and

his father had taken him to stand in the crowd beside the
tracks as the train with its black bunting passed through
Newark.[39]

I didn't dream Rothian dreams after Patrick died, but
back in Sydney at the table that had moved with me from
the house on the corner to the flat on the hill behind
Bondi, when I talked of his death I'd recall the first time
I saw him cry. We were watching Churchill's funeral on TV
in the sitting room of his house by the river, and I can still
muster the sensation of shock as silent tears rolled down
his cheeks and were wiped away as they emerged beneath
his glasses. The only other time I saw him cry was the
evening I sat at the table in his kitchen while Betsy watched
Days of Our Lives in another room and I told him how
Poppy had died, how she'd asked for Janey, and soon after
she'd arrived had surprised the nurses and us by opening
her eyes with a slight turn of the head as her breathing
slowed. There was no line to mark the end of her life;
the final breath became the final breath only when long
enough had passed for there to be no other. For Patrick,
too, the end, the very end, came quietly. When I returned
to Sydney after his death, there were no tears. The tears
were done. The death was done. Ambivalence was not
banished, the story was not elaborated; it was as it was;
and ambivalence, at least in regard to Patrick – father and
mortal being both – was also as it was. Maybe analysis had
done its work. I mourned him, of course I mourned him,
but I was not undone; it did not leave a festering wound.
When I woke with a start thinking, Who will rescue me if

I end up in some foreign jail? I could recognise this late-night horror for what it was: a spectre of the protecting Father, now dead, who in his mortal form, for all his experience with English law, would not have been able to rescue me from a jail there was no reason to think I'd find myself in. I came to understand that it had been his absent presence, this ideal of the Father, that had freed me to climb those mountains into the moss forest, to cross the world and re-create myself not as the daughter nor, as it turned out, a wife, but as myself, whoever that person 'I' was who emerged through the tries, the stories, the testing. Of course those letters to Patrick were veiled; what else could they be? I was performing for him as I was for myself, as if auditioning for a play, testing a role that might be mine, or for which I could – and did – prove only an understudy. I couldn't perform for Poppy, but for Patrick I was another *storymasta*, which was what the Duna of New Guinea called us long-haired ones who were neither church nor government. *Storymasta*, psychoanalyst, anthropologist, writer.

I did write an essay called 'The Death of the Good Father', but not until many years later, prompted into it by reading a 2008 collection of essays and stories from *Granta* called, simply, *Fathers*.[40] Many of the contributors were young enough to have fathers my age, or not much older; not all of them were bad fathers, but many were: drunk, self-regarding, irresponsible, sometimes outright criminal; at best inconsistent and inadequate. Nor were all the writer-children angry, but many were; not all the angry children were sons, but again many were. And with good reason. Since then there's been *Breaking Bad* and if ever there was an ambivalent portrayal of a twenty-first-century father, it'd have to be Walter White. Good father or bad? How come it's even a question? The categories collapse around this anti-hero father, and I can't be the only one who, despite it all, longed for Walter's son to turn back towards him before the inevitable end. Is it only a case of clever filmmaking, of narrative control? Or does it (also) touch some desire in us? What's going on in our crazy upside-down world?

'What is it that we've done to make so many children's hearts so hard,' Obama asks in *Dreams from My Father* when he returns from Kenya to Chicago's 'decaying' South Side, 'and what collectively might we do to right their moral compass?'[41]

A little over a century ago, in 1907, when Edmund Gosse published *Father and Son*, his friend Henry James felt its 'audacity' had gone too far; 'not too far, I mean, for truth, but too far for filiality, or at least for tenderness'.[42] To read it now, audacity, or lack of filiality, is as nothing compared to the angry twenty-first-century sons. As to tenderness, there is a painful twist of love – if that counts as tenderness – to the story of Gosse's ruin of a father. Edmund was eight years old in 1857, the year Philip Gosse, his devout, scientist father, was crushed by the humiliating response to the book he'd laboured over for many years. As a bible-reading Christian and also a respected (until then) naturalist, he had made it his task to reconcile two irreconcilable rivers of thought: the theory of evolution – the evidence for which, as a scientist, he couldn't ignore – and the creation of the world in six days – which he understood, literally, as six days each of exactly twenty-four hours. He called this book, the great work of his life, *Omphalos*, the word for navel or belly button in ancient Greek – chosen for its symbol of the dilemma. Adam had no need of a navel, being born of God not woman, and yet he surely had one. Why? To give him the appearance of a human past. Fossils were part of God's creation; like everything else, they came into being during those six momentous days. Why? So that the world, too, would appear to have a deep history. Certain that 'he alone possessed the secret of the enigma', he offered Omphalos, his son wrote, 'with a glowing gesture, to atheists and Christians alike'.[43]

Instead of accolades, Gosse was lambasted by both scientists and Christians, lampooned and humiliated. God the liar! God the trickster! Planting fossils to test man's faith! Even his friend Charles Kingsley, from whom he'd been sure of support, wrote to him saying it was the first book that had made him doubt, and he feared many others would doubt with him. 'Shall I tell you the truth?' Kingsley began. 'It is best.' For Philip Gosse, truth was the bitterest blow; he left London that year, 'closing the door upon himself', and his colleagues at the Royal Society. Recently widowed, he took his young son to live on the cliffs above the sea in a remote part of Devon. It's quite a story, and the son's account, *Father and Son*, is said to have ushered in the modern memoir, published at that turning point – Virginia Woolf put it at 1910 – between the Victorian age and 'modern life'. It is the portrait of the fallen Father, a 'noble' figure of the past whose 'soul was on its knees'. Certain that his terrible failure was the result of having displeased God, the father was determined to save the son from a similar fate; he remained solicitous, a word that is frequently used of a good father and that too often merges with censorious. Like Walter White destroying his family in the process of saving it, Gosse the father, thinking to protect his son from the wrath of God, precipitated the bitter break between them. Edmund closed the door on his father's house and left for 'modern life' in London.

'God the father, land of our fathers, forefathers, founding fathers,' Siri Hustvedt writes in an essay on her father, 'all refer to an origin or source, to what generated us, to an authority. We fall into the paternal line. Patronymic as identity.'[44] How do any of us, she asks, find our own shape in the shadow of the father? She was born in 1955, midway, more or less, between *Father and Son* and the *Granta* anthology in which her definitely-not-angry essay first appeared. Her father was much like mine: kind, attentive, reticent. Why are fathers so hard to talk to? she asks. Her dance between steering her own course and wanting the approval of her father, between resisting and complying, is a story I recognise, the story of our generation of clever, post-war, educated daughters; she had a breakthrough of tears, as I had, right at the end, in her case when she showed her father the manuscript of her novel *The Sorrows of Men*. No, Siri Hustvedt is not angry: maybe such fathers were 'good enough' for daughters like us; maybe it is the way of daughters to protect rather than confront the fathers whose wounded nature they know; at least for daughters of our era, or some of us. I don't know, but I knew I had nothing to add – she'd said it; and so had Sharon Olds in her poem sequence *The Father*, an almost perfect rendition of the turning that comes when the daughters who have revolved around the father, the sun to their lives, sit beside the dying man.

> Maybe his terror is not of dying,
> or even of death, but of some cry
> he has kept inside him all his life.[45]

Our fathers kept the cry in. The fathers the men of our generation became let the cry out. Was it better, or worse? And when the fathers departed their posts, and Fathers too, often enough, or never even knew there was a post, what then? It's the trajectory I'm interested in. A friend of mine became pregnant just as she turned forty; it was a surprise both to her and the man with whom she was in a relationship she thought good enough for the raising of a child. He was thrilled at the prospect of being a father, but not, as it turned out, by the reality of a dependent child and a mother who worked. The child was barely two when he left the house, and not much more than three when he left the country. No more pick-ups from preschool, no more baths and stories while the mother, my friend, worked late. His inner child, this man said, couldn't handle a real child; the choice, he explained, had to be for his own growth and a time of travel – was that so hard to understand? Truly. It's a good thing there are gun laws, or there could be a lot of dead men on our streets. This is not an isolated story; extreme, I admit, but wind it back a bit, substitute a reason less laughable, and who cannot bring up examples?

I was in a bookshop not so long ago, and there on the table of new fiction was Dave Eggers' *Your Fathers, Where Are They? And the Prophets, Do They Live Forever?* What a title; I saw it almost before I was through the door. I bought it, of course, drove home, made a pot of tea and started reading. If I were ten or fifteen years younger I'd have read all night, but I'm not and an hour after midnight I turned out the light. Written entirely in dialogue, which is impressive enough, Dave Eggers answers the question I've pondered off and on this last decade or more – longer really, right back to Poppy's work with her boys. What happens when the fathers are missing, the actual fathers, and the Fathers? What becomes of the sons? Well, Eggers tells us. Thomas, a fatherless boy-man, takes six hostages over six days and shackles them to posts, each in a separate building on a disused military base. Crime? Yes. Crime novel? No. The helicopters come, inevitably, and there's no mistaking what Thomas's fate will be when the book closes with the SWAT teams outside the door. This is not a story of clue and chase, that satisfactory tale of order restored. It is the social cure in savage form. Thomas is killed and nothing is solved. It is the story of why a young man, who thinks of himself as moral and has no intention of hurting his hostages (despite the shackles), wants answers to the question: what's happened? What's gone wrong? You follow the rules and the rules change; or there are no rules, and no one to explain them. You want a reason to live, a mission, something to bring you meaning, or praise, and there is just the blank tedium of nothing. You want something grand, a big proper war, and instead there's only the small everyday war against the fate of being discarded. 'There are millions like me,' Thomas says to the hostage congressman – a Vietnam vet with both legs blown off in a stupid accident, not even in combat. He's the Father of the story, shackled and legless. 'This'll keep happening,' Thomas, discarded and superfluous, tells him. 'If you don't have something grand for men like us to be part of, we will take all the little things. Neighbourhood by neighbourhood. Building by building. Family by family.'[46] A twisted logic, true, but should we not listen? Angry sons like Thomas can do a lot of damage.

When we asked Poppy why she was working with men, why she was putting so much of her time and herself into 'her boys', who were often angry, she'd say, Because it matters, because men are the problem. The petty cash would go, tables would be overturned, some of them resenting having to be at the centre all day when they used only to have to show up for an appointment once a week. But most came, most stayed, and reoffending rates dropped. When she was first diagnosed with the cancer that killed her, some of her 'boys' from the day centre turned up at the hospital with limp flowers picked over fences from gardens, a fitting gift for the dying woman for whom their eyes turned red as they sat beside her bed.

Back in the 1990s, when the conversation at my Bondi flat turned to the problem of men, it was not always to our lovers, or lack of them, but to the social problem that was becoming apparent around us: rudderless young men who drove in from the western suburbs and smashed the windscreens of cars parked along the beach, or near the Opera House – random revenge against those of us who were eating in the brasseries above the beach, or sitting in the audience of plays and concerts, the satisfied classes, who inhabit the beautiful part of a city that is a lot less beautiful as you move west, away from its harbour. One evening an anthropologist friend said that if she were to generalise, which anthropologists are reluctant to do, she'd say that in any society you look at, going back in time, anywhere in the world, chances are you'll find that attention was given to the problem of how to turn boys into men – until, that is, our industrial, post-industrial world, in which we don't articulate it as a problem at all. We are shocked when there are riots and disaffected young men travel to war zones in search of a cause; we toughen sentences and build more jails as if that will solve the problem. Girls, my friend said, speaking anthropologically, become women through menstruation and childbirth. But boys, what marks their transition to men? And if they do not become men, if they do not take their role in the group, the tribe, the village, the town, the consequences can be severe for everyone. Men are necessary; they can also be dangerous. So, to continue the generalisation, societies find ways of marking – easing? forcing? – the transition: initiations, quests, wars, sacrifices; the methods are many – some brutal, some less so – but always emphatic.

When I returned to Papua New Guinea a decade or so ago, it was to visit the barkcloth painters of Ömie, high on the mountain the maps call Mount Lamington. The initiations had stopped after the Second World War, but we heard the stories, still told, of underground 'nests' built for the initiation of their not-yet-men boys, caves dug into the mountain. The boys would live there for a year or more, with the senior men camped on the ground above them. They'd learn the history and traditions and knowledge of the tribe handed down from the ancestors; they'd endure the rigours of this long separation from the life of the village and the company of women; they'd learn the skills they'd need as men, and prepare their bodies for the tattooing that would mark them as men. The word for this initiation is *ujave*, meaning egg, and when the elders considered the boys fit to return to the village as men, the smallest boy-man, wearing a headdress shaped like a beak, would sit on the shoulder of the tallest boy-man and peck though the woven leaves that made a roof for their nest. Boys hatched as men, tattooed and resplendent in their feather headdresses, returned to the village, welcomed as ready to marry and to fight. In 2004 we were shown a deep, dank hole far in the bush, an old nest where once the *ujave* had taken place. One of the old men looked doleful. Time before, he said, as we looked down; it was lined with leaves and grasses. It was comfortable, he said, not like this. A long time ago, the young guide said. No more.

The bookshop where I bought Dave Eggers' novel is in Newtown, not far from the house on the corner where I used to live. It's a suburb where you see fathers with babies strapped to their bodies, or pushing children in strollers. You see men in the supermarket comparing brands, or sitting in the cafés with a book, or with a friend and his child. Is this the other side of the coin? The new-style, new-age, good-father homemakers? What hatched them? Also in the bookshop, alongside the novels and memoirs of hopeless or absent fathers, were piles of the latest volume of Karl Ove Knausgaard's vast memoir-novel *My Struggle*. I was in London when the first volume came out in English in 2012, and like everyone else I was swept along by the energy of his prose, the audacity of the pages of details that held my interest even when they bored me, which they often did, the point being that most of daily life is boring, but still worthy of our attention. It was summer and I'd sit in the square near where I was staying and read under the chestnut trees, or lie on my bed with the windows wide open. One evening with friends, the talk turned to Knausgaard. Was he a genius or a narcissist? Both, or neither? In the first volume, *A Death in the Family*, he gives us in excoriating detail what it was to have been the son of an inadequate father, growing up with little guidance, and then to watch him die an alcohol-sodden death. Early in the book there are pages about the first time a girl, Suzanne was her name, lets him see as well as touch her breasts, and then the soft hair beneath her pants. He was fourteen years old, and he transports you there, to the girl's bedroom where they are lying on the bed while her parents are out. And he takes us into the mind and body of a boy mesmerised by the astonishment of it, until he ejaculates, though he doesn't realise it, a pain in the groin he thinks might be the death of him, and the breasts, so recently all his world consisted of, become as nothing, just skin and nipple; and afterwards, the confusion and the shame, and no one he could ask whether what had happened was normal or some terrible pathology. To a woman, though maybe not to a male reader, it is a revelation, not boring at all, even as the pages go on and on.

In the next volume, *A Man in Love*, Knausgaard takes us through 528 pages of how such a son becomes not only a father, but the house-husband-father who does the childcare while his wife works. Early in this volume, there are pages on the humiliation of taking a toddler to a rhythm-time class, the only man, lusting after the woman playing the guitar and putting on the awful tapes for the children to bounce to – another electrifying scene of the cross-currents of desire and shame. There is page after page of domestic tedium, the scraps and irritations of a marriage, the moments of connection that seem few in comparison. He's tough on himself, true, but he's tough on his wife, very, when she falls short, which of course she does, how could she not? And all the while the question is simmering of how he's ever going to get to his desk with all this going on, the difficulty that has for so long been the fate of the woman as writer, getting up at four in the morning – that 'still dark hour before the baby's cry', Sylvia Plath called it. And here is Knausgaard giving us hundreds of pages on the frustrations of not getting to the books he would be writing if he weren't in the supermarket aisle with a stroller! I read it in another hungry gulp, and all the time with a growing unease. *Min Kamp*, the series is called in Norwegian, a title that takes it much closer to *Mein Kampf* than the anodyne English title, *My Struggle*. The publisher was against the title, but Knausgaard prevailed, certain it captured 'the intensity of his personal and artistic endeavour'. Okay, we all struggle, and I suppose a man should be applauded for taking on the domestic, though there's something galling about a man becoming an *international sensation* for writing the fine detail of family life and its constraints on his writing. Reverse the genders and it's not exactly new; I'll spare you the list of the bad reviews, going back for more than a century, suffered by women for doing just that. Lily Briscoe had good reason to fear the reaction of men if she let her feminist views become known; Virginia Woolf removed the word from the final draft of *To the Lighthouse*.[47] Knausgaard is not taken to task for being too personal, or complaining, or kicking against his nature; he's called the Norwegian Proust. Well. In interviews he's said that he wrote *My Struggle* as a way out of a writer's block. Sickened by the surfeit of fiction, all those DVD box sets, he turned to his own life for a subject as an antidote to the hard work and poor results of his own labours with fiction. 'My writing became more and more minimalist,' he told the *Observer*. 'In the end I didn't write at all. But then I had a revelation. What if I did the opposite?' After years of paring everything down, he reversed his method to see what would happen if he put in more; more and more. And here we have it: *My Struggle* over six volumes and many thousands of words.

The editor of the *Paris Review*, Lorin Stein, has said that by creating a narrator 'who is a real person and is in charge of the story', Knausgaard has 'solved a big problem of the contemporary novel'. Has memoir pushed all the way through its formal constraints to rival fiction? Write autobiography, Virginia Woolf asked, and call it fiction? No, for her that was not the way; but the lines were clearer then, the rules, and maybe also the ethics. Read as a novel, the portrayal of Knausgaard's wife, his children, his father, his mother-in-law, have the freedom of characters. But what if we know that they are not? Feminists have criticised Knausgaard's portrayal of people, particularly his wife and ex-wife, who are not only alive – you can google them – but living their own struggle, which, from their perspective, doubtless makes his look rather different. His birth family no longer speaks to him, which is not surprising given that one in ten of his countrymen have bought his books – only slightly more than the proportion of Australians who bought *Fifty Shades of Grey* at its crazy heights. And spare a thought for Suzanne, who came from the town where tourists now go on Knausgaard tours. And what about his children?

'It's my nightmare,' he said in an interview with the *Guardian* in London, 'and one day I expect it will come true. I have documented their parents' inner life and that could be problematic for my daughters and my son when they become teenagers. Maybe I shouldn't have written about us but I felt I had to. I just hope there's more to us than this.' When it came to writing *My Struggle*, he said in another interview, 'I was kind of autistic.'[48]

What is the pact of love? Of family? Of friendship? Bad luck if there's a writer in the mix. Many of us do it, and I'm in no position to speak; here I am doing it right now. 'Don't write about this,' Helen and I used to say in mid-story over the table at the house on the corner. We'd laugh, make a joke of it, and meet each other's eye; we were serious. Sometimes a detail or moment would make it onto the page, more or less disguised, and years later I breached a line that wasn't articulated, but I knew was there, and she was angry, hurt, and it was some time before we were at ease again, our boats nudging up to each other once more. And when I've found myself on someone else's page, I've felt the stab of betrayal, no matter how well I was disguised, even if I shouldn't, given

what I've done myself. In such matters we are nothing
if not contradictory and inconsistent. As the years have
gone by and I've got older, with each passing year valuing
family and friends, that ground of my life, I look back on
this younger self unsurprised at the upsets, the fallings
out, the repair work I had to do. Friendship does not
rest on a *pact* of intimacy; its spontaneity, its depth, its
radiance depends on the unspoken as much as the agreed.
We should not have to say: don't write about it, as Helen
and I did – and as two writer-characters do in a David
Lodge novel before they get into bed at a conference.

When I wrote *Poppy*, I could – and did – look back
to *The Golden Notebook*, in which Doris Lessing broke
through the 'dilemma' and 'unease' a woman felt about
writing of 'petty personal problems', by which, of course,
was meant the petty personal problems that women have.
She came 'to recognise that nothing is personal in the sense
that it is uniquely your own'.[49] *The personal is political* was
the slogan when we were young, us next-wave feminists,
picking up our pens in the rooms of our own. I was in an
honourable tradition, I thought, and I was on the other
side of the world. I didn't forsee the consequences when
I pressed ahead at my desk in this antipodean country
where so many English had reinvented themselves. Not
a reinvention exactly in my case, more a reimagination, a
line of engagement with a private history, a zone of play,
and I stepped right into it. I didn't think about how *Poppy*
would be read by the family in England; but news travels
and so did books, even in the days before the internet. My

mother's father's third wife, Elky, took me to task. I liked
her and always visited when I was England. If you don't
know what you're talking about, she said, you should
keep quiet. She'd loved my Tory grandfather and knew
he was not the stock character old-style blimp of a father
I'd drawn. She was right; I hadn't thought to talk to her
about him before I wrote the book. Did I think she'd
congratulate me now? I tried to explain: Doris Lessing,
the history of the memoir, the importance of making the
personal political, and so forth.

'He was a literary device,' I said.

'Then write a novel,' she said.

'Well, it is a novel, sort of,' I said. 'I changed the
names.'

'That doesn't mean anything.'

'Well, it protects you.'

'No, it doesn't, not from the people who know who
you are, and who knew your grandfather. They know well
enough. The name isn't even a fig leaf.'

'I say in the acknowledgements that nothing should
be taken literally.'

She wasn't having it. 'He used to stand up for you
when Patrick scolded you for the stories you told. You
were a good storyteller, he'd say, you probably got it from
him, like Katie.' By Katie she meant Katie Mitchell, my
cousin. She was a toddler when I left England so I barely
know her, but I see her occasionally and follow her work
as a theatre director, and among the many plays of hers
I've seen was her excellent adaptation of *The Waves* at

the National Theatre. Martha and I went together, and afterwards when we walked along the river to a small bar behind Waterloo, we were whooping with pleasure. Martha did a little jig looking across the river towards the Embankment and the Temple where Patrick, her grandfather, had worked. Katie, being on Poppy's side of the family, certainly didn't get whatever it was that produced that version of *The Waves* from the Medds. They were very earnest, Elky said. But your grandfather could get Patrick laughing. They were marvellous, his stories.

I don't remember my grandfather's stories, only the scolds, and Poppy's word for mine: embroidery. Write memoir and call it fiction? Or write fiction and call it memoir? With Knausgaard, have the two become one? And if they have, does it matter? And if it matters, to whom? To us? To his readers? To his family? It's a story people want to read, so maybe I have my nose too tight against the windowpane of history to see clearly. What is the bigger story? Can there be a bigger story when nothing happens outside the confines of his own thoughts? For all its fascination, *My Struggle* is the personal stripped of the political. There's a narcissism at the heart of this indeed somewhat autistic, page-turning memoir that puts him at the centre of the entire six volumes, and keeps him there for three thousand pages.

Is this the memoir for a neo-con age?

Karl Ove Knausgaard and Walter White; are these the fathers of the neo-con age?

When, in *Dreams from My Father*, Barack Obama asks his grandmother if she has anything left from his father or his grandfather, she gives him 'a rust colored book the size of a passport, along with a few papers of different colors, stapled together and chewed at an angle along one side'. The 'rust colored book' was his grandfather's domestic servant's pocket register. The stack of letters were from his father, addressed to American universities asking for application forms and information regarding scholarships. 'This was it,' Obama thought to himself. 'My inheritance.' He was at the rural compound where his grandmother still lived, on the plot of land where both his grandfather and father are buried under the same 'pile of rocks'. Obama weeps there, alone in the dark. Having pieced together their stories, he contemplates the inheritance of fear as each successive generation sets out into a world unknown to the last. He imagines his way into the confusion of both men as his father left the place that gave him life, yet must have seemed obsolete when the offer from Hawaii arrived. There's no shame, he muses, 'in the fear, or in the fear of his father before him. There was no shame in the silence fear had produced. It was the silence that betrayed us. If it weren't for that silence, your grandfather might have told your father that he could never escape himself, or re-create himself alone. Your father might have taught those same lessons to you. And you, the son, might have taught your father that this new world that was beckoning all of you involved more than just railroads and indoor toilets.'[50] And the paragraph segues into the ruminations of the man

who will become the American president, the political
being who knows how to weave complex cloth from the
threads of the personal. Which might be why there was
such hope across the world when he was elected, and such
disappointment now.

I was in Papua New Guinea in November 2008, the
month of Obama's election. When I arrived at the village
in the fjords of Cape Nelson, where I had been going for
several years and still go now, there was a larger than usual
crowd waiting to greet the dinghy. They were calling out,
I thought, for me, a ripple of pride at receiving such a
welcome – but no, it was *Obama! Obama!* they were
calling. Had I brought *Time* magazine, they asked, as I
usually did – the only time I buy it – and fortunately
I had, several copies. Though I was indeed welcomed, it
was Obama they wanted to know about and talk about.
He is president for us, for us here in PNG, one of the
elders said, as the old women clucked over the photos of
Michelle and the children. I had *Dreams from My Father*
for the school teacher, who read from it to the men of the
village over the coming evenings. I felt rather the same,
the sweep of hope that was surely more than political,
an impossible projection, a magnifying glass beyond all
others. He offered us the hope, the glimmer of possibility,
a new form of authority, a moral compass to serve our
crazy, upside-down lives. He was the one who said to us,
Yes, maybe there is a way we can move forward together,
find a new form of authority. 'The new president . . .
doesn't just speak for his people,' Zadie Smith said at

the New York Public Library in December that year. 'He can speak them. It is a disorienting talent in a president, we're so unused to it.'[51] How could he not disappoint? What does it say about our world that in his memoir he could see so clearly the role of 'men', of 'governments', of 'western ideology' and interests on the poverty and inequality he knew from Chicago and from Kenya, and yet in power he could do so little to counter exactly those forces, their 'messy histories'? Now when I go to the village there is no mention of him. The loggers are still nearby in Collingwood Bay, the government is still corrupt, high-school education is still beyond the reach of their children. .

A Dangerous Road

10

On the morning of 1 March 2004, I was on a plane from Brisbane to Port Moresby. A window seat on the right-hand side as we flew north over the reef and ocean – turquoise, green, blue on blue – New Guinea coming into view, a shape against the skyline slowly revealing its mountains. The plane turned left, as it had all those years ago, and tracked along the coast towards Moresby. There it was, the dream landscape, known and also not. Were the mountains steeper? More jagged? Or was the angle of the sun lighting the ridges? Cliffs dropping into the water, small curving bays, tracks and villages, rusty tin roofs under the palms, occasional water tanks. The plane turned again, coming down to the runway in a valley with round hills. Yes, the hills of memory, and behind them the mountains.

Green. In memory it is burned dry, earth colours, a landscape of heat.

'Green,' I said to David in the seat beside me. 'I don't remember it *green*.'

'It's the end of the wet,' David said.

Ah. A memory from thirty years ago, the sudden thump of rain, the crash of it on the tin roof, and afterwards the ditches beside the roads running with water. But green? No, no memory of green. Steamy heat, yes, the air, the edge of lime and sweat and smoke, tattooed faces, tall hair, babies on hips, the crowded street outside the terminal.

Yes, we were there.

I was travelling with two Australian men I barely knew. The one who'd invited me was David Baker, an imposing man with a moustache from another century. He was the then director of the no-longer-existing New Guinea Gallery in Sydney's Surry Hills. He'd made his money in advertising; he'd been a co-founder of the company Schofield Sherbon Baker, which had among its credits the 'It's Time' campaign that had swept Whitlam into power. I was newly arrived in Australia in 1972, and it was only later, in retrospect, that I understood the roars from the election party at the ANU college where I was living, a bystander out of place in a college where most of the students were fresh from school, while I, alone, was fresh from marriage and four years in Papua New Guinea.

Thirty-one years later, sometime towards the end of 2003, I had a phone call from Murray. Do you still want to go back to PNG? he asked. *Want*, I said. I *must*. I had a research grant to write about that place, that time leading into Independence; I'd been in the libraries, I'd spoken to people who'd been there then; I'd been lent manuscripts, diaries, copies of the student newspaper; the room where I worked had become my own small research library. It told me a lot, but it didn't take me back. I'd met Papua New Guinean writers and historians in Sydney for their research, and occasionally seen old friends from the university when they were down on government or diplomatic business. I was well ready to return. But how? And to do what, exactly? Did I need to go? I was asked – a form of concern from people who knew of PNG only through bad stories in the press. I wasn't fool enough to think there were no dangers, but for me it was a point of principle. Hadn't R. H. Tawney said that a historian – and by extension a writer like me – needs strong boots? That was a more empirical age, and though the idea of walking in the footsteps fell from fashion in the theorised 1980s and 1990s, I hold to it still, even as I concede that the boots we wear and the roads we must walk can be of the imagination as much as, possibly even more than, of tarmac and mud. It's not as if I thought there was some sort of unvarnished reality waiting to be seen, I wasn't that naïve – the fresh flower plucked from the vase of artificial; these days is it not more likely that the artificial is taken for the real? Even so, not going back to PNG was emphatically not an option.

But how to go, and with whom, and where? The bad stories were all too real: car-jackings, hold-ups, rapes; guns and *raskol* gangs. I met a woman whose biologist husband had been killed at a roadblock; she'd been a young woman at the time, a new wife. She went back some years later to do postgraduate research in criminology. She found her

way into the gang that had killed her husband, and lived
with them in the settlements of Port Moresby; she adopted
a child orphaned in another killing. He was about eight
when I met him, with her, here in Sydney. And nothing
happened? I asked. No rape, no violence? She shook
her head. How did you manage that? She stared them
down, she said. Melanesian men, like men everywhere,
can turn nasty when alienated and angry. True, she had
a protector, but there's a softness too, she said, especially
in those who were raised in a village; an empathy remains
somewhere, underneath. She found it. The danger will
become greater, she said, when the anger and the poverty
becomes entrenched, generation by generation, with no
subsoil of the village.

I met this woman and heard her story long after
Murray rang to say his friend David Baker was looking
for someone to go up with him to see some barkcloth art,
and maybe write about it. Even if I had met her, I'd have
said yes. A reason to go, and with someone who'd been
many times; a large, confident man at that. It's a tough
walk, Murray warned. They're on the top of a mountain.
Was I up to it? Me? Of course I was up to it!

Murray didn't know much about the barkcloth, he
hadn't seen it himself. He'd had a coffee with David, who
told him how he'd made the long walk up to Ömie on
the invitation of a man he'd met, purely by chance, in a
town on the plain beneath their mountain. Having time to
spare, David went out of curiosity, and was astonished to
see the cloth still being made, and used, and painted, when

so much of this ancient art form had been lost – or had become a debased item for sale to tourists. Yet there it was, hanging from the walls, still in use as a textile, and painted with the colours of the forest. As far as David knew from his researches there was none from these people in museums anywhere, nor in colonial collections where other examples of barkcloth art are plentiful – though few as exceptional as this. Does he want it for his gallery? I asked. A moment of caution. There are bad stories of collectors taking art from villagers who have no notion of its value. No, Murray said, he thinks it should be in major galleries and museums; that's what he wants to achieve. He's not doing this for his own gallery, he's an honourable man. Then he told me how David had run the company, his reputation as a man who didn't rip off employees, didn't dodge taxes – He plays with a straight bat, Murray said – and when he didn't like the way the corporate world was going he got out, put on his boots and went to PNG.

So there I was, on the plane that March morning in 2004 with David and an old friend of his, Grahame, who was coming to film the trip. We'd seen some of the barkcloth at David's house in Sydney, and photos he'd taken in the villages at Ömie. I have no expertise when it comes to Oceanic art, I'd warned David; if that was what he wanted, I was not the one. But if it was a journalistic task, if it was a matter of writing about what happened and what we saw, I could do that. And I liked David, as far as I could tell on a few short meetings; there was a humour to him that softened the largeness and the confidence of a man with a moustache such as I hadn't seen since childhood, and then only on the faces of great-uncles and strange, ancient men.

We landed that afternoon in a barely recognisable Port Moresby. The colonial town I remembered had no tall buildings, and the map of the town was marked then by how far you were from the old colonial centre on one of its few well-defined roads: four mile, six mile, nine mile; now there's a sixteen mile, and the suburbs and settlements stretch a good deal further than that. The dirt road (not much more then a track) that once ran into the valley where the university was built – which I could have described tree by tree – had vanished under a maze of roads, new suburbs, government buildings. The roads were potholed, the roundabouts and intersections a confusion of trucks, people hanging on the back, horns blaring. Markets with men in bright t-shirts calling out, young women shading their babies with umbrellas in the colours of the PNG flag; old women sitting cross-legged along the road with betel nuts and mustard pods laid out on a mat, bilums hung on the fence for sale; highland gardens dug in straight lines down hills that once were bare, precarious-looking mounds of sweet-potato vines. All of it, so green.

Two days of memory, a strange overlay: the shape of the harbour, the memory of flame trees, a freeway cutting through the suburb where once our friends had lived. Gone.

Two days of supplies: medicines over the counter at the pharmacy – there'd be sores and ulcers in the village,

I remembered them from before, and everyone coughing; lamps, blankets, kettles, a tarpaulin; a long diversion for a back-up battery for Grahame's camera.

Two days in Port Moresby, and two evenings of long-ago friends, and new ones, David's and mine, writers from the university, whom I'd read but not met. On the first night it was beer and fish and chips in the hotel bar. I was on a high, and I don't drink beer. On the second, a dinner at a house on Paga Hill overlooking water and reef, the road winding up, fragrant vines hanging over the wire-mesh fences, a guard-post at every gate. Our hosts were Roslyn and Mekere Morauta, she an Australian whose freckly skin had accommodated the sun, he a senior and respected politician, once Prime Minister and then, in 2004, the Leader of the Opposition. Among the guests at the long table overlooking the water, was a man whom I'd once sat next to in history classes, still as charming as ever he was, now Foreign Minister, and a Sir, like our host. Again the strange workings of memory, the young figure of memory there in the face, in the eyes of this portly man. Memory fading, reorganising itself, catching up, the overlay that lets us be all those things at once; not like a town, where one thing replaces another, at first a breach, a shock, until you realise that maybe that long-ago town does exist still, a palimpsest, an underlay with the new buildings growing tall around it, its roads multiplying, but still, somewhere, itself. That was what I wanted to see, and in the faces around me that is what I saw. I was drunk with the pleasure of it, for all that the conversation would drift away from us visitors back to the politics of a place I hardly knew any more.

The next day took us in a small plane north over the mountains to Popondetta, an exercise in Second World War history, flying over the Kokoda Track, more or less, not that it can be seen through the canopy of rainforest; half an hour in the air over mountains that would take days to traverse by foot – strong boots the least of it – until the land eases, undulating towards the coast where the Japanese landed. Maybe they are our friends, a Yorkshire-born missionary had said when he saw the warships that had made their way through the reefs. He was mending a deckchair he used on the local outriggers that took him from village to village.[52] I often think of this when the coast comes into view and the plane lands, as it did that day, on a long military strip, a remnant from the war, like the machinery rusting in tall grass and encroaching wild sugar cane. More green, but this time a lush, extravagant, tropical world, not the savannah around Port Moresby.

From the runway we could see Mount Lamington, where we were heading, its great bulk clear against the sky with only the highest peaks gathering cloud around them. I looked at David. Up there? He put his hand on my shoulder. Up there, he said. When we get there you'll be pleased. If I get there, I thought, but did not say.

The town of Popondetta is built around a flat grid of streets with utilitarian buildings, corrugated-iron trade stores, warehouses with high counters where you hand your money through metal bars, men with guns standing guard as you look through to the cavernous interior stacked with boxes of biscuits, bully beef, dried milk, tins of cocoa, axes, blankets, candles, kerosene. On the streets a dull surliness, piles of rubbish, betel-nut sellers, eyes averted, cigarettes for sale laid out singly. Groups of people loaded with bags of rice waited under wide trees for the trucks that serve as buses, PMVs they're called.[53] More supplies. I stood back as David negotiated, notebook in my pocket, wary. Then to the police station – I wasn't expecting that – a demoralised two-storey building where we were met in the scuffed yard by a senior officer. He shook David's hand enthusiastically, asked when we'd be back and assigned Thompson, a reservist, to accompany us to Ömie. Was it really necessary? Or a kind of leftover colonial gesture? Either way, something about it made me uneasy. I could see the prisoners in a wire enclosure, a cage, some of them off their heads with something – drugs? anger? despair? – a glimpse of a dangerous underbelly. Then there was a woman at my side. It's okay, she said, they can't get out. She was in uniform, the most senior woman in the district, she said; her name was Roma, and she was the wife of Thompson, our reservist escort. She was pleased, she said, to see her husband *doing something*. Make sure he comes back four kilos lighter. How was I to do that? I laughed, and she laughed, one of those womanly sighs. *Men*. What to do with them, she didn't know. Look at him, she said. We looked across in time to see her overweight husband issued with four bullets, two cans of tear gas and a pair of boots. He knotted the bootlaces together and slung the boots over his shoulder, which is where they remained for most of the trip.

In the dark hotel dining room that evening, over a meal enjoyed only by the three Ömie men who'd come to meet us, David told a story about a man working in the town's tourism office who'd ripped him off on a dinghy trip. It was an expensive price but David had paid up, thinking it'd get him where he was going, a day's journey along the coast. The man had been full of helpful advice: yes, there could be problems, but he'd make sure, for David, very good his work in the villages, he could count on him, etcetera. But when David got to the coast, there was no sign of this man, and the men who had a dinghy waiting at the wharf had only enough zoom – fuel – to get halfway, which is where they expected the journey to end; it was all they'd been paid for. A complicated story of negotiations and looking for the man who'd done the original deal, and finding a relative, and another dinghy waiting, another relative, more money, double the cost he'd paid to the man in the tourism office. Michael, from Ömie, shook his head. He knew of this man. No good true. And he grinned when David reported that on his return to Popondetta he'd written a letter to be circulated round town, naming the man, shaming him. It was a warning, David said. He wasn't getting ripped off again.

That was only the year before, and all I could think was that we'd been all over town; the man from the tourism office would know we were here. Was David crazy? We were about to get on a road – the one and only road going north – and the man would know that too. He'd have us held up – if not tomorrow, then on the way back. Is that what Thompson was for, and the display outside the police station? Popondetta had spooked me, the four bullets had spooked me, and large, cumbersome Thompson's boots.

It was not a good night. A small hot room, bed bugs, the guards, with their guns, smoking under the light that shone in through my window. In my head, keeping me from sleep, was just one phrase, over and over, *a dangerous road*. I couldn't shut it down, I couldn't reason it away. I knew it was Martin Luther King, though not then where it came from exactly. *A dangerous road*, again and again, until it morphed into the yellow brick road from *The Wizard of Oz*, and strange dancing figures were tapping their way into the room where I lay alone with the bed bugs, all courage gone. All I could see was a dream image of a man with Martin Luther King's face dead on a track. Then David was banging on my door. I must have slept; it was morning. The truck's arrived, he said. I opened the door, and there was the sky, the sounds of a town starting its day. The night horrors retreated, but the road remained, and we were to travel it; no turning back.

The truck, an open-backed utility, didn't look too knocked around. A solemn driver stood beside it. He was to take us north towards Kokoda until we reached a side road that turned eastwards into the mountains. On David's map this small road went for a few kilometres past the village at the junction, but Michael said no, the driver would take us all the way to the river which, on the map, was a long way from the end of the road. Michael's English was good, he'd been to the mission school in Popondetta, he hadn't had to pay. Not like now with fees, he said. It's hard for children to go to school. On the open tray of the ute, two plastic chairs were tied with rope to the back of the cabin, their seats about level with the low wall of the tray, nothing to stop you bouncing right out. No way was I sitting there, and when Michael gestured to the rather collapsed-looking seat in the cabin, I took advantage of being the only woman and got in with him and the driver. David and Grahame sat on the floor of the tray in among the piled-up cargo, Thompson poised himself on the rim, a bunch of men who needed a lift climbed on, and off we set at a stately pace.

The driver leaned forward over the wheel, circum-navigating potholes, corrugations, creeks that had washed the road away. Very good, Michael said each time we went up on the bank to let a crowded PMV thunder past. No danger there but dust and grit. Sometimes a driver coming towards us would stop to talk to our driver, horns blaring behind us – which is how we heard there was a sick woman in the next village. Yes, we'd call in to see her, and yes, the ute would take her to the hospital on its return. And so it went, all morning, through patches of forest, over bridges, past densely planted palm-oil plantations, until we turned off the road towards the river that marks the boundary of Ömie.

Just as on the map, the road became a track as soon as it passed the village near the junction, and disappeared into a walking path through thick undergrowth. We lurched down a steep bank, crossed a creek, wheels spinning, the men jumping off to push, and on we went at a steep angle until the driver stopped. Finish, he said. I saw his point, but the Ömie who'd come whooping through the trees towards us were pushing at the ute, slashing at the undergrowth to clear a path, arguing with the driver. No further. Finish. We clearly had to walk and, besides, there was the sick woman to consider; she hadn't looked good with her hard swollen breast and a tiny baby who couldn't suck.

It took more than two hours to reach the last village. Just to get there had been a long, slow climb – not steep but relentless. At the village, green coconuts were tapped open with the back of a bush knife. I sat on the platform of a shade house, lay back, closed my eyes and could have slept for a week. But no, we were off again, down a steep bank to the river, Michael holding tight my wrist as we waded across onto Ömie land. Ömie ground. The start of their mountain. Steep. Forested. Beautiful. Daunting. Above the river were signs of once-cleared forest, grown over. Coffee, Michael said. What happened? For a while it was good, then the coffee prices fell. No good. No? No. Up we climbed, and then down, one ridge after another, and at the bottom of each was a stream – the next welcome soak in cold water – then up the next ridge, steeper, higher. The sun was way past its midpoint. Michael's brother Andrew, who'd met the ute and seemed in charge of everything, kept saying, Walk faster, Walk faster, as if it were possible, which it wasn't, although David reached the top of each next ridge way before me, sometimes before Grahame as well; he'd be sitting there with the men smoking their trade tobacco, and he'd stay with me as I caught my breath before they were all off again, whooping through the forest. Reduced to the muscles of my legs, I followed step by step, notebook forgotten, attention only to the next foothold, the next steadying tree root. Two hours, more, three, the forest canopy above, the path below, that's all I saw; maybe the brain closes down when all that's required are our feet. I noticed nothing as we walked – *faster, faster* – through Na´apa, the first of the Ömie villages, though not a barkcloth village.

Where I most needed to attend, I saw nothing.

The light had almost gone when we arrived at the first barkcloth village. Clouds that had been wisps on the peaks had thickened in the valleys. We'd heard a roll of thunder, and then the drums as we climbed the last ridge before the land opened out to gardens and pathways lined with flowers. Smoke from the roofs of houses was drifting up behind a hedge; the gateway to the village was hung with a large painted barkcloth. Small girls with dots of ochre across their cheekbones came through the gate, took my hands, clasping the hem of my shirt. They were wearing the painted barkcloth wrapped around them as skirts. The gate opened. David and Grahame went through into the village. The men who'd walked up with us dropped their cargo and joined the dance. Then it was my turn, led by the small girls to the women dancing inside, every one of them dressed in barkcloth – ochre and black, dull red, orange, a surprising yellow – their voices rising over the drums. As we approached the houses, a woman of about forty whom I'd come to know as Pauline tucked a handful of herbs into my sleeve, drew me into the dance, my feet in wet boots clumsy as she beat the time on my arm, and somehow, I have no idea how, I was danced into the rhythm of another world.

We woke the next morning to the sound of birds and a village waking for the day. The clouds had gone, the sky a pale dome stretched tight above the peaks, a wash of yellow towards the east. It was hard to believe Popondetta and its anxieties were but a day's journey away, so still and calm and beautiful was that morning light. Outside the guesthouse two older women were sitting on mats painting. One had her cloth spread in front of her; the other had hers folded on her lap. Lila and Dapene. They called me across to them, patted the mat beside them, inviting me to sit. These women were the *duvahe*, a word Michael gave as chief, inadequate as a translation, for their authority came not from lineage but from wisdom, *uehore*, a *moral* clarity, an authority that, when you are sitting beside them, is strangely palpable. I sat where they indicated, and they took my hand, put their noses to the inside of my wrist, then to my elbow and breathed in with a long sniffing noise. I came to love this greeting, their noses pressed higher along my arm until by the time I left, they breathed into my neck and shoulder as if to smell the sweat of me. Several years later, when Dapene was in Sydney for the opening of an Ömie exhibition, I saw how unerring she was about whom she greeted this way. In a crowded gallery, when she needed me as close by her as she or Pauline had been by me when I was in their world, she greeted few people like this, Jo Bertini, and writers Beth Yahp and Gail Jones among them, Janet Laurence when they went to visit her studio, artist to artist. For the rest she took the custom of our world and accepted a hand with nothing more than a touch of hers. But with those few, she lifted their hands to her face, turned them and breathed into their wrist and elbow.

That first morning we didn't speak, or rather we spoke words that were mutually incomprehensible: a look, a smile, a frown, a painting stick gesturing to the cloth, a language of movement and sign. I could, and would, have sat with them all day and let being there wash over me, making the wonder real. But no. Andrew came bustling over. He was like a tour leader. He'd done a business course for eco-tourism in Moresby, and must have been told that tourists need constant activity. So began a round of inspections and demonstrations. We were taken from garden to bush track, from river to stands of sago-palm trees; we were shown how to make fire with bamboo, and traps for pigs; we had orations from the men *duvahe*, histories of the war that had brought the Australians up to these villages enlisting men and boys to work on the Kokoda Track. And then, soon after the war, the mountain, a volcano that had been rumbling for years, erupted, burning the forests, destroying the villages and gardens – and somehow this catastrophe was all because of the war. Michael's translation was vague, as if he were apologising for the old men *duvahe* who clearly wanted us to understand a story, a causality that Michael dismissed as the old ways – legend, that's all. There was no time to absorb what the *duvahe* had said, or to sit with them and ponder, we were on to the next thing: demonstrations by the women of how the inner bark of a selected tree is beaten flat, and how the dyes were made.[54]

The only time I got off from all this was when Pauline and Michael's wife, Naomi, a Popondetta girl who'd been to school and had good English, took me to the women's wash place. Andrew sent a security guard with us – for what, why, he wouldn't say. Another display like Thompson, who spent most of his time on the veranda of the guesthouse? But Andrew's guards, with their bush knives and machetes and the yellow labels he'd written for them with their name and role proud on their t-shirts, were with us wherever we went – even to the women's wash place. The guard would stay at the top of the path down to the river, his back discreetly turned, while I joined the women. They washed the vegetables from the gardens there, huge piles of sweet potato and yams; they talked and laughed, the children splashing in the small pool downstream where we dipped under to wash. It was there that I got to know the women from the cookhouse,

Cecilia, Penny-Rose, Josephine, but when I tried to help they shooed me away with a hilarity I can't say I shared; and when they did relent, they'd pick up the sweet potato to see that I'd got all the earth off it, nodding approval. When I said, Of course I know how to wash a sweet potato, and Naomi translated, such was the laughter that the guard turned to look.

Likeness and difference. I felt it every day, a dance of expectation, misapprehension, goodwill, and a self-consciousness that was entirely mine, as I resisted the white woman *Missis* role. No, no, not *Missis*. Drusilla. Dursula. I became Dursula, that's fine; there was a Dursula in one of the higher villages – your namesake, you'll meet her soon. Very good.

Whatever the confusions and uncertainties, one thing was clear, and that was the quality of the art itself. Each day women would hang the cloth across the dance ground for Grahame to film. Andrew would stand in front of it, with a snail shell, or a hooked vine, or the bone of a river fish, pointing to the designs on the cloth that originated with the item he held up. We might baulk at Andrew's lessons, and we mightn't understand the cloth hanging there in the sun, but we agreed, all three of us, that the barkcloth we'd climbed all this way to see was indeed remarkable. It hung from the walls of the guesthouse, a conservator's nightmare as the clouds swept in leaving them sagging from their nails, still vibrant, without pride or vanity: the music of the forest, mountains, fishbones, thorny vines.

Modest, simple, encompassing the complex meanings of clan history and daily existence. Even with Andrew's snail shells and vines there on the table, I learned more about the Ömie by living beside that cloth, that art, than from all his demonstrations. Dapene's spider web, Pauline's fruit of the forest, Lila's mountains – a visual language, as National Gallery of Victoria (NGV) curator Judith Ryan would write five years later, reverberating 'with an aura of women's inner power, blood and spirit . . .'[55]

But that was way in the future. At the time, when we were in Ömie, it was not at all clear what should happen next, and on this Grahame and David didn't agree. Should the cloth be taken out of Ömie at all? Was it a form of cultural imperialism for David to think he, we, could 'discover' and then 'save' an art form that had survived for hundreds of years? We interfere, and we change the art. Take the art out, and we expose these people to bargain hunters and exploitation. How will they defend themselves when the buyers come up here offering water tanks and lamps and take the art and sell it for thousands? All the more important, David said, to get it into museums and galleries where it will be safeguarded and a standard set. But once prices were known, went the counter-argument, the rumours would start. That was why David was working with Andrew and the men to set up a business that would be registered and structured to benefit only the community. How secure would that prove? David would be the sole agent; the carpetbaggers would have to deal with him! But would he be there when

they came into the village with their swagger and their
offers and their guns? And if we do nothing, David asked,
will the cloth-making last another generation? Will it join
the long list of lost arts? How many of the young women
are learning its rigorous practice? Some, yes, and more
than when David had visited two years earlier, but even
now, not many. Why? They want their husbands to bring
money. They want clothes for their children, and school
fees, medicines. They might have lived for thousands
of years without, but times change, things change, the
modern world isn't going to leave them undisturbed.
Which, from the other perspective, was all the more
reason not to draw attention to them.

And what did I think? Acquainted as I am with the
ambivalent – too many planets in Libra, an astrologist once
told me – it wasn't hard to see both sides. It was a puzzle,
a true dilemma, and we weren't the first to encounter it.
The critical question, I ventured, wasn't what I thought,
or what David and Grahame thought, but what the Ömie
thought, and not just the young men – we knew what
they wanted. What did the women want? The women
duvahe? They were the custodians of the knowledge and
the trees, and the dyes, and the designs, and the stories
told through the cloth. If anyone was to ask, of the three
of us it'd have to be me – but how, and when, with Andrew
rounding us up for the next lesson, and Lila and Dapene
never at the wash place. And even if I had the chance,
how would I set about it, with no language, and only the
smallest acquaintance with an art I knew had deep roots,

though what those roots were I had little idea. I couldn't even read the sky; the shortest walk turned the sun this way and that through the high canopy of trees.

All in all it was something of a relief when, on the morning we were to walk on to the next village – another five hours up the mountain – Grahame said he wasn't going any further. Like me, he'd lain awake that night listening to rain drumming on the sago-thatch roof. The path would be slippery; how many times had I lost my footing on my way down to the wash place, and it hadn't even been that wet. My night horrors hadn't been about the wet, or the leeches – I had come prepared with salt – or the dangers of the road. It was my own physical capacity, or lack of it, that had me awake. The walk up this far had pushed me to an edge that had taken days to come back from. I wasn't sure I'd make it, and then what? While I listened to the rain thump down, I'd imagined strokes and heart attacks, helicopters, thick cloud, insurance disputes. So when Grahame announced he wasn't going further, coward that I was I said that in that case I'd stay too. We could meet David when he looped back round from the highest villages to one a mere four hours away, where dancers from all of Ömie were to gather on the night of the full moon. Thompson, also looking relieved, said he'd stay to keep the *Missis* safe, and settled himself back down on the veranda with his block of tobacco and deck of cards.

I spent most of those unscheduled days with the women, not only at the wash place but in the cookhouse and in their houses when they came back from the gardens. With Naomi to turn the talk, and Dapene sitting with us painting the pathways of her folded cloth, instructing the younger women to paint between the lines she'd drawn, I learned new words, struggled with new concepts. I went with the women into the forest to find a tree ready for its bark to be cut and pounded flat into fabric for the art. I watched as Dapene put her hands on one tree, felt around it, and then moved to another until she found one that was indeed ready. How could she tell? That was not a question that made sense to her – any more than I could see the difference, quite clear to her, between this tree and that, let alone their readiness. But I did begin to understand that our Western notions of art as something separate, to be hung on the wall or seen in a gallery, were far removed from a world in which the cloth, its art, was woven into every aspect of their culture, their environment, their daily lives.

Back in the village, sitting on the platform of a house where the women were painting, I'd ask more questions, notebook open, as if that way understanding would come. I'd think I'd grasped something, and then realise that I hadn't. How do anthropologists do it? Words are hard to find when they come from one way of seeing the world and are carried across to another, where even the experience of forest and sky, everything we share in the physical earth we tread, can shift register and meaning. Sometimes Dapene would become firm and cut off my next query, back and forth over the same point as I watched her paint the cloth, folded on her knee, turned this way and that. She'd tell me the name of the design as she painted, no explanation, just a name, which I was coaxed into repeating until my tongue worked its way around it. How did she decide where to start? Did she have a pattern for the whole when she folded it to paint in sections? Was there a pattern to folding? I couldn't work out how she did it. The design when it was finished didn't break into the small sections of the folds. Dapene put down her stick. She held me tight around the wrist, no breathing in: this was a rebuke that told me how dumb my questions were. The cloth, it knows, she said. The answer of an artist. 'The landscape thinks itself in me, and I am its consciousness.'[56] That's Cézanne, and with him too I only dimly comprehend its import.

It was time to close my notebook, and for a good bit of that unscheduled time I did. Instead of trying to get every word, everything transcribed – a process that mostly showed me how much I had wrong as I re-encountered what I thought I had grasped – I gave in to doing nothing more than sitting, watching, being. For someone of my disposition, given to over-thinking, it was not easy, just to sit – that failure with Zen – and I can't say I succeeded entirely. The days passed so slowly, the hours, the minutes, my attention could lapse and I'd be mulling again: thinking, ordering, rethinking. I suppose the Ömie were too as they tried to get the measure of this white woman from a world that was at once powerful and woefully ignorant. What did they say when I was not there? What did they make of what I said, translating my words into their ways of thinking? More impossible questions, which set off another round of pondering, interpreting.

Back on the veranda where Thompson was playing cards with the men, his rifle propped in the corner, Grahame and I would compare notes, or just sit quietly with the barkcloth on the walls around us, not trying to interpret. His days were spent with the young men he hadn't had a chance to know while Andrew had kept us on the hop; we relaxed, both of us, into the pace of the village. When the food came over from the cookhouse, the table Andrew had built became an easier place. David had told us that on his previous visit the men had eaten on the floor, everyone in together. With the table – another innovation from *bisnis* school – came a formality, without enough room for everyone. And so had begun a muted tussle about who could and would eat with us. I wanted some of the women from the cookhouse to join us, but that upset the men; the women shook their heads and went back to the smoke and the cooking fire. Grahame had thought David let too many of the young men eat with us; David didn't want to be the one to decide who was there, or not. Those who had English took one priority; those who were quick to sit down took another. I didn't like the exclusion of the women, while I, being white, got to eat at the table, and was stopped by Andrew if I went to eat in the cookhouse. Stay, David said, or it will shame him.

In compensation, on the night before David left for the high villages, I arranged a special dinner with the women. We ate on mats on the veranda, and for this meal I had saved the last of the packets of tuna we'd brought from Australia – most of which had been eaten by the men crowded round the table. The women gave the tuna close attention. Yes, it was good, but where did it come from? It was like tinned fish, I said, from a shop, a trade store. They looked dubious. Which river was it from? I did not know. They asked about my garden, and I tried to describe my Balmain courtyard. No! They tutted and laughed. A garden smaller than the size of the guest-house? It was not possible! Like Popondetta I said, some people have small gardens beside their house, that's all. No laughing this time, a sombre tutting. That night was the first time I heard us called the 'new' people. They, with their gardens and their mountain and their cloth, are the 'old' people.

It was also that night with the women that I heard again the story of the war and the volcano. Lila, the *duvahe*, had been a small girl when the mountain erupted in 1951. She had walked for two days with her grandmother to the government camp further north along the road to Kokoda. She'd learned to paint from that grandmother. The mountain had blown in the other direction, to the north, to the other side, but thick ash and flying rocks had landed on Ömie land. For a week before the eruption, the sky had been dark and the bush animals – cassowaries, bandicoots, snakes, even wild boars – had come in from the forest, into the villages; the rivers were sucked back up into the mountain, or ran too hot to cross. The mountain was angry. Unhappy. Naomi and Pauline translated. Lila named the Ömie who were killed, not as many as there were on the other side of the mountain, where the missions were and the land less rugged; many, many people were killed there, Lila did not know how many. On the Ömie side, the forests had caught fire, the gardens were covered in ash; it was a year before the rivers ran a normal temperature. Old people died in the camp, away from their land. It was not good. And all because the mountain had been unsettled by the angry spirits of soldiers killed in the war, lost and wandering about, unable to find their way back to their own ancestors. Too many of the men who knew how to look after the mountain had been taken away to work on the Kokoda Track. All those white-men soldiers, some no more than boys, left dead, carried dead, and the Japanese, dead men lying in the forest, dead souls upsetting the mountain. Yes, it was very big work for the *duvahe*.

This was not legend; this was history, another view, another interpretation, which, told by Lila that night on the mountain, made perfect sense.

And afterwards? What then?

This was what Lila wanted me to know. Her hand had hold of my wrist, her eyes didn't let me move. The women were very quiet, the children leaning against their mothers were still. It was then that I understood the division between these villages and the Ömie at Na´apa, the village to which I had paid no attention on the long walk up. There they had understood this cataclysmic eruption as a rebuke, a punishment, for not having gone fully enough to the missions. In contrast, I understood Lila to be saying, the Ömie we were visiting had moved their villages higher, where the missions would not come, higher and further; their appeasement was to paint. Our mountain. Our art. At Na'apa there was no more painting. The missions came, the people there, our relatives, Lila said, do not like that we paint; they wanted trade stores, oh it was no good, and they planted coffee, and their rivals across the river, some of them married to women from Na'apa, took the money. No good.

And now? I asked. We are very happy that you have come. Would they say otherwise? But I understood why the security guards were there, and why there'd been a disturbance a few nights before which had woken us, only briefly, but not Thompson, who snored through it all. Andrew had passed the event off as *something nothing*, but no, it was not nothing; it was men from Na'apa, relatives some of them, wanting money. Have they gone? Yes, for now, they have gone. That night with the women I asked if this trouble with Na'apa altered how the *duvahe* thought about the cloth leaving the village? Maybe, Pauline translated. Lila and Dapene nodded their heads. Na'apa was a problem. But their own young men, they, too, were a big problem. Not the old men, the young men. They're all stirred up. Gardens, fences, hunting, it is not enough. They are shamed in Popondetta, *bush kanakas nothing*. They are shamed when they walk on the road and do not have the money for the PMV. They want pride. They want a *bisnis*. David says *bisnis* can come from the art. Is this so? Pauline asked. Maybe, I said, an answer that was no answer. David a good man, she said, a strong spirit. And I understood that they needed an answer from me, which I couldn't give. I couldn't tell them that an art *bisnis* would bring money and solve the problem of the young men; nor could I cast doubt on an option that was well in train, a possibility that existed only because of David and the resources he had to make it happen – were it to happen. I sighed, I said general things – that there were many people in Australia who were interested in art from PNG, that David was a good man, he wasn't here to make money for himself. The women sighed. The young men, they said, a big problem true.

And the young women? I asked. Do they want to learn the art? Before David came, before Andrew went to Moresby, did the young women learn the painting? Some, maybe. And now that David's come, do the young women learn? They'd been dressed in painted *nioge* for the demonstrations, though often enough Dapene slapped at them, a correcting hand. Some like the cloth, yes. For some it is the old way, and they do not want. They want warm clothes, they want trade-store cloth, it is better for the babies. It is cold when it rains, which it did that night, thumping down, keeping Grahame awake, deciding not to go with David on up the mountain.

In the morning, after that dinner with the women, the men were surly. Our meal had shamed them, it seemed, and there was the matter of the tuna; there were many

men who had not had any. The women looked as they
always looked; I heard them laughing in the cookhouse.
One of the men called up to them and the laughing
stopped, a lull, then the talk began again. Grahame, after
his bad night, said the dinner had been a mistake. Maybe
it was, an inappropriate feminism, but, Hey, listen to what
I learned, it changes things. Another legend, David said,
not taking what I had to say seriously, charmed, he said,
by my response. You're such a writer – as if my way of
seeing was all imagination, and therefore lesser. It was a
Greenwich Mean Time situation, and in response anger
flared in me. Furious, I walked to the edge of the village to
calm down, and was about ready to turn back when David
joined me. As we looked over to ridges he was to cross,
I told him again what Lila had said. It's not sentiment,
I said, and if we are serious about the arts of this place, we
need to comprehend what it means – as you should know,
I added; an intended barb. To David's credit, he nodded,
his face serious this time. I think he took it in, and that
when he said he was sorry, it'd been a tense morning, it
was not a sop – or not only – to a woman he felt responsible
for. Was I sure, he wanted to know, that I was okay to stay
in the village without him? If I had any doubts, he'd call
off the visit to the high villages. No, I said. Of course you
must go.

While David and the men travelling with him made
their noisy preparations for the journey, I retreated to the
cookhouse where the women were feeding the children.
I leaned against the smoky wall and the thought that came

to me was of Sophie and how we used to walk between
the high tide and the low, and that was hard enough to
judge, a wave catching us, the sand hard beneath our feet,
then giving way to unexpected sinking. Land on one side,
ocean on the other, and Sophie and me picking our way
along the tiny strip where they cross each day. Here, the
strip between the overlap could narrow and vanish, and
then again it could widen out, a broad horizon, which
is how I'd felt that evening with the women. Something
had happened that night, and it had changed how the
women were with me, and how I could be with them, just
there, a presence they need not perform for.

Pauline went with David and the men, up to the village
where her children were. I was sorry to see her go, a
surge of anxiety; with Pauline I felt safe, in every way safe,
and she was going. Had I made the wrong call, staying
here in this village so close to Na´apa? The short answer
is that I hadn't. They were good days, those next days
in that first village, excellent days; without them I would
have understood even less. It took walking the forest
with Dapene; it took sitting and watching as the women
painted; it took just being, alongside the women, part of
their days. As to Pauline, there she was when we climbed
up to the village where we were to meet David, arriving
in time to see him stride in with his boots and gaiters.
There she was, waiting by the gate: strong, safe Pauline. It
would be churlish to complain of the climb Grahame and
I made, a mere four hours, taken slowly with Thompson

setting the pace. If my legs were trembling when we arrived at the gate to the village, there was no stopping to rest them – for there was my namesake, Dursula, with a barkcloth skirt and a headdress for me to wear; in photos I look ridiculous with an ugly blue singlet beneath the festoons of necklaces. But when we went through the gate led by Pauline, dancers were pouring in, drums beating, women singing.

One afternoon Pauline came to sit with me on the covered platform where I'd fallen asleep. The rain had started, blowing in from the valley. It was cold. We sat looking into the rain, and I unzipped my sleeping bag, spreading it over us both, *very good*, and asked her how it had gone in the high villages. She liked it up there, she said, and she liked a man up there. Just a little, maybe. She was the only woman who'd admitted to liking Popondetta, let alone a man; the others would shake their heads and laugh, hands to their faces. Pauline found the town interesting. If you know what to do, it's okay, she said. She doesn't mind the shame of being a *bush kanaka*, she's a strong Ömie woman. She prefers it here in the villages, but the town is good too. She goes to the market, takes vegetables from her garden, women from the government houses buy them. She saves the money for school fees. She has many children, and an old husband. Her face tells me what she thinks of him. No good, I say, you're young yet. She laughs. A young man, she says, yes she'd like a young man, but that means babies. And trouble? I ask. Big trouble, she says, and laughed. Did I have a husband?

Once I had a husband, not any more, I say. But, yes, there is a man. His name is Jeremy. When I go back to Port Moresby, he'll be there to meet me. We were going to go to a place near the salt water. Why does he not come here? I didn't have an answer. The walk had put him off, and the time away, and a son who was not well; he'd meet me for the last two weeks, that was enough. And my husband, Pauline wants to know. Where is he? It was long ago, I say. I was young yet. Did he die? No, we divorced. He divorced? No, me too. A woman can divorce a man? Send him finish? She is astonished. They sit down good, and you go? Really? Some men get violent and beat the woman, I say, sometimes a woman is killed. Pauline is not surprised. But mostly it is okay. More divorces come from women than men in our world, I say. She is impressed. *Sister-friend.*

The next morning the sun returned. Women were hanging more barkcloth on the lines Andrew had strung across the dance ground at this next village. The iconography was different, the designs looser, the cloth paler so that the dyes seemed stronger, the yellow more yellow, the black a dark smouldery blue-black. There was work to do: Grahame's camera; my notebook; David's tape measure. Across the valley, the bare rock of the peaks was visible above the forest. The ancestors had come from a stream up there, Lila told us. A man and a woman. The woman did not have a birth canal until the man cut one for her. In exchange she cut the first bark and beat the first cloth for him. Babies and art. Our mountain, our clans, our art.

This was a story that could be told. Other stories, Lila would say, or Dapene, did not want to be told. As we worked, measuring and documenting the cloth, Andrew translating for David, Naomi or Michael whispering for me, the talk went back and forth as we waited for Lila or Dapene to say, Yes, okay, or No, not this story, not this cloth. David thought we should write down everything; we didn't have to use it, but the record would be there, and if need be we could. But I didn't, not with Lila's sharp eye on me, and anyway, without the translation, I couldn't. Not exactly the method of an historian or an anthropologist; a start, no more. There was the camera to testify to the complex beauty of an art that five years later would be exhibited as *The Wisdom of the Mountain* at the National Gallery of Victoria. But that was way ahead. Right then, before we left, there was a crescendo of events as the village filled with people coming in from the high villages. They had come to dance to the mountain on the night of the full moon, beginning at dusk with everyone on the dance ground – old men, new mothers with their babies, small children, everyone – until dawn when only a few strong men were still dancing to the exacting rhythm of the drum – and Pauline, strong Ömie woman Pauline. The essence of that night, as magical as the Popondetta night had been threatening, worked its way into my novel *The Mountain*, an experience I gave to Jericho, a character who exists only there, and was never anywhere near the mountain, for all that he remains a presence, palpable to me, and I hope to readers. No, David, Grahame and

I were the outsiders that night for a dance that took its
own rhythm and shape, disregarding us. We might as well
have not been there, which was part of the power of the
experience, for all the attention we'd receive when it came
time for the feast that had steamed all day in long earth
ovens: pig and stringy chickens, pumpkins, yams, sweet
potato. And again the next day when the *duvahe* gathered
for the meeting that would decide the fate of the cloth
and Andrew's *bisnis*.

I wrote about that meeting for the NGV catalogue, and
when I showed it to David he said it was another fairytale;
not that it hadn't happened, but that I credited the *duvahe*
with a decision that was, more accurately, an agreement.[57]
And in a way he was right; it was his decision – not theirs,
not Andrew's – that had put everything in train. And it's
true the outcome was never seriously in doubt. I knew
that from the groups of men gathered around David and
Andrew, and from the cookhouse, where the talk was
of school fees and warm clothes, men no longer going
to Popondetta and coming back angry. Sometimes the
women got beaten. The *duvahe* would stop the beating,
but the men would be shamed, and sometimes they'd
return to town and then there'd be no husband.

On the afternoon of the meeting of the *duvahe*, the
dance ground filled with anticipation, all the dancers,
everyone, there, children leaning on the steps to the house
where the *duvahe*, dressed in splendour, had assembled.
Yes, the *duvahe* said, David could take the cloth, Andrew
could start his business. The news was carried out to the

crowd. Children on the steps leaped in excitement, and were hushed by their fathers. Yes, the cloth could leave Ömie, but there were conditions. The *duvahe* were to approve every cloth that went, and they would say which must not go. They would say which custom story could be told, and who was to translate. Outside, we could hear excitement rippling through the crowd. Inside, Andrew had more to say. Was he demurring? No one translated. Lila was sharp. One of the men held up his hand. Andrew became quiet. A murmur through the crowd outside.

Then David spoke, a round of translation, explaining the diagrams. The money would go into the community: half to the business Andrew and the men would run, doing all the work of taking the art to Popondetta, sending it to Australia, a long way. The other half would go into an account for the artists that the women *duvahe* would have control of. Pauline and another woman would go to Popondetta with the mark of Lila and Dapene, and to give their own signatures. More talk. More details. Pumpkin and yams were carried over from the cookhouse.

It was an exhilarating day, all tensions evaporated into the high, light sky. How could it not be so when Wellington, the *duvahe* of all Ömie, walked out onto the dance ground and reported the decision, if decision it was. The outcome. For the rest of that day, and into the evening, there was dancing, and Ömie songs, a great swirling excitement.

Pauline took my arm and breathed in. She was clapping. Sister-friend, she said, now I will visit you in your place. Standing there with her, looking into the crowd, I thought: what have we set up? What expectations? Will we meet them? What would Na´apa do when they heard of this day? What were we doing here? Should we have left well alone?

I was back on the terrain of anxiety, and as it turned out, with good reason.

11

Jeremy had been at school with my cousin Philip. Six years older than me, Philip could stand on his head and make shapes of animals with his fingers. He'd cheer when my sisters and I walked along the tops of walls and fences. He'd take our hands until we were balanced, and he'd catch us when we fell, which by the time I was twelve I made sure I did, as often as possible, straight into his arms. He'd put me back on the ground, upside down, standing on my head – and then he, too, would be on his head, and we'd look at each other and collapse in a heap. He was glorious, and because he was a cousin and because his father, a close cousin of my father, almost a brother, had been killed in the war, while miraculously Patrick with his thick glasses had not, there was a tragic mystery about him. Long before the wall-walking, head-standing years, I'd dance in praise when he – with his mother and brother – were coming to lunch. So there I was one summer day, dancing on the lawn outside the house, swirling, toes pointing, arms above my head, when Philip, half an hour early, looked over the gate. Don't stop, he said, as I froze in mid-swirl, my toes square pegs. He wasn't meant to *see* the dance, it was just for me, a dance of private joy. The day was ruined. Was it at that lunch, as memory would have it, or another when the grown-ups talked in grave voices? Philip was in some sort of trouble at school, I don't remember what – smoking maybe, or talking back to a master; such things were serious then. Should Patrick speak to his house-master? Philip was saying nothing, his brother was eating. When my sisters were excused from the table, my mother said why didn't I go with them and play. As if.

Jeremy and I had been together for several years when a childhood friend turned up in Sydney and we discovered the connection with Philip. Caroline's father, like Philip's, had been killed in the war and their widowed mothers had holidayed together with the children. Caroline had been born as the war ended, and when it came to Philip, she too had been entranced. She, Jeremy and I had dinner together in my small flat on the hill above Bondi, and as Caroline and I pondered this early enchantment, Jeremy asked, Was he at Clifton? Yes! The school Jeremy had been to. Philip who? Philip Parsons? Jeremy had recognised him from our talk, our memories, our fascination – which, it transpired, Jeremy had shared. Marginally, he said, careful of his words. Marginally, that was all. No dances of praise, not that kind of smitten; a schoolboy crush, no more.

That night in my bed Philip was there with us, not as an erotic third but as another blessing; such coincidence, such connection. Jeremy and I had grown up within miles of each other, we knew the names of towns and villages that no one else in Australia knew, or if they did, it was as a name on a map, that's all. We still couldn't believe we'd both lived here in this distant land for more than twenty years with no idea of each other's existence.

We had met in December 1996, two months after my fiftieth birthday, a little more than a year since Patrick's death. We were set up in the most discreet way, and neither of us had any idea until long afterwards. We were invited to a dinner by our mutual friend, the journalist and writer Anne Deveson, who sat us opposite each other at the end of her long, narrow table. Jeremy was just back from two months in England. I was recently back from a month in the Kimberley with a friend whose birthday was within ten days of mine. So I had been camping out by waterholes on the Drysdale Plateau while Jeremy was visiting the graves of his parents in an English churchyard at the village of Bramley – one of thousands of villages in southern England. Bramley! Exactly where my maternal grandmother is buried. Our mothers had shopped in the same market town, we knew the name of the same butcher; we took our Christmas book tokens to the same branch of W. H. Smith. His parents retired to a village so close to the house with the walls I walked along with Philip to catch me that I could have ridden there on my pony. Imagine! Who else, these last twenty years, had understood what it meant to be born in that particular there and live in this particular here. It was as if a light switched on and we could see each other in our childhood houses; we knew the names of the trees in the woods, the rivers that meandered through the villages, the station where we caught the train to London. We'd both spent more hours than anyone could want waiting for connections at Reading Station; we both knew the strong and bitter tea from the platform kiosk.

The week after the dinner at Anne's, we met for a drink at the Dry Dock Hotel in Balmain, and later, when we'd return for an anniversary drink, Jeremy would say there should be a blue plaque to mark the occasion. We'd talked about England, and the split between a past there and a present here. It was a split that, to him, had always been burdensome, and to me had become, I thought, merely a condition of life. Yet at the Dry Dock that night I felt something shift in me, some submerged longing make itself known. As we talked around each other, I could tell from his eyes, the flick of his hair, that he was drawn to me, and also afraid. That old familiar vulnerability. Patrick, I suppose. Who better to hear our vulnerabilities than those who know them best? I'm not going to be hurt again, he said, a warning even as he took my hand. Goodnight, I said, as I got into the car and rolled down the window. He put his arms on the roof and leaned in towards me, put his hand on my head. Your hair, he said.

On New Year's Eve 1996, we were back at Anne's house in East Balmain. At the start of the party, when there were hours to go before the clock struck midnight, we'd talked of Thomas Hardy, a writer who'd deeply influenced Jeremy, and about whom he'd written and published. He was disappointed, I think – or maybe surprised, given that I was English and had been at school in Hardy's Dorset – that I hadn't read more of him, and nothing for years. Maybe it was that I'd read *Tess of the d'Urbervilles* too young, I said, describing to him the afternoon I finished it, aged thirteen, standing at the edge of the tennis courts at school. I was barely able to breathe, unable to watch the match, wanting only to bow my head to the ground as Angel Clare does on the final page of the novel as he heard the clocks strike eight that terrible morning, and watched the black flag run up the tall staff on the tower of the prison – a 'blot on the city's beauty' (a city I knew well) – that told him Tess had been hanged. Jeremy looked at me long and hard. Yes, he said. You were too young. I don't remember much else of the evening before we all poured out into the street to watch the fireworks over the bridge. He's a good man, Anne said as we embraced for the New Year. Afterwards, in the early hours of the morning, we walked back to Jeremy's house in Birchgrove where my car was parked. As we walked, hands together, we talked about the comma; as we cut through the park at Mort Bay, we stopped for a tentative first kiss on the grass that covers where the dry dock once was.

The comma. That cracked up his sons, both of them at home, one at university, the other in his last year at school. How good to be fifty, we said to each other, with the children more or less grown, an age when they were more fun than trouble. These next years will be ours, we said – those first easy summers of picnics and reading in the garden, those first winters by the fire burning in the grate of his rambling weatherboard house filled with books and furniture from England. And we said it again at the Adelaide Writers' Week a few years later, in 2002, when we stood at the edge of the river, the noise of a publisher's party billowing out behind us. Our good fortune, oh, it was boundless; it might have come late, but it had come, and there we were, still in our prime, congratulating ourselves, watching the boats on the river, and raising our glasses to others who came out to escape the noise of the party.

What we didn't know that night, but would in the morning, was that back in Sydney the younger of his sons was spinning out in what would prove to be the first bipolar episode that would land him in hospital and cast a cloud across his and his father's sky.

One of the things Jeremy and I did well together was travel. Jeremy enjoyed the planning, the maps, the research, but when it came to the moment of packing and leaving the house, he baulked. I put it down to being sent away to school too young. Like my father, like the boys of our class and generation, he was sent to board at seven. A fastidious chap with no interest in sport, he was a target, as my father had been, for the bullies. The boys in Jeremy's dormitory took to snatching the plug from the bath or the basin and turning off the taps, so that he would go for days, even weeks, without being able to wash. Yes, getting Jeremy out the door was taxing, but the odd thing was that as soon as we were on the plane he was cheerful again, looking ahead, and when we arrived wherever it was we were going, I'd be the one who'd think, What now? but Jeremy had it sorted, whatever it was that needed to be sorted. In Hong Kong the hotel room we'd booked through the travel agent was so unpleasant there was a spring sticking up through the mattress. I said we could make do, put towels over the spring, sleep around it, but the next morning Jeremy was up at dawn and before I'd surfaced had found a better deal in a much better hotel – close enough to wheel our bags – and a comfortable room with a view across a park. We had a fine breakfast that day. Between us, we made good travel companions, in Australia, in Europe, in the Pacific. Even as the skies darkened at home, travelling, elsewhere, was a realm we made our own.

There is a lot I cannot say about the years I spent with Jeremy. Or rather a lot I will not say. If I were a Knausgaard I could write a thousand pages on living in proximity to mental illness, but there is a life outside the page for the young man, who is making his way to a clearer future – and that, as Jeremy would say when tensions rose, trumps everything. So travel, when we could, was our escape, our balm, and we could feel ourselves back on the road we'd thought we were travelling when we'd stood by the river in Adelaide, congratulating ourselves on our good fortune. I'd published *Stravinsky's Lunch* by then, which I'd begun as Patrick was dying, part of my long quest to understand that vexed question of love and independence. Through the lens of two most different artists – Stella Bowen and Grace Cossington Smith – the question had morphed into the conundrum of love and art. Could a woman have both? Must her art and her life of the heart be always in tension? The irony, I realise now, is that exactly as I finished *Stravinsky's Lunch*, certain there was a way through the conundrum, I found myself up against it in a way I was not prepared for. I'd thought of it in terms of whether a woman could write – or paint – and have the support of a lover, a partner; an equal relationship. Well, Jeremy liked my work. He didn't always agree: I could tone it down, make it less personal, which I didn't; and we argued, amicably for the most part, and he kept abreast of my research. He read his way through the novels of Stella Bowen's lover, Ford Madox Ford; he came with me to galleries and archives; he read my drafts paragraph by paragraph. And when his son fell down and Jeremy needed my support, loyalty switched his way as we did what needed to be done. At night he wept, and in the morning he was still filled with the thoughts that had kept him from sleep, lamenting for his son, loved and a stranger both. I cooked, and I fed them; I took Jeremy for walks; I read up on treatments and therapies not only for his son's condition, but also for his, as the depression he'd held at bay, more or less, rose to crush him. And still I cooked, and still I made phone calls, and I did it willingly, certain we'd find a way through. Somehow, some way.

For the first time in my writing life I was late for a deadline, a small piece of writing, and I had to ring up and apologise, the fee gone, and I was never asked to write again for that editor.

Mornings, I said to Jeremy. That's all I ask, uninterrupted mornings. For him it was another abandonment.

I had first encountered Stella Bowen at an exhibition in Melbourne.[58] It was 1993 and I was there visiting Helen and Murray, who were married by then and had moved to Helen's home town. Murray came with me to the exhibition, maybe Helen too, I don't recall; the significance of the memory is that standing in front of Stella Bowen's 1928 *Self-Portrait*, Murray said, You should write about her. Born – like him – in Adelaide, Stella Bowen had gone to England just before the First World War began, and during those dark days she'd begun a 'long intimacy' with the writer Ford Madox Ford. She'd painted the self-portrait ten years after the war ended – as she and Ford separated. It was an image of herself, I'd write, 'that acknowledges the pain of parting but refuses to be reduced to it'. Ford was an H. G. Wells figure, and to a modern eye even less attractive, his mouth slack in photos, the result of being gassed in the war. Like Wells with Rebecca West, Ford took Stella seriously, this young Australian woman fresh from art school in Adelaide. And like Wells, he treated her badly. But that was not the story she told. True, though she bore him a child, she could not marry him – there was a past wife and no divorce; true, she was wounded when he moved on to another, and by the affair that preceded the final break. Yet she refused to speak ill of him, or to regret an intimacy with a man who *listened*, she said, and from whom she learned a great deal and by whose side she became the artist she was. 'Her eyes,' I wrote, 'tinged red, meet ours in a challenge which invites not the admiration of the world but its attention. This, they say, is the condition of the woman as artist. Woman? Lover? Mother? Artist? The distinctions are false. A woman is all of these, and reduced to none. To be an artist is not a matter of surmounting, or refusing, or even of juggling, but of bringing the values and knowledge of heart and belly into the work, into the image, into the paint.'[59]

I wrote that during the early years of my life with Jeremy. In retrospect it seems naïve in its confidence, yet at the time it was a realisation that had been hard to reach. Do you hear the echo of Dorothy Green? I do. She died in 1993, the year I first saw Stella Bowen's self-portrait. I went with Hilary to the funeral that was held at the chapel at Duntroon, the military academy in Canberra where Dorothy had taught after many years of teaching at ANU. When I knew her well enough to ask why she'd made that move, she'd said that it was work that mattered, teaching literature – the humanity of reading – to young men who'd go on to lead our forces and make military decisions. Her funeral was on the day American ground troops went into Iraq in the first Bush war – one of those strange synchronicities that are no more than coincidental, but can carry the weight of a life. Her coffin left the chapel on the shoulders of uniformed cadets, and I'd swear, and so would Hilary, that one of them was close to tears. Afterwards, after the wake and the speeches that spoke of her as poet and teacher, writer and mentor, Hilary and I went to the National Gallery. We were sparing in the paintings we saw, choosing those that resonated with Dorothy; among them was Grace Cossington Smith's *Interior with Yellow* (1962), the artist's bedroom with a single bed and wardrobe mirror. Then we sat in the café, looking out into the trees, talking about Dorothy and the lives of women who'd gone before us, and whom we could glimpse only through the legacy of their work.

Looking back, I sometimes think I wrote *Stravinsky's Lunch* in answer to Dorothy's challenge when I was fortifying myself with all those anecdotes for my city of women. If so, it was there that I answered – or had a go at answering – her question about what matters when we tell the lives of women. What matters in their lives? What matters in our telling, our reading? In the work they bequeath to us?

There were some who thought Grace Cossington Smith was mismatched with Stella Bowen; to me she was the perfect complement, exactly because she was such a very different woman, and artist. Unmarried and with no children, Grace Cossington Smith had lived, or so it was said, without love. But such a notion is, or can be, and in her case was, more a matter of blindness, seeing only the spinster, and not the lived experience of loves which come, as we should know but mostly forget, in many and unexpected forms. She did, however, paint one of the great paintings of a woman living with the absence of love. It is *The Sock Knitter*, painted while she was still at art school in 1915, the year of Gallipoli and that particular wartime slaughter of young Australian men.[60] The sitter was Grace's sister Madge, knitting socks for soldiers, not for the babies she'd never have, a retrospective observation, I know, but Madge, even then, was suffering the fate of a young middle-class woman constrained by circumstances, both domestic and world-political. She would become one of those 'superfluous women' Vera Brittain wrote of; unlike her sister Grace, there was no redemption, no art, no grace, nothing but a curate in England to attach her hopes to, and he married elsewhere.

For Grace, not marrying was as much a matter of choice as circumstance. It wasn't that she made the best of it, or that her art was the compensation of a woman who found herself superfluous. She found a way of living a rich life of art and work and friendship in what has too often been seen as the narrow confines of a house on the northern edge of Sydney; a full life that paid attention to what lies beyond consciousness and convention – a life revealed in an image of a jug, a vase, a window opening onto trees. It was not a life without love, or without passion, and while we can't know – and don't need to know – what that meant in the sex-conscious terms of our world, I made the argument from letters and paintings that her emotional orientation was towards women rather than men. *Preposterous* was the response from more than one critic. Jeremy was not surprised; he, too, thought I'd overreached. But actually nothing about Grace Cossington Smith is preposterous except for a view of her that insists on her spinsterhood. Dreadful word.

'Emotion without knowledge is the mother of all sentimentality,' Grace wrote and I quoted. 'Knowledge without emotion is cold and sterile.' It is a way of speaking against the split, the many splits, that Stella Bowen also spoke against: thinking and feeling, inner and outer, public and private. Again the echo of Dorothy Green, and of Poppy, too. Both long dead, I mentioned neither in my three pages of acknowledgements. But I did thank Jeremy, 'who barely knew me before this book grew to become a presence in both our lives, and who showed me that there need not always be a conflict'. It's a foolish woman, I've heard it said, who boasts of her happiness.

Towards the end of the editing, when there was much to check, pages to be reconsidered, Jeremy, himself an editor, had been helping me for days when his sons came home early from a trip away visiting their mother in the country. His kitchen table was covered in piles of pages that couldn't be easily moved without losing track of where we were. By the fridge was a table brought in from outside and on it reference books lay open in precarious piles. 'Books suck,' one of the boys said as we cleared the table, as fast as we could, but still too slow from their point of view, hungry, of course, from a long train journey. By then I was living nearby, along a laneway lined on one side by the wheelie bins of the houses on the street below, and on the other a high bank up to the back gardens of the houses on the street above. When I first moved there, in 2001, to that small house at the end of the lane where I still live, the bank was a tangle of lantana with old tyres and other junk thrown into it. Since then it's been cleared by a woman from one of the houses above, and replanted into a garden of frangipani, lime and lemon trees; lavender, lilies, bottlebrush; salvia, pumpkin and parsley. Early on I helped her plant out a row of small rosemary plants – what a border they'd make, full and bushy so that one day everyone would be able to pick a sprig. But no, we lost almost all of them in a single night – gone, dug up, stolen. Another neighbour made a sign asking for RESPECT, for the community and for the plants. I said it'd do no good, this hippy-dippy respect business; if you were into stealing plants you'd just scoff. I wanted a sign that said THIS BANK IS LANDMINED. It was taken as a joke, which it was, I suppose. Sort of. Now, a decade later, everything's well enough established to be safely rooted into the ground; we don't have thefts like that, though drivers have been seen getting out of huge shiny cars and hacking off a branch from an overhanging frangipani or soft, whispery bottlebrush.

The first time Jeremy came with me to the Pacific was in September 2001, just after 9/11. His pipe knife, a blunt object for scraping out the pipes he insisted on smoking, was taken off him for the flight to Fiji – our first experience of the new security regimes. We were going not on holiday but to visit old friends from PNG days, to collect diaries and research materials I was being loaned, and to visit the University of the South Pacific's Oceania Centre for Arts and Culture on the hill above the campus. Poet and writer Epeli Hau'ofa, who'd been a tutor at the University of Papua New Guinea with Nick, was the centre's founding director, a large Tongan with a smile to match. It was he who'd shifted thinking about the Pacific, Oceania, from a view that saw specks of land as islands separated by a vast ocean, to a way of seeing the encompassing ocean as shared, holding the people of its islands together.[61] The same shift of perspective could, of course, apply to the rainforest with its scattered villages, but that was a thought for later when I tried to conceive of Ömie not as separated but conjoined by their mighty forests. At the Oceania Centre, Jeremy and I spent many hours sitting at the edge of its wide, open-sided studio, watching a choreographer at work with his dancers, talking to singers and musicians, artists and writers: a new generation of Islanders reinterpreting their world, as Epeli had done in his youth thirty years before. There was the sophistication of those who'd travelled and studied in Auckland, or Sydney, or New York, and yet the sensibility, the power of everything we saw, was based in a history and culture that were entirely of the Pacific, that resilient ocean of islands. For me, it was the first move towards a return that would take me back to PNG, and it was good, very good, to have Jeremy there, responding with a full heart to the strong island rhythm of music and poetry.

Mike Monsell-Davis, the friend who was lending me his diaries, had also been at the university in Port Moresby when Nick and I were there, but unlike most anthropologists – who base themselves away, returning for research and conferences – Mike had lived in PNG for the better part of thirty years, keeping a diary that tracked not only events in his life, but the profound changes that came with Independence. For someone like me, who wanted to write about that place and that time but had lived thirty years away, the diaries were an invaluable and generous loan.[62] There was serious talk to be had between Mike and me, about the terms of this loan, and there was a lot to catch up on, a lot for me to learn that took me way past the urge simply to reminisce. As dusk fell and we talked on into the night, the conversation would shift into the banter of friends. It turned out that Mike and Epeli, like Jeremy, had been born at the start of the Second World War, which meant they could remember the planes. Jeremy had watched for German bombers above Newbury, while Epeli had run along the beach at Samarai – an island off south-eastern Papua where his father was a missionary – watching fighters tumble out of the sky in the Battle of the Coral Sea. Mike wasn't into the insignia of aircraft, but the other two, literary men both, advocates of culture, were laughing with pleasure as they outdid each other with the names and makes of war planes they'd seen as children.

It was a good trip for all that it'd been more than usually exasperating getting Jeremy on the plane, not so much because of 9/11 as his stubborn prejudice against palm trees. He hated the way they were planted in the centre of Sydney roundabouts, and the way the ones in a neighbouring garden dropped branches onto the roof of his kitchen. As prejudices go, I suppose it was minor, and the intimacy between us was sufficient to accommodate it; I could laugh when I saw him see them in place, where they belonged, liking them as I'd hoped he would. He drank beer with Mike and Epeli under them, and when we weren't at the university he sat beneath them outside our hotel room – where at night we listened to news from the BBC World Service – and read William Trevor and Robert Louis Stevenson.

The second time Jeremy visited a land of palm trees was when he flew up to Moresby in 2004 to meet me after the Ömie trip, and never had I been so pleased to see him. He came through from customs and I leaned into him, his hand on my head as I breathed him in. Safe. I'd spoken to him from Popondetta while he was still in Sydney so he knew that our walk down the mountain had run us into trouble that had come in the shape of an arrest. We spoke briefly, given the distance and the dollars ticking over, and apart from anything else, of which there was a lot, I was concerned about him coming to join me, especially as Oliver, his elder son, was coming too, with his girlfriend of the time. We were going to Tufi in the fjords of Cape Nelson – different people, different history, different ways –

but still I was unnerved. Endangering Jeremy was one thing, but endangering the young – that wasn't on. What do you mean *arrested*? Jeremy asked. By police? How? Why? It makes no sense, he said, as I tried to condense what had happened into a few short sentences; it wasn't until he was there with me that I could tell him the whole complicated story.

After the meeting of the *duvahe* and another round of dancing, though not all night this time, we'd walked down to the village where Grahame and I had spent our peaceful interlude. People from every clan and every village came with us, a long line of us snaking through the forest, Thompson and me at the rear, patient Pauline walking with us. The forest seemed particularly rich that day, the canopy protecting us from the sun, intact spider webs beside the path telling us, Pauline said, that no enemies had been this way. When we arrived back at the village, a journey that was only slightly easier coming down, the guesthouse had the familiarity of home. Frogs were croaking, smoke drifting up from the cookhouse roof, children running ahead to call out that we were there. Thompson settled into position on the veranda, and after a meal of yams and pumpkin tops, I went to bed and slept the sleep of the virtuous. All was well; I'd squared up to the rigours, hadn't died on the climb; I was at ease with the women around me, and with my two travelling companions. The task was done, and as to whether we'd made the right decision, what other path could have been taken with the build-up of the last weeks? Whether we would meet the expectations was another matter. There would be nights back in Sydney when that anxiety would keep me awake, but that night in the village I slept easy.

In the morning I lingered on my sleeping mat, and when at last I went onto the veranda, there were three policemen outside in the sun talking to a group of curious people. What's going on? I asked David. A pep talk about keeping the village clean, it seems, he said. Odd. Oh well. When the police finished, David invited them into the guesthouse to join the large group squeezed around Andrew's table for a breakfast of sweet potato and the last of the instant coffee we'd bought in Moresby.

Well, David said, getting up from the table, conferring with Andrew about the schedule that had been organised, putting his hand out to farewell the police. We'd better get started. It was then that the atmosphere changed; we felt it at once, a breath taken in, silence, as the senior of the three police handed David a sheet of paper. David turned pale and sat down. He handed it to Grahame, who passed it to me. It was a warrant for our arrest on charges of *Phonography*. Pornography, David translated. I laughed. David and Grahame didn't. Later, when we were back in Moresby, I asked people why such a ludicrous charge? We were all in our fifties, for goodness sake, and if we were into pornography, which obviously we weren't, we'd have been better off staying comfortably in Sydney. The answer, which made a certain sense, was that there had been trouble in the past with white men going into villages with cameras and using the girls, and boys too, in ugly ways. The mere presence of a camera could lead to suspicion. So the charge was plausible, which was all that was necessary for a shakedown. Shakedown? I'd never heard the term until naïveté and good intentions walked us slap into an ambush. Pornography was irrelevant – it was a means to a different end, and that end – which should have been obvious that morning, but wasn't – was money, a lot of it. Maybe David knew, but I didn't, and I don't think Grahame did, when his camera was confiscated and our bags inspected. We were told to pack up; we were to leave with the police right then that morning and walk down to the village at the junction with the Kokoda road, where a police van was waiting.

In some strange way I wasn't afraid; it was so off-the-wall ridiculous, I couldn't think it would be taken seriously by anyone anywhere. I was still thinking in terms of justice and evidence. Patrick, I suppose. I am fifty-seven, I told the sergeant who was searching my bag, and a Fellow at the University of Sydney, as if that had anything to do with anything. He shook his head and apologised, polite as he riffled through my notebooks with their diagrams of designs from the barkcloth, names and measurements, charts of families and clans, stories from Lila and Dapene. It was a bad way to leave the village, with everyone upset, the women weeping, the *duvahe* remonstrating with the police – Good spirits all, these white people *tahua* – to no avail. We were under arrest. Everyone wanted to lift our hands to their faces, the women clasping my arms as

I breathed into them, children watching with astonished eyes. David looked terrible, pale, lined, as if he'd aged ten years in a morning. Andrew was beside him, and the security guards with their yellow labels and bush knives, carrying sheets of paper, exercise books filled with diagrams and agendas. Evidence. Proof of our innocence. Pauline walked with me every step of the way, five hours down to the road, silent through the village of Na´apa, holding me steady in the river we had to cross, and that was running fast that day. When we were ushered into the police van and the doors were closed, her hand was on the outside of the glass beside my head. It was the only time I shed a tear, and that was a great deal more to do with her than the van we were squeezed into. *Sister-friend.*

There'd been storms down on the plain while we were on the mountain; rivers were swollen, chunks of road collapsing, bridges precarious. It was a slow return to Popondetta. Thompson got out of the police van at the edge of town, and we continued on to the hotel with the bed bugs where we were to stay until we were charged, the sergeant said. The hotel had few vacancies with only two rooms available. David took the one that would fit him and Andrew with space on the floor for the Ömie accompanying him. Grahame and I took the small room with narrow single beds, which compared to the cage at the police station looked positively luxurious.

David had said nothing in the van. I'd put my hand on his knee, a gesture of sympathy, and he'd smiled, that's all. At the hotel, while Grahame was on the phone to Sydney, he and I sat in the small, hot bar, and he apologised. When I said it wasn't his fault, we couldn't have predicted it, he said he'd brought me here, I'd trusted him, and by that logic he was responsible; he had endangered me. Not you, I said. The situation has endangered us; not you. It didn't matter that I wasn't – at that stage – frightened. We'd ring the Australian High Commission in Moresby; they'd sort it out, I said. We're in PNG, he said, his voice sad and low, his eyes glistening – tears perhaps? – and I saw that for him who'd given so much, it was an assault on his honour, his good name, though he didn't use those words: they are Patrick words. A random hold-up on a street in Port Moresby – when young men from a settlement had tried (unsuccessfully) to stop the car he was in – had not diminished him; nor the wrangle with the man from the Popondetta tourist office over the price of a dinghy ride. But this sudden loss of control – of which David had so little experience – had humiliated him.

And what did I feel? Protective of course, as I had so often of Patrick, shielding him against knowledge of his own fragilities. I could stand up to David when he was being boorish and unthinking, but when I saw him reduced, that perverse feminine instinct to protect kicked in.

When Andrew's crew, barred from riding in the police van, turned up, they joined us in the bar. Grahame was off the phone, and there were beers all round. The Ömie men were certain the arrest was a stitch-up, the work of some men from Na´apa who had married into a family in Popondetta. When the delegation had come to protest their exclusion and to bargain with Andrew that night of the disturbance, they'd been sent away empty-handed and shamed. Why had Andrew not told us? Would it not have been better to settle it then? Useless questions. One of the Na´apa in-laws, Andrew now said, was in the police. Which? Not one of those who'd come to arrest us, it seemed; I never did work out who, or which, or whether. I ordered a bottle of Australian red, and hang the expense.

By then we had rung the Australian High Commission. A consular official, a woman with a calm voice, was reassuring in a general kind of way, but said they couldn't interfere in PNG's justice system. On no account, she warned, were we to offer any money, for that way we could legitimately be charged with bribery. The High Commissioner, she said, would ring the provincial police chief the next day. All we could do was wait. After that long walk down the mountain, and the wine, at least we slept; no night terrors – at least not for me – no dreams, nothing.

In the morning we were escorted back to the police station and told to wait outside. We joined a group of men under a mango tree, the only shade in the scorched yard. Whatever troubles had brought them there, it seemed they knew all about us. No good, they said, shaking their heads and filling ours with stories of malfeasance of one kind or another. Were there police involved in this shakedown, if that's what it was; and if so which? If not the ones who'd come to arrest us, then who? No one could, or would, say, though the sergeant we were taken to see that morning was the obvious choice, or would have been were it not

that in Papua New Guinea the obvious is almost always
not. The police station was curiously quiet as we were
taken down a long corridor of closed doors to this
sergeant's room where, in the course of the next hour, we
were asked questions, which David answered, or Andrew.
What were we doing on the mountain? Why would we
be interested in the barkcloth? It was *tapa*, that's all, we
could buy it in Popondetta. He offered to bring some, to
show us; we could buy from him. Another hour, another
set of questions until the talk went back and forth only
between Andrew and the sergeant. Were they negotiating
a price? It was too fast to follow, too much in language we
didn't have. David was asked to hand over his passport.
No. Not his passport, and not his wallet either. Andrew's
explanation of his exchange with the sergeant was evasive.
And still there was no sign of the officer who had assigned
Thompson to us. The police chief was not available. No,
there was no one who could speak to us but this sergeant,
with his patchy English and rapid Tok Pisin, who sent us
back outside to the yard.[63] A crowd had gathered on the
street to watch. The prisoners in the cage were turned
our way. Under the mango tree, with no water, nothing
to drink, it was hot, and the stories kept coming, none
of them reassuring. How much was *mauswara* – a vivid
word that means mouth-water: bullshit.

It was well into the afternoon when we were taken
back, yet again, to the sergeant's room. This time he was
beaming, and on the desk in front of him was a porno-
graphic magazine from 1996, chewed by cockroaches and

stained with betel-nut juice. Evidence, he said, his own teeth red and black from chewing betel. At that moment Roma, Thompson's wife, came into the room. Come, she said, looking at me. Where? Why? Better you come, she said, and David nodded. Looks like we won't be going anywhere, he said. So I let her lead me up the stairs to her office in another silent corridor of closed doors. This is not true, I said. *Mauswara*. The evidence is serious, she said. What does Thompson say? I asked. He knows it's not true. Evidence, she said again, shrugging off her husband. Where else could it have come from but us? If we'd brought it, I said, wouldn't we have brought a more recent magazine, not one eight years old and covered in betel stains? She was unconvinced, and of course she'd have had no idea what was available on the shelves of newsagents in Australia and would have been shocked if she had. Very bad, she said. If she weren't in the police she couldn't have looked at it. Bad, yes, I said, but it did not come from us. Not you, she said. It is David they want, not you. But I was there, I said. I am the same as David. She shrugged. Evidence.

Oh Patrick, *daddy-oh*, it was happening, just as I feared; an arrest in a foreign jail and you're dead. Gone.

No, the consular official told us that evening, they had not managed to get onto the police chief. My student friend, the foreign minister, had they contacted him? No, they said, it was too soon; the High Commissioner would be seeing him the next week, he might be able to mention it then. Next week! There was the matter of interfering,

she said. That's when we rang Ros Morauta, who'd
had us for dinner that night in Port Moresby, a friend
of David's, now a friend of mine. I don't know why we
didn't ring her first up, as soon as we arrived at the hotel.
A classic shakedown, she said. The man we needed was
an Australian lawyer who worked weeks in Moresby. She
gave us his name. Ring him now, she said. He'll be going
down to Brisbane for the weekend on Friday. So David
rang, and within the hour the fax in the hotel juddered
into action with a letter addressed to the arresting officer,
informing him that he, this lawyer, was acting for the
three of us. His advice, he said in the letter, as well as to
David on the phone, was that if we were not charged,
we should leave Popondetta on the morning plane. If we
were charged, he would be on the lunchtime plane over
to Popondetta. He was known in the town, we heard,
having recently won a high-profile corruption case there.

Oh Jeremy, I said on another expensive call to Sydney.
I thought I wasn't afraid, but I am. Of course I'll still
come, Jeremy said, and it was one of the few times he
got on a plane without having to fight the countervailing
impulse to stay at home.

'And Oliver?'

'I'll speak to him when we know more,' Jeremy said.

The next morning, within twenty minutes of handing
the fax to the sergeant – who smelled of home brew;
I suppose for him too it was a dangerous situation –
Grahame and I were told we could leave. There would
be no charges. David insisted that we go straight into

town and change our tickets. I accepted, and agreed, and wished I hadn't. I felt it as a failure of courage. So much for protecting David; there I was saving my own skin when he and so many others were left unprotected. Andrew had seen men from Na´apa in another room that last time we'd been taken into the sergeant's office. He knew exactly who was in town, and what it meant, even if we didn't. More Ömie men had arrived, bringing news from Ömie women who'd married into Na´apa, their loyalties not so much divided as earthed in their birth clan. Yes, the women had said, it was all true, and worse; it was pay-back. Ömie honour was at stake, the men said, and yes, it was this sergeant, he was the relative. Up it ratcheted, true or not, who was to know, certainly not us. Out under the mango tree, where Grahame and I were saying goodbye, all was heat and rumour and warrior shoulders raised. I was leaving, leaving David to the prospect of that cage; what would become of him with that out-of-time moustache I'd become accustomed to, even fond of? Strange what you can come to like in a man. He held my hand in his. I want you to go, he said. And I want Grahame to go with you. It's my decision, not yours.

We were about to walk back to the hotel, collect our bags, when a car drew up outside the police station. Several men got out, among them – finally – the officer we'd seen the day before we'd left for Ömie. They walked into the building without a glance in our direction, and some minutes later a well-spoken official in a yellow mufti

shirt came across the bare yard towards us. He was so
sorry, he said in perfect English. It seems you've been
caught up in a land dispute. He handed Grahame his
camera and congratulated him on the work he'd done,
documenting traditional art. David, too, he said, was
free to go. The police van was ready to take us to the
airstrip. But David had no ticket. Even if he had, he said,
he'd have stayed. There was Andrew to consider, and the
Ömie; their honour. He couldn't walk away and leave this
fight brewing; was it not due to us, to him? he said, taking
on the responsibility. No, he'd stay, talk to the senior
officers, to the police chief, if he could. For it was not a
land dispute – we knew that and the police knew that –
and should they not take some action to solve the tensions
among the villages and avoid a war on the mountain?

David spent another day, another night, in Popondetta.
He did speak to the senior officers, but to little effect. The
feud simmered on for another year before Andrew gave in to
David's persuasion, and there was a meeting of the villages,
a pig feast, compensation (paid for by David), a settlement
that ensured at least some form of involvement, and reward,
for Na´apa in the barkcloth *bisnis*. It can still be uneasy, even
now, and there are occasional ambushes along the road,
though more likely by people from other tribes, other places,
hoping they can take the cloth, make the money.

Back in Sydney I looked up Martin Luther King and found,
as I should have known, that *a dangerous road* comes from
his last speech, given in Memphis, Tennessee on 3 April

1968, the day before he was assassinated. The road he
meant, in a literal sense, was the road that winds down
from Jerusalem to Jericho, the road on which Jesus placed
the parable of the Good Samaritan. Martin Luther King
drove it with Mrs King, he says in the speech. 'We rented a
car . . . and as soon as we got on that road, I said to my wife,
"I can see why Jesus used this as the setting for his parable."
It's a winding, meandering road.' A road that drops 3000
feet, a road of ravines and rocky passes. A road that is
'conducive for ambushing'. It's a fine speech that takes
the metaphor of the road through many turns: the road
through history, the road against injustice, the dangerous
road of civil rights; the roads we walk and how we walk
them, together or alone; whom we assist, whom we pass
by. As with the man of the parable who was left wounded
by thieves while travelling the Jericho road, do we pass by
on the other side and leave him to die, as the Levite and
the priest did; or do we stop, as did the Samaritan, 'a man
of another race', and lend our help? The Samaritan was a
great man, a good man, because, Martin Luther King says,
'he had the capacity to project the "I" into the "thou", and
to be concerned about his brother'. He thought not of the
danger to himself were he to stop, but of the danger to the
injured man if he did not stop.[64]

'Let us develop a kind of dangerous unselfishness,'
King says, for there is reason for us all to be afraid. Bad
things happen on dangerous roads, and in dark times
many a road can turn dangerous. He hoped, he said that
night, that he'd live to walk the road of justice and civil

rights further into the twentieth century, undeterred by threats from 'some of our sick white brothers'. Such were the threats that the plane he'd caught from Atlanta that morning had had to be under guard the previous night. He was thirty-nine years old when he gave that speech – and when, on the evening of the following day, he was shot dead by a single bullet from a white marksman.

I cannot leave you in Papua New Guinea with only the image of ambush and danger. Such shakedowns are rare, though many a well-intentioned whitey will tell you they've been taken for 'chickens to be plucked', as Bob Connolly puts it in his account of being caught up in a Highland tribal war while filming *Black Harvest* in 1990.[65] There are indeed roads on which you must travel with care. There are settlements around the edges of towns filled with people – many of them young men – coming in after a slice of the wealth, or because of land pressures at home, and finding only poverty, unemployment and *raskol* gangs. There's money being made in that country, a lot of it, not least from logging and mining, but while some grow rich, ostentatiously so, many more are left in poverty, disaffected and without land. If there is violence, which there is, is it a 'primitive' instinct, a legacy of pre-colonial tribal warfare? Or is it a response to the divergence between a Westernised economy of wealth, capital and corruption for some, and the degradation that is the lot of many, and not only in the settlements? You might think me an apologist if I put the emphasis on the response to the inequalities of the new. I don't doubt the legacy of the old, or those warrior enmities, especially in the Highlands. But I also know, and have seen, another PNG that belongs to neither extreme, either in daily life or aspiration; it is to be seen in villages across this rich and diverse country where culture remains strong, authority structures sufficiently intact, where land has not been lost to logging or mining, where there is rich gardening and rich fishing. The challenge for this Papua New Guinea, at once vulnerable and strong, is how to live in both, combining and reconciling the world of the village and the world beyond, without losing control of the land, the 'soul' of the country's culture, and the way its people can live day by day.[66] It is not easy, and the challenge is great, the tide can pull against them, but there are many parts of the country – on the coast, on the islands – where a walking between, or with both, is articulated, and where visitors are welcomed and made safe.

And so it was with us when we flew back over the mountains, David, Jeremy and I with young Oliver and Maya. We landed at Tufi, the plane coming in over a landscape of deep fjords and vivid green peninsulas, circling out over a shimmer of reef, before landing on the sloping grass strip. The men who met us greeted David with high fives, their baseball hats worn with the peaks to the back. Already joking with Oliver, a language of references the young understand, they took us by dinghy to their villages further east along the fjords. David was bruised, brooding – when we were alone, which wasn't often – on what had happened, and how it might have been different. He should have got up that night when the men from Na´apa had come to the village; he'd heard voices and thought it was young men trying to wake the girls. But for the rest, it was the buoyant David who turned his face to the village, and I alone saw that he was unable to relax into the ease of that beautiful place – which Oliver and Maya enjoyed so much, learning traditional dances, and tapping to a fjord reggae, that they decided to stay on after we left.

I've been back to those villages many times. I've been back alone, and I've taken many people, not only friends my age, but their daughters, some as young as thirteen or fourteen, and I've taken Martha, sanguine when she went back alone with another young woman. The safety of this Papua New Guinea, its beauty, the strength and gentleness of its people, is a view that runs counter to everything we read. The first time Hilary came with me, we were swimming in a fjord late one afternoon. Lying on our backs in the calm, silky water, kicking gently to keep afloat, looking up at green curving into the distance, the mountains beyond, a dreamy blue-grey against the sky. Why didn't you tell me it was like this? Hilary said. How come I didn't know? *Hilary!* I said, and we laughed, pulled our goggles back down and returned our attention to Evie, who'd brought us to this part of the reef and was diving down, pointing to a bright blue starfish.

And if you were to go to Manus right now, you would not find the hellhole you read of. The detention centre, Australian-run, is a hellhole, built of the wrong materials in the wrong location, but Manus is not. It's an island with a strong and proud history. It has produced many of the best leaders of an independent country; it has an ethos of education and cooperation.[67] It has been rocked, like so many places in the Pacific, by the seismic events of the twentieth century, not least of which, for Manus, was the American airbase built on that small island during the Pacific War. A wave of money washed in, and then washed out again. And now the next wave washes in with the detention centre, bringing complicated and contradictory consequences for the island population.

In villages and markets hundreds of miles away, on the north coast of the Papuan mainland, you'll hear people say that as well as the insult that a rich country should use a poor country so, it is an insult to the ground of Manus that people from a distant place should be imprisoned there. They have seen photos on social media of rubbish tips spilling outside the detention centre. Digicel reaches into most of the villages, though not to Ömie, which remains as remote, in that sense, as it ever was. But in villages with Digicel people know of the plastic that blows into the sea, the clouds of flies, the stench that reaches nearby villages. No, it is not good, they say. It is bad for Manus, and it is bad for the ground of its ancestors to have lost and angry people imprisoned there. And this doesn't even touch the question of the asylum seekers themselves, or the context of the dangers they are fleeing, the refuge they are seeking. That is a matter of concern to me as an Australian citizen and resident, though I rarely hear it spoken of in those villages and markets. Lost, far away from their land: on those grounds alone asylum seekers should not be on Manus.

In February 2014, early in the writing of this book, a young Iranian Kurd called Reza Barati was beaten and killed in that detention centre. Like most Australians, I knew nothing of Reza Barati when the news of the riots and the violence came through in grainy images on news reports. And other than his death, I know very little about him now. Who was this young man, an architect, twenty-three years old? What had brought him on the hazardous journey away from the country of his birth? Do any of us know him by anything other than his death? Little information gets out of this distant camp. We hear of the flare-up of violence when riots occur, but we rarely hear the voices of those detained by a system that keeps journalists at bay, requires confidentiality from those who work there, and refuses those seeking asylum that most basic of needs, to have their stories heard.

No, Manus is not a hellhole. The hellhole of the detention centre is Australian-made, and while the material conditions are woeful, the true hell of that hole is psychological for the people detained there without trial, without voice, without hope, with all certainty removed, their stories questioned, their names replaced with numbers. The shame is ours, here in comfortable Australia. It is also the shame of a colluding PNG government. It is not the shame of that country's people, and certainly not the shame of the people of Manus.

12

When I stood beside Pauline after the meeting of the *duvahe* on the mountain and she imagined the day she'd visit my place, anxiety had punched through me. Pauline in Sydney? What had we set in train? What else was being imagined in that rejoicing, dancing crowd? But five years later, in July 2009, there she was, indeed in my place. She had come down to Sydney with Dapene for the second exhibition of Ömie art at Annandale Galleries. The first at the same gallery had been in 2006, and in preparation for it Andrew and Michael had come to Sydney. David and I had arranged for them to spend time with a young linguist – a postgraduate from Sydney University – drawing up lexicons, Ömie word lists, standardising spellings, for use in catalogues and essays about the art. Watching them work, David and I were astonished at the subtleties of vowel sounds that the Ömie and the linguist could hear but we could not. O. Ö. Oe. Other days were spent with Mike – the anthropologist friend I'd visited in Suva, who'd lent me his diaries, and was now living in

Sydney – going over the stories of the *duvahe*, names of the clans, their interconnections, the iconography of the designs.

Not much more than a year after that visit, Andrew was bitten by a snake. He had been in his garden and, with no one there to help him, had walked back to the village, where he'd died. David heard the news on the phone from Popondetta. It was hard enough to grasp what had happened. Why was there no one else in the garden? Why hadn't they carried him down to the aid post on the road? It was harder still to comprehend the ramifications of this next disturbance. Was it a warning? Was the mountain displeased? Who would pay the compensation? The questions swirled as a dreadful event gathered conflicting meanings. A batch of art had arrived in Sydney a few months earlier – Andrew's last. David and I looked at it and knew at once that something wasn't right. But what exactly? It wasn't until later that we learned there'd been a dispute with the women, over what we were also never entirely sure, but it had to do with them feeling pressured in ways that were no good for the cloth – and as a result they'd refused to paint. So Andrew got the men on the job and had them drawing the lines with rulers he'd brought back from Sydney. Not every line was ruled, but enough to kill the music, the movement of the cloth. After more calls to Popondetta, long negotiations, Andrew's replacement, a man called Alban, came down with another batch, and among them, as well as cloth painted by Dapene and Lila, were *nioge* by some of the young women who'd returned to the old knowledge, giving it new shape. We were on the road again.

Pauline and Dapene were the first women, the first artists, to visit Sydney. It was July when their plane landed after dark, and it was cold. Waiting for them at the airport with David, I was jittery. Half an hour, an hour, and still no sign of them, a long lull with no one coming through, as if every plane had emptied. And then there they were – Pauline and Dapene, with Alban, undiminished by a journey every bit as daunting to them as our climb through the forest had been to us. I had jackets and scarves for them, but all they had on their feet when we walked out into the night were the rubber thongs Alban had bought for them in Popondetta. Walking to the car, Dapene stopped, but no, it wasn't the cold. She was looking up at the sky, exclaiming in her Ömie language. Pauline and Alban looked up with her. David and I did too. The stars, Alban translated, the stars are changed. They do not shine. Yes, they were dim indeed compared to the constellations above their mountain. A different world, this new people's place.

The next day David drove us all to a shopping mall to buy shoes and warm clothes. I thought a local second-hand shop would be easier for Dapene, but Alban had been to this mall before, and David said that at Big W they could also buy for people back in the villages. So off we set, through the suburbs of Sydney, Alban in the front with David, and me between the two women in the back.

Dapene held onto my hand in a tight grasp. Pauline was interested in everything she saw through the window, until we turned into the car park with its low concrete ceiling, dim light, and lines of silent cars. No good, she said as we walked towards the mall. Not a good place. Inside she rallied and let go of my arm, but Dapene remained subdued. We found shoes and jackets and filled the trolley with t-shirts for the children in the villages, and with packet after packet of underwear. For women reliant on moss and leaves during menstruation, a pair of pants to hold them in place allows mobility, a degree of control. Into the trolley it all went. David raised his eyebrows. It's okay, I murmured, I'd explain later. The mall had shaken the women, the queue was slow, I had a headache myself, but Dapene, though subdued, no longer needed my hand. We had only to get back to the car and we'd be out of there. But as we walked past the food outlets, surrounded that day by particularly large white people overflowing their chairs, Dapene suddenly slumped. Her shoulders folded over, she shrank, visibly, and the light went out of her eyes. Another whack of anxiety, David this time as well as me. Had she had a stroke? (She hadn't. We took her to a doctor the next day even though we knew by then that it wasn't that.) Not sickness, Pauline said, holding her up. It was the bad spirits on the escalators. They'd stolen all her strength.

Back in the car Dapene slumped against Pauline. I put my hand on hers and there was no response. What should we do? Even David was at a loss. Best we go to your house, Pauline said, adding *Missis* in a voice also gone limp. Best we go to your house, and Alban go with David to his. For Pauline, it was the obvious answer, as it should have been for David and me, knowing the gendered nature of life in Ömie. So that's what we did.

'Will you be okay?' David asked as he pulled up at my house. 'Ring if you need me.'

In this crisis, David wasn't an option. I made a pot of strong tea, heaped sugar into the cups, opened a packet of biscuits and again turned to Pauline. Certain, strong-voiced Pauline.

'Where is your ground?' she asked.

Outside. Yes, of course, they needed to be outside.

At the oval at the end of my street, they scuffed at the hard earth with toes in new shoes. They leaned down and touched the grass, pressed their fingers through to the earth. Yes, they supposed it was ground, of a sort.

'Your gardens?' Pauline asked. 'They are where?'

'In the cities we have no gardens. We have shops,' I said and Pauline translated for Dapene. It clearly wasn't an adequate answer. Pauline looked at me again, her face a question mark.

'There are markets,' I said. 'The people who have the gardens bring the food to the market. The people from the shops buy the food from them.'

Pauline nodded, translating for Dapene again. Not much better, but sufficient this time, and yes, we could go to a market, they could see it for themselves.

We walked on round the oval, along the front of Snails Bay, and out onto the jetty to taste the salt water, *sol warra*, they'd seen from the plane but had never encountered hand and foot. We walked around to Mort Bay, and as we walked Dapene regained something of her stature; by the time we returned to the oval, she and Pauline were singing Ömie songs. It was dusk, joggers were jogging past, the lights were coming on.

Back at my house they wanted to lie down, which they did, on my bed – a good spirit bed, mercifully – while in the kitchen I brooded on that *Missis*. Was it a default position? The result of being here in the 'new' people's city? An indication of the stress of the moment? A rebuke that I should be able to look after them – protect them – as they had me while I was on their ground? That's when I wished David was in my kitchen, and not across the city at his house with Alban. I rang, the next best thing, to let him know how we were going. Alban, he said, was fine. He had all the cloth out on the floor and had refused a beer. Yes, we agreed, right then we could have done with each other and a bottle of red. I'll check in tomorrow, I said, and rang off.

When Pauline and Dapene came downstairs to eat – sweet potato and pork that didn't convince them as pig – Pauline reported that Dapene's strength had returned. She took my hand, put her nose to the inside of my elbow, leaned into my shoulder and breathed in. *Sister-friend*, she said.

Where is your ground? It is a question that has stayed with me. Where was our ground? Ours in the sense of a highly asphalted world, and ungrounded culture? Where was *my* ground? Mine in the sense of the PNG novel I was – or rather at that stage was not – writing. And where was my ground as the terrain beneath Jeremy trembled and shook? In the spiral of his life with his younger son, where did I stand? Where could I stand? Did my love for him, tattered but not gone, my commitment to a relationship made late in life, require of me the sacrifices he was prepared to make – and couldn't not make?

Books suck. Books took me away. Books kept me sane.

Jeremy had come to PNG with me one more time and after that I returned alone, or with friends, or a combination of both. David didn't come again – in part due, I think, to the injury of the shakedown, in part to a shifting interest to Vanuatu that had already begun; he had art projects there that needed attention. I went with him once, towards the end of 2006 when things were at a low ebb with Jeremy and with the still-stuck book. You need a change, David said, a break; it'll do you good. Come as my guest, he said, and I did. Jeremy was put out, very, but I went anyway and David was right, it did me good. Though I couldn't not feel for Jeremy, still it was a wonderful trip: islands, banana boats, masked dancers, deep water and clear light. Why don't you set the book here, David said, it'd be a whole lot easier, and maybe it would but my allegiances – my heart – were in Papua New Guinea, and the book only made sense if it was there.

A few months later I was back on a plane to Port Moresby. I didn't climb the mountain again, for reasons that mostly had to do with legs and strength, but I returned many times to the fjords. On the way, I'd sometimes stop in Popondetta to take messages to the Ömie who were down from the mountain, before flying on to those bountiful villages, where I spent weeks at a time sitting with the women, with the elders, in the cookhouse, or on the platform of a *winhaus*, an open-sided platform built beside the beach or on a ridge to catch the wind. I'd learn from the women as they made their bilums and wove mats; I'd walk with them up to the gardens, canoe with them to the next village; I'd visit the schools where David was still paying the fees of many children. I took up sketch pads and crayons and scissors and glue. Most went into the school, which from an Australian perspective was chronically under-resourced. Chalk and board, no power, workbooks for the older grades but very little for the younger children, who'd come to the *winhaus* after they'd canoed home from school, wanting a page from the pads, a crayon. These were children I'd seen draw in the sand, diagrams, maps, pictures, all along the beach, and the older children teaching the letters, stories, wending their way around the drawings; and the waves lapping in, and the children laughing, running into the water, and back out again to draw some more. And there they were, sitting beside me drawing on their paper until the light went.

There were occasional whispers, hints, that David hadn't always chosen the right students to sponsor, and all of them were boys. I'd try to persuade him to support others and

I made the case for the girls, which was not difficult given the amount of research demonstrating that the education of girls is the fastest route to development. Sometimes he did as I suggested; but when I asked if this was the best way of supporting the village – should we set up something that gave the villages, the schools, more say – he'd defer: later, he'd say, we'll think about it later. Like all of us, his strengths and his weaknesses were interlinked. The other side of his generosity was his need to control. I didn't press; that was my weakness. I didn't have the money to do what he did – though I sponsored a few girls – and there was something in David – that vulnerability shadowing his masculine certainty? – I didn't want to cross. Besides, there was too much to lose – for me, and for the villages. So I did what I could, and in the villages I placated and soothed, and for the most part it was no more than a ripple on the surface of visits as calm as the water; canoes gliding in, crayfish from the reef, a meal as the sun set, an evening of story and bad tea, mosquito nets.

It was Sydney that returned me to anxiety: Jeremy, the book, the Ömie. Actually, the fortunes of the art – though they were costing David a lot, a responsibility I was all too willing to let him keep from me – kept moving well, better than we could have imagined. Three exhibitions – the two in Sydney, another in Perth – was an achievement in five years from a halt-start. It was David who did it. I was there, but it was David who knew the world of business and of selling. Was it like this in advertising? I'd ask, curious, never having given those skills – that industry – much credence. Rather the contrary. Back in radical student days we'd scoffed at those who sold things that weren't needed to people who couldn't afford them – and wouldn't have thought to want them if it weren't for these slick advertisements. Yes, David said, some of it is the same. You have to know how to get the interest started, how to follow up, how to make a deal. But it also wasn't the same, and not only because it was art we were promoting. When he'd sold the company, it wasn't because he was disenchanted with advertising – which, he'd say, can have its own ethical framework for the accounts it takes on – but with the way the corporate world was going. A Labor man of an earlier era, businessman though he was, he despised the elevation of profit above all else. There'd been complaints from the accountants, I remember him saying, that he provided food for anyone working in the office, many of them young people who were saving to buy a house, or had small children. Not lavish food: good bread, cheeses and jams, fruit, tomatoes, decent coffee. That can't have been a reason for getting out, but it stuck with me, this story from David's past. He was a man who thought about what people working for him needed, a man with a sense of exchange, a recognition, in this case, of the hours put in. Quite Melanesian really. It had never surprised me that he had loved the Pacific, Oceania, its islands, its exuberant cultures, and the art he'd immersed himself in. I could see it met something in him that hadn't found a place in Australia. A kind of antithesis to advertising. Although, yes, it did take skills learned in the industry he'd left. It also took his determination that whatever happened with the *nioge*, it would be in the interests of Ömie, not of someone else's profit. Having money, I came to see, meant that in his negotiations he could withhold it as well as bestow its benefits.

But skill alone wouldn't have done it if it hadn't been for the quality of the cloth. Critics and curators were quick to see its significance, and by 2009 it had been acquired by the state galleries in Victoria, Queensland and Western Australia as well as the National Gallery of Australia in Canberra. So by the time Pauline and Dapene arrived in Sydney, Ömie art was beginning to be known, there was a buzz, a small buzz, but enough that the omens were good for *The Wisdom of the Mountain* exhibition that was to open at the National Gallery of Victoria that November. It would be the gallery's first major exhibition of contemporary Papua New Guinean art, and was given a premier space at the St Kilda Road gallery. As well as being in Sydney for the exhibition at Annandale Galleries, Pauline and Dapene were here that July to be filmed painting as part of the supplementary material for the NGV's exhibition. It was a significant undertaking, with two curators and a cameraman flying up from Melbourne. Alban had brought dyes in small jars; Dapene and Pauline spread mats on the floor, unfolded the beaten cloth, sharpened their painting sticks, and dressed as proud Ömie women sang as they worked.[68]

While they were in town, there wasn't time to worry about the sticking point I'd come to with the book that wasn't yet called *The Mountain*. And Jeremy rallied in support, if not of me then of the visitors. He'd enjoyed being in the fjord villages, playing football with the boys, sitting with the old men, smoking his pipe on the beach, giving everyone, including spluttering children, a puff. Of all the people who have been to the village with me, his was among the most immediate and intuitive response. It was reciprocated. Though he only ever went there twice, people continue to ask after him, and there is now a small namesake Jeremy running around. Also a Drusilla, much the same age, a shy girl who is pulled forward to sit beside me, poor child, for yet more photographs. Jeremy found a similar ease with the Ömie who visited Sydney. He'd taken Andrew and Michael for drives around town, caught the ferry with them, visited galleries and the Opera House. He gave them sausages and ice cream in his leafy garden. And so it was when Pauline and Dapene were here. He came to the gallery for the filming; he cooked more sausages. Janet Laurence and Jo Bertini also came to the gallery, and Jeremy took Alban to the museum while I took Pauline and Dapene to Janet and Jo's studios. At Jo's they drew on paper with wax crayons; at Janet's they looked at her images of trees and forests on glass, partly concealed by pours, those veils of paint. As they touched and looked, and looked again, walking round the studio with Janet, I watched – the only one of us who didn't use her hands as they used theirs. I saw a connection between them – for all that was different, hugely different – which I did not share. If Janet had been in the village, Dapene wouldn't have had to tell her that the cloth, it knows.

Does the page also know?

When the writing goes well, as it has, largely, with this book, I think perhaps it does. But with the draft of the book I was still calling 'the PNG book' when Pauline and Dapene visited, the page seemed as unknowing as I was. Or else the book and its problems were trapped inside my head and there was no movement through the hand to the page. I was watching myself, the sternest of the critics, some kind of internal post-colonial border policewoman. How could I, a white woman, write of Melanesia without appropriating, or projecting, or sentimentalising, or mistranslating the un-translatable? If I wrote black characters would I get them wrong? If I didn't, would I be rendering them part of an exotic background as colonial writers – and too many since – have done, 'a distorting lens' as the writer and critic Regis Stella has written, not only to the way Melanesians are understood by readers outside, but a distorting lens onto their own perceptions of themselves and their culture?[69] Despite everything I'd learned through the lives of women, everything I'd written and stood for, when it came to the vexed issue of race and the legacy of a colonial order that had first been under the control of England, and then Australia, I'd boxed myself into the binary opposition of either/or – same or different, like or unlike, their culture or ours – shrinking the ground between.

Yet in the twenty-first century there are few of us, Papuan or Australian, tribal or globalised, who stand on just one ground. For Dapene in her sixties, who'd only twice been down to Popondetta, Sydney – with its escalators and obese people, its homeless men on the streets with no family, no village to go to – was incomprehensibly strange. From her point of view this world of ours was as 'other' – and a great deal more savage – than anything a resident of Sydney would encounter in Ömie. But it was not so strange for Alban, a younger man, who'd done several years of school in Popondetta and knew Port Moresby. He was an explorer, an anthropologist in our world, talking to the bus driver who took him round the bus at the end of the route (one stop from my house), accompanying the postman round the block, questioning everyone, taking dozens of photos with his digital camera. Pauline was somewhere in between. She didn't like the shopping mall, but she liked the local hardware store, where she stocked up on scissors and wooden spoons to take back to her village.

On the first morning of filming for the NGV, I could see something was wrong. There we were at Annandale Galleries, Dapene and Pauline dressed in nioge and feathers, Alban in his headdress, everything in place, and yet every time Pauline's cloth touched Dapene's, Dapene would push her, and it, away. The cameraman wanted them to work closely together; he wanted their cloth to touch, to overlap, but Dapene wasn't having it. When I called for a break, the cameraman – who was

French and dramatic – wouldn't hear of it. I tried again, with no success. Even David was waved aside. Dapene continued to pull her cloth away from Pauline, and when at last David insisted we stop and Pauline reluctantly stood up, it was clear what the problem was. Her period had started. I took her downstairs to the bathroom, shot round to the chemist, and arrived back at the gallery to find Alban and Dapene adamant that Pauline must stay away from the barkcloth, and therefore from the filming. There was even a suggestion that any of the *nioge* on the wall that Pauline had touched, some with red stickers, some going to major galleries, should be taken down. I left that one to David and the curators – destruction was averted – and took Pauline to my house, where we could be secluded from men. We closed the door, turned on the heater and settled in. Dapene would return to sleep in David's much larger house.

The next morning, while the filming was continuing at the gallery and I was expecting a quiet day of seclusion, Pauline asked if, instead of staying indoors, we could take a ferry out on the salt water. Sure, I said, but there'll be men on it. She shrugged. Were there more pads? Would there be toilets? With the answer to both being yes, we took the ferry to Circular Quay and walked through the Botanic Gardens – relatively secluded, I thought – until we were hungry. When I suggested that we go home, she asked if we could stay in town, eat in a shop, look at the tall buildings. Sure, I said again; we were close to the art gallery, we could have lunch there, but there'd be men eating as well. She smiled. They don't know, she said. And of course they didn't. She was a sufficiently modern woman to judge that it was the sensitivities of men that caused the fear of contamination she already doubted. We had lunch in the café and then a long afternoon, much of it in the Indigenous gallery, where she was particularly interested in Kitty Kantilla, looking closely at the mark of her paint stick. At the Sydney Museum we stopped to see the pillars and poles that make up the courtyard sculpture of Fiona Foley and Janet Laurence's *Edge of the Trees*. We walked around the poles, some made from sandstone, some from steel, some of grainy timber from a demolished colonial warehouse. Pauline put her hands on them, taking in their texture, walking slowly, feeling each one, stopping with her ear to the whispered sound of the Eora language that comes from a recording set into one of them. Twenty-nine poles. Twenty-nine clans of the Eora people. She liked that. Where are they now, these old people? Another hard question. Or perhaps not; all too simple with the city buildings rising above us. The analogy she drew was with the palm-oil plantations around Popondetta, the impoverished villages, lost land, people living on the edge of the town where rice and tinned fish were considered a feast. Ground. It was all a matter of ground.

The next day Pauline declared her period over and we returned to the gallery and the filming – to no ill effect. The only person who knew what was in the bag she carried was me; that day I was indeed sister-friend.

When the Ömie returned to their mountain, Jeremy and I went for a drink at the Dry Dock Hotel, where we'd had our first date. On the walls were pictures of the working dry dock that had once been across the road, with steep steps down to its base beneath the hulls of the cargo and navy ships, a nether region long gone. I liked those photos and always looked at them; how tidy our lives seemed in comparison, all that history concealed under a park for children to play and dogs to be walked. Jeremy and I were there that evening in an attempt to remind ourselves how we had come together, why it was that we were still, just, sleeping in the same bed. Not often, by then, but enough. And yes, we could connect to our shared England. We could reminisce about the journeys we still made together, our overlapping visits to London, the last one only nine months before, in the summer of 2008, when I was there to greet Amy's first baby, my great-nephew Sam, the first of a new generation. A glorious, milky moment. Jeremy had joined us for a family holiday at a cousin's rambling house in the hills behind the coast in the south of France. We had a large, slightly sagging bed overlooking hills covered with olive trees. It was Jeremy who looked on the map and saw that we were not far from where Stella Bowen had visited and painted in the 1920s while still in love with Ford Madox Ford. 'A landscape full of little, separate accents,' she wrote in her memoir, with a dry light 'which hits the ground and reflects upwards, to fill the shadows with a bubble-like iridescence.'[70] Stella had caught a tram to shop at the Nice markets. At the end of

our family holiday, we drove to Nice along the motorway
that skirts the coast with buildings as ugly as any you'll
see in Australia swamping once-small towns. When my
family returned to England, Jeremy and I took the train to
Genoa, and then to Florence, enjoying each other again,
and no, it didn't matter that I didn't get up at dawn when
he went off to walk the city streets before the crowds.
He'd arrive back at our room with the *Herald Tribune* and
we'd go to the place he'd found for breakfast. At the Dry
Dock with the racing on the TV screens beside the bar,
we could see ourselves in that café in Florence, and in the
room in the quirky hotel he'd found, but it was like a film,
with little to do with our life shared between two houses
up the hill from the pub.

Even that reconciliatory night, we tumbled back into
the bitter argument that had arisen between us. No,
I couldn't give up the ground of my writing life; and
anyway I was far from convinced that even if I could,
and did, it would change anything. It was magical
thinking, I'd say, as if I could wave a wand and become
a fairy godmother. And there was the question hovering:
would it have been different if I'd had children of my
own? If I'd been a mother? It was a line of thinking that
made me angry – and also defensive, touching as it did
that deep-seated cultural notion that a woman who does
not have children is lesser, missing something. When the
editor of the *Sydney Morning Herald*'s *Good Weekend*
had rung some years before to ask me to contribute to
a feature called 'Childless by Choice', telling me who

else was contributing – all women, of course – I'd asked whether he'd thought of inviting some men writers, like David Malouf, perhaps, or David Marr? That'd be radical, I said. He laughed, nicely enough, as if I hadn't grasped the nature of the issue.[71] I rest my case. But I wrote for the column, making the point – as I have so many times in interviews ostensibly about writing and books which inevitably segue to this question – that not being a mother does not leave a woman without close relationships with younger generations. In a world as complex as ours, for a child to have someone else on their side in addition to their parents can often be a benefit, especially, perhaps, someone without their own competing children. It was for me growing up, with Poppy's friend Gillian a confidante and rock-solid support during my difficult teen years. Poppy said I'd have made an awful mother, and she was probably right. I'm glad I wasn't tested on it. Given the circumstances of my fortieth birthday I can't say it was entirely a choice. But for me, as for many other women, it was right. I do not apologise for it. I love being an aunt, I wrote for the *Good Weekend*, and my life would be unimaginably lesser without Amy and Martha, without Obelia. Jeremy said the article proved his point that I favoured the girls and was tough on boys. What about Oliver? I asked, holding up two fingers close together. We're like this. That's because you gang up on us, Jeremy said. On him and his younger son, who was so often living at home, tough for both of them.

Being an aunt, or an aunt figure, is an entirely different matter from the relationship a woman is thrown into with the children of a partner. As an aunt, one is in addition to parents, a rather glorious supplement where there need be no divided loyalty. But that is far from the situation a stepmother finds herself in, caught, often, between the guilt of the father for being divorced in the first place, and the anger of the child, whose hope that the parents' marriage will be restored is dashed by the presence of this new woman. Accept her and it is a strike against the mother, which only serves to triangulate the situation further. While the child may be far from wanting another mother, the father often enough wants a mother figure to ease what is not easy and shield him from the discomfort of conflict and guilt. I'm not saying it's always a disaster, for clearly it is not; but I am saying it is structurally difficult. Those who find their way through to an inclusive ease should be saluted. Those who do not, or cannot, should not immediately be blamed. The evil stepmother is a trope of myth and fairytale, deeply embedded in our culture and consciousness. And it's not made any easier when the resentment can so readily run the other way. When an adult child who's out for the first time in weeks comes home unexpectedly, just as the candle has been lit, the wine opened, and turns on the light asking, What's for dinner? do you say, as Jeremy would, Get yourself a plate. Or do you say, as I would want to, but almost certainly wouldn't, Why don't you go and get a pizza? A bad atmosphere; a night slept back to back. In such a situation, it is not a matter simply of who is at fault but something much larger and more difficult.

How easily small incidents return when resentments build. I don't recall how we reproached each other at the Dry Dock that night, only that we wrangled until the wrangle lost its energy and we eased up on each other, had a meal and talked of other things. We walked to my house, arms together. I made a pot of tea, Jeremy had another glass of wine, amiable again, but as we got ready for bed the argument rekindled. Why did he always have to sleep in my bed? he asked. When was the last time I'd slept in his? When was the last time you washed your sheets? I countered. And so it went, until he put his shoes back on, his jacket, and walked home.

The intimacy that had carried us through earlier irritations stretched and strained. His house that had once pleased me with its English furniture and shelves overflowing with books became an irritant: dark, dusty, untended. Once I'd cleaned out the kitchen cupboards; now I couldn't so much as look inside them, cockroaches everywhere. Jeremy didn't believe in baits or sprays; he believed in coexistence. There'd been a time when I was amused by a cockroach in the salt, but now I wasn't eating another meal off those plates. Every small thing, every plan disrupted, every extra meal needed, every deadline met, or not met, every night at my desk catching up, every call that took me from my desk – each one of little significance in itself – frayed not only those old bonds, but something of our selves.

Look what it's doing to you, first one friend said, then another; and still, somehow – for reasons that I knew had to do with a distant past – the tie remained, less a bond than a strap.

By the end of August that year, I was worn down not only by the impasse with Jeremy but with the PNG book, which was still stalled on my desk. Nothing was happening. I was stuck in some sort of energy drain. Pity I'm not into cocaine, I'd grumble to friends. I needed a shot of energy, something to get me back to that part of myself that was once able to write, to act, to *risk*. Well, I got a shock, if not a shot. In fact, I got two in the space of two months.

The first came in September with a diagnosis of an early breast cancer after a routine, no-reason-to-worry mammogram. With it, the last remnants of my strength went. Gone. Stolen, maybe. But unlike Dapene, it'd take months, not hours, for it to return. While it was gone, the shock was such that I couldn't even read the breast cancer book I'd been given at the clinic. I could see that it was informative and well presented, exactly what I should read, but when I tried, it was as if my eyes, or my brain, couldn't lift the words from the page. Fortunately my friend Liz, whom I'd known since the house on the corner, was with me for the consultation in the surgeon's rooms. She'd taken over the book – which that morning fluttered with her yellow stickers. While I sat dazed, she went through her notes and queries with the surgeon. It was her mind, not mine, that got me through that day. At pre-admissions, Liz had to tell them my address. It was as if I'd taken flight and vanished.[72]

In this crisis Jeremy was no help at all, and maybe under the circumstances I shouldn't have expected him to be. And maybe it's not fair to say that he wasn't, as I stepped back from him as much as he did from me. He didn't come to visit me at St Vincent's; I didn't visit him when depression next returned him to Concord Hospital. He said he couldn't deal with me weak, and anyway he had enough to contend with. I said I needed a break, which I did, time to myself, and for myself, time to let my brain come back. I couldn't remember what I'd done two days before and was unable to write even an email. In my diary, a blank. No, the oncology doctor said, I didn't need testing for dementia. You're in shock, she said. Stress hormones play havoc with your memory; they take a while to settle. So, no, I wasn't cooking any more meals. I wasn't listening to any more of it. I wasn't doing any more research on depression for solutions that weren't followed up. I backed right off and stayed at my house at the end of lane. He closed his door behind me, turned up the music, opened another bottle and rang round his old girlfriends. There was no generosity in either of us.

Generosity came in the form of the little boats, my women friends sailing alongside. Anne Deveson was with me before the operation, and afterwards Liz was by the bed, on the phone to England, to Jane, and to Sophie. When I was home again, Gail and Robyn brought food, and suggested movies which we saw and I promptly forgot. People rang from all over, sent books and messages. I never felt alone – afraid, yes; alone, no – and as my mind regained its capacities, it was these friends who helped me recover. And the women doctors who saw me through the aftermath of radiotherapy and medication. From them, I learned that 50 per cent of women diagnosed with breast cancer will, like me, be in the five years either side of sixty. We are likely to have had few children, or late children, or no children. We've had oestrogen surging through our systems for decades, which was not, in evolutionary terms, what breasts were designed for. You could say that for women like us, breast cancer is a predictable, physical event. But I don't subscribe to the idea that the body is separate, unaffected by mind or emotion. And nor did the doctor who was in charge of my radiotherapy. She wasn't saying that stress causes cancer; nothing so simple. But she knew – how could she not, she saw it every day – that those of us in that 50 per cent faced this diagnosis at a time when, as women, we become invisible, when children, if we have them, have left home, and the men in our lives, if there are any, do all the things that men our age do to avoid the spectre in the shaving mirror. For many of us, it can be a time of domestic turbulence. I told her about Jeremy, and the hard, stuck place we were in. She listened, brushing nothing away. She knew that the door onto our lives that is opened by the shock of the diagnosis doesn't just close. You can try to shut it, give it a good slam, or you can use it as a spur, she said, to make some changes. It was a doctor I was talking to, not a therapist. I wasn't back in the stone house, though I thought of it often enough. There were times I wanted to return, came close to picking up the phone, but I didn't. Something had happened there, and even if I couldn't say what it was exactly, I could feel it somewhere underneath, steadying me.

Through all this, the one man to whom I could, and did, stay close, was David. There was a lot to do in preparation for the NGV exhibition. There was reason to be in each other's company, and until my brain began to regain its old capacities he was patient. Sometimes we sat quietly with his books, catalogues of Oceanic art dating back decades. Sometimes we just sat. There were stresses in his life too, and I was one of the few people outside his family who knew of them, though even to me he spoke tentatively. That he could at all, I think, was because I knew the hidden side of him, and to his credit he had not turned away, as men so often do, when a woman sees them weakened and afraid. And he knew, and saw, the situation I was in with Jeremy, though of that too we spoke tentatively. His response was to protect me, to save me, which he couldn't, of course, and I saw the pain of that too, for him more than me. What I did try to emphasise to him was that living with long-term, unresolved stress is not good for us. Let what's happened to me be a warning, I'd say. But he was not a man to speak of ailments, and certainly not to be slowed by them. When his gout played up and his leg was painful, when he took four codeine, or six, on the principle that if two were good, more were better, I'd tut and cajole, as women do, insisting that he went to a doctor. Don't you start, he'd say, turning it into a joke. If he did go to a doctor he'd manage to find one who thought concern over high blood pressure was exaggerated. Did he *say* that, or did you *hear* that? I'd ask, exasperated. It became a game for him as it ceased being one for me. Teasing was one thing, a form of affection I could, and did, enjoy. But when he ran stupid risks and played dumb about his health, when he took my reaction as that perverse kind of affirmation men get when women worry about them, I became cross. He'd flex his arms and laugh. Look, he'd say, there was nothing wrong with him that codeine couldn't fix. And indeed he was a large, strapping man, nothing frail about him. His mother was still in good shape at ninety; his father was in less good shape, but alive. He had their genes, he'd say, hopping from one foot to another, arms raised in mock fight. He'd live at least that long. I was the one with dodgy genes, both parents dead from cancer – not that David would have said that, even if he'd thought it which I doubt he did. But I did.

When I told him I was about to start radiotherapy, which would mean going to St Vincent's, across town, every day for a month, he put a thick envelope on my desk. Don't look at it now, he said, and I knew that inside would be a wad of cash. You might need to take taxis. Dear David. I felt cared for by him, and right then it meant a lot. Dear, maddening, self-sabotaging David.

The last time I saw him was on 31 October 2009, the day he flew to Vanuatu. As well as the Ömie exhibition, he was sponsoring and facilitating another – of art, this time, from North Ambrym where I'd been with him in 2006, so I knew its rigours, its steep hills. That alone was tiring, let alone the negotiations to be made with the community and at the Cultural Centre in Port Vila before any art could be taken out of the country. And then there were the practical arrangements to bring carvings, slit gongs taller than David, to Sydney; this was not barkcloth to be rolled up and posted.

It was the last day of October when he boarded the evening flight, as we had three years before, taking off into a night sky and landing in Port Vila while the bands were still playing. This time he'd be gone a week, and when he returned there'd be a week before Alban and the three Ömie new to Sydney – a man, a woman and a boy – would arrive. Then it'd be down to Melbourne for *The Wisdom of the Mountain* opening.

'Rest well,' David said as he left.

'I wish you weren't going,' I said, not meaning I'd miss him, though I would, but that I thought it was too pressured, too tight. Couldn't he have put this trip off until the New Year?

'I'll be fine,' he said.

But he wasn't. What happened I don't know, only that on the night he returned, he stayed up late working, and was found dead in his bed the next morning.

That afternoon I was driving from Balmain to Glebe, a route I often take, and though I don't know why I was doing it that particular day, I remember the exact spot where I was when I heard the ping of a text come in on my phone. The lights changed to red. The message was from one of the curators in Melbourne. 'How terrible about David,' I read. 'We're all shocked, and thinking of you. He was a good man.' That tell-tale past tense. No. The lights changed. I drove on. No. David couldn't be dead. I'd spoken to him when he came off the plane. I drove into a side street and parked. I got out of the car, re-read the text and rang his house. No! *Yes.* The ambulance had been, the police, the undertaker. David was dead.

I've only been in an earthquake once, and that was long ago, in the Highlands of PNG, at Kopiago with Nick. Nothing fell over, houses built of materials from the forest bent with its force and righted themselves; there was a landslide up in one of the gardens, but no one was hurt. We all ran out of our houses, jumping around to keep our footing. People coming up the path lurched from one side to the other as if they were drunk. I sat down on the ground where at least I could feel it was the earth that was moving, not me who couldn't stand straight. It was, to state the obvious, deeply unnerving to find the ground beneath us and the way our bodies move across it so profoundly disrupted.

I thought of that earthquake when David died, and in the aftermath when his sponsorship stopped, when it was me, not him, on the phone to Popondetta, listening to the alarm from the mountain. What had caused this death?

What would become of the art? Of them? I thought of it again the next January when I was faced with forty children, more, in Ömie and in the fjord villages, waiting for their school fees to be paid. But it wasn't an earthquake like that. The analogy was wrong. The ground under my feet had given way when Poppy died and I stepped into the arms of Ross, landing in freefall. That was an earthquake. This time, hard though it was, weep though I did, it wasn't deep ground that was shaking. I had been stopped in my tracks; that's what had happened. I was lurching, and had to find ways to walk differently – with Jeremy, with the book that would begin again in 2010 and become *The Mountain*.[73]

As to my connection to that beautiful, heartbreaking country that lies to Australia's north, did I walk away from all that David – and I – had set in train now that he, and all that came with him to make it work, was no longer there? Of course I didn't. But what to do, and how, was very far from clear.

Now

13

If a book can be said to have a now, a present moment that lasts for the time of its writing, then the now of this book has been as strange as its beginning. Every other book has come in the wake of events in the (once lived) now of my life, after a death, say, like *Poppy*, or after re-encountering the unlikeness of Papua New Guinea, a country that has turned the course of my life. This book, though it has the title of *Second Half First*, indicating that it, too, is written in the wake of events I could turn to as memoir, came uninvited, so to speak, without me setting out to write it, without a trigger more significant than a sleepless night at the end of 2013.

I was a third of the way into a novel at the time. The novel was – and maybe still is – called *Vanity*. It is the story of Hannah Frost, told in three parts: the year she turned forty, then fifty, then sixty. That was the now of my writing in 2013. Forty was fun to write, I had no trouble with it at all, and was full of cheerful confidence – always a mistake – telling everyone how in love with fiction I was. Hannah Frost's story was not mine. She was a journalist on the arts pages of one of the big Sydney dailies, close but not too close, distant enough to ring Susan Wyndham, a friend who was literary editor at the *Sydney Morning Herald*, to ask her to take me through the working day, the working week, of my Hannah Frost. One of the great pleasures of writing fiction is imagining one's way into the lives of others; and the research you have to do for these practical aspects takes you to places you would otherwise not go, or if you went, as I have on occasion, into a newspaper office, all you see is the chaos (the seeming chaos). Susan made sense of it to me, making it possible for me to write Hannah at work – which is not to say there is anything of Susan in Hannah, or that Hannah works for the *Herald*. Nor is she me, and not only in the detail of me not being and never having been a journalist, or because by and large journalists don't make themselves the story. Hannah does have a philandering man, called Adrian, but he doesn't leave her as Ross did me. On the contrary, when she has an affair – a love affair, not a philander; an impossible love affair – Adrian gives up his infidelities and suggests they move in together. Wish fulfilment, you might say, an alternative version of what life might have been had I been Hannah Frost and not me. And if you're wondering about Ben and his fugitive appearance in this book, well that's where he is, transmuted into Isaac Meltone – Hannah's all-too-possible, impossible love – an altogether different figure, suspended in a file now somewhere in my study. There are some stories you can't tell direct, and in this case I have no desire to. What I remain interested in are the dilemmas, the emotional cross-currents, the love – intense and real, and also fractured – and these resonate far beyond the lived actualities I shared with Ben.

By the middle of 2013 Forty was finished, with both Hannah and Isaac's wife pregnant. Fifty had made a hesitant start with Adrian and Hannah living in London, when, with the same cheerful confidence, I packed up my notebooks for three weeks on the Greek island of Skopelos with my friend Helen from up the road. She'd lived there, almost a neighbour, for as long as I'd lived in the house at the end of the lane – a good deal longer in fact. But the first I knew of her was at a Christmas party further along her street that awful year of 2009. I don't know why I went, seeing as I was still fragile, fit only for the company of friends. But it was Christmas Eve; Jeremy was in good spirits and wanted to go, and though I couldn't take much part in the festive cheer, it was okay being there, with enough people in the garden for me not to be noticed, standing back, observing. Over to one side of the garden there was a woman my age with pretty loose brown hair, no sign of grey. I chose a chair a few away from her; perhaps she was in the same frame of mind, and I didn't want to intrude. So we sat there for a while, until one of us said to the other, So you're not in party mode either. Not really, was the reply. It's been a difficult year, one of us said. Yes, said the other, for me too. And before we knew it we were talking, one of those rare party events of a real conversation. Helen Mueller is a printmaker, an artist who works in black and white, the many shades between, and although her art practice with its heavy presses and etching tools is far from the pen and paper that's all I have to show for the making of my work, there was a lot we understood in common, and it now seems unimaginable that we had lived so near each other for so long without meeting. Since then barely a week has gone by when I haven't seen her. That June of 2013, when I was writing *Vanity*, she was going to Skopelos to work in a print studio she'd been part of setting up with, among others, the master printer Basil Hall, and being in London that summer, I joined her. We rented a floor of a house at the top of the old town, and while Helen went to the print studio I sat at the courtyard table with a view over roofs to the harbour. Shaded by the vines, I returned to Fifty, or tried to – though, in fact, I was doodling more than writing. Something wasn't right. I didn't know what, but I didn't worry that much. After all I was on a Greek island; maybe I should give myself a break and enjoy the dry hills and the water and the old churches with their icons, evenings in the tavernas with the people from the studio. It'd resolve when I was back in Sydney, I told myself.

But it didn't. My time was fragmented; I was teaching a semester at the University of Sydney. The year rattled past, and then it was December, and Martha went back to England and I sank into the sorrowful decline that ended with that strange night of remembering. I hadn't thought about Ross for years, or thought I hadn't, though I suppose he was there somewhere in Hannah Frost's Adrian. And I suppose my own very different forty was in there too. Though I felt I'd been riding the crest of a fictional life, the unconscious has a way of tripping us into exactly what we are enthusiastically rearranging. And so I woke that night, just before Christmas, when I looked up Ross on the internet and this book began. Some books come easily. *The Mountain* did not. It took years. This book, as if in recompense, was written in not much more than a year. But the really weird thing has turned out to be less how it started than how its writing has proved a time in which many strands of the stories, the recollections of my life since forty, have drawn themselves into strange concluding patterns of the sort you couldn't get away with in fiction. It's almost as if this book I never set out to write came in anticipation of events I could have known nothing of at the start.

January 2014 was hot. My small courtyard garden shrivelled under a relentless sun; thyme dried, oregano browned at the edges. Only rosemary thrived, and the bamboo. I stayed indoors and wrote, tracking back to another house, on a corner in Enmore. I drove past it one afternoon, just to have a look, remind myself. It has windows in the long side wall. Nice. I would have done that if I'd had the money. Should I have stayed there? How different would it have been with Jeremy had I lived a twenty-minute drive away and was not at the end of the lane? Since the bad year of 2009, little by little he'd become lost in depression, barely recognisable as the man I had loved. Not all at once, of course; these things are incremental and cumulative. The line I'd drawn, or tried to draw, was scuffed. There were times when I crossed it because I couldn't not, and times when I crossed it because I'd get a glimpse of the man I'd once known. There were moments of harmony, when we swam in a nearby harbour pool and lay in the shade to read. And there were times, not many but a few, when he'd walk into my house and there he'd be, arms open, and by way of apology tickets to a concert. I have a photo of that Jeremy – 'the good Jeremy' my nieces remember with affection – taken in London in 2010 when he and I and Martha were in Hyde Park after visiting the memorial for the victims of the 7/7 bombings. With a pillar for each person killed, Martha's friend Laura Webb among them, the memorial is simple, clear, uncluttered. Martha was weepy, Jeremy was calm, kind, and we walked on through the park: a hot day, almost Australian.

So yes, there were moments, and I am glad for them, but the movement of those years was downwards for Jeremy as his depressions became more frequent and he sank into periods of despair that left him profoundly alone, drinking too much, alienated not only from me but from all but his most stalwart friends. At his worst, he'd appear at my door, sometimes barely capable of speech. I'd feed him, ring Oliver, who was managing his hospital admissions, and send him back to his cluttered old house.

Some ruthless part of me performed the care without letting it touch the part of me that was writing again. The sliver of ice that Graham Greene said lives in the heart of every writer? Not that I wanted to write about Jeremy's depression – which is what Greene meant; where others weep, we watch and write. I didn't want to write about it then, and I don't now, and not only for Jeremy's sake and his sons'. What is there to say about witnessing depression, the daily pall of its inertia, its stasis? When there was forward movement, or what appeared to be forward movement in Jeremy's case, it was the effect of ECT hauling him out of despair and overshooting him into a manic high. And when that happened he had no interest in being around me; the coin flipped, and where there'd been dependence there was resentment.

When that happened early in March 2014 I was frankly relieved, and the relief was entirely for me. Jeremy would spiral back, I knew, and I also knew there was nothing I could do to prevent it even if I'd been the most wifely of women. If it took a sliver of ice, I'm glad of it; never mind writers, there are times when every woman could do with one – 'in the interests of freedom', Virginia Woolf wrote in her diary the year she was writing *To the Lighthouse*. She'd refused to agree with Leonard that they hire a gardener, not wanting to be tied to a house away from London, all their money spent. 'L. was, I think, hurt at this, & I was annoyed at saying it, yet did it, not angrily, *but in the interests of freedom*. Too many women give way on this point, & secretly grudge their unselfishness in silence – a bad atmosphere.'[74] And so I stayed home and wrote, day by day, *Second Half First* arriving first in a scrawl in my notebook, and then on the computer, chapters printed out into a neat pile. There it was each morning, returning me each afternoon to the books I'd read all those years ago, when 'the conundrum love propounds',[75] to take a line from the wonderful Elizabeth Bishop, was a live and potent question; this time I was reading more like an anthropologist studying a tribe of clever young women and their strange misshapen longings. And in this way, for the first months of 2014 my life was quiet, almost too quiet, with friends away, Gail in Berlin for a year, Robyn having moved to Melbourne as Helen Garner had years ago, another friend moving back to Perth, another in London. Helen Mueller was up the road, a felicitous presence, an unfolding conversation, but otherwise, for the most part, the days passed, slowly expanding to meet what was required of them by the book on my desk.

There was one welcome interruption early in the year when Libi Gnecci-Ruscone was in Sydney. Italian with an Australian mother, Libi is an anthropologist who has done fieldwork in the fjords, on a peninsula between the villages I visit and the airstrip at Tufi. I'd met her in January 2012, in Milan where she lives – I'd flown over after Christmas in London with the family. There was snow on the hills beyond the city where we walked, talking of tropical fjords that were as present to us as the city's churches and theatres. I'd read her thesis about the ways in which traditional practices and the new ways of Christianity intersect. It wasn't a case of one supplanting the other, but of the two co-existing, with each coming to the fore in certain situations and for certain reasons and benefits. So while they could appear contradictory, it was not confusion so much as a canny use of competing rhetorics and discourses, a nimbleness of argument that made a lot of sense to me, having seen it in action in the villages where I stayed. And not just in terms of Christianity, but more broadly the world of modernity that was pressing on them. There'd been no Digicel when Libi did her fieldwork; now there are mobile phones in the villages and the internet in Popondetta. The challenge for these villages and villages like them across the country is how to integrate, or reconcile, these two realities. It isn't a matter of choosing one over the other, any more than it was a choice between love and career for many a young woman of my generation, or today.

I'd read Libi's thesis after David died and my visits back to PNG became radically altered. Never again would I be the writer with her notebook and clean hands dreaming of fiction. It had been pleasant enough coasting along with David, leaving the decisions to him, retreating to the shade of a tree when the dinghy didn't arrive or the plane was late. Let David sort it out. It was a part-formed way of being. I thought I'd understood the dilemma of post-colonial Papua New Guinea – I'd certainly read enough – but in truth I'd barely begun before I was slapped in the face, which is how it felt at the time, by the question of what to do now that David was dead and the money to support all that he'd supported was gone. Without him, what was going to happen? It was a question that came in myriad forms, many of them addressed to me – as if I had any answers, as much in shock as anyone.

Fortunately, just months before he died, David had found the young man who would take over the running of Ömie Artists. He'd been looking for a while for someone younger who could help him with the work that was gathering pace with the success of the art, someone who'd be able to do what David and I could not do again, and climb that mountain. I met Brennan King just weeks before David died, and maybe only someone as young as Brennan would have stepped in with no financial backing, no income, nothing but his wits and his youth. Being the age he was, there were those who doubted he had what it took to negotiate the tough world of galleries and curators. But David had been no fool in his selection. Brennan had worked with Aboriginal art centres before his interest turned to the Pacific, and after David died I saw him with Alban and the other Ömie who'd come down to the NGV opening. He took them to live in his house. I was still having radiation, and while those who've had chemo scoff at the burns and the exhaustion, with David so recently gone I was in no fit state. Brennan was young, welcoming and full of interest. He was with them every step of the way, at the opening in Melbourne with its lights and cameras, and on the buses in Sydney. He was at ease with them, as they were with him. In the two short weeks they were here, he soaked in everything they had to say, and arranged his first visit to the mountain, where news of David's death had had a predictably destabilising effect. Was the mountain displeased again? Was the pride the young men had taken in their *bisnis* to be pulled from under them? If the art was to survive this next disturbance, I knew it'd take someone young enough to walk that mountain not once but many times. What gallery owner was going to do that? There's a story to be told here, a long one, and I hope one day it is told and told well. As to Brennan, his achievement speaks for itself when I tell you that the art has more than survived. A new generation of women is painting, a movement of vision that is grounded in the lineage of their grandmothers, as younger artists reinterpret their world both within Ömie and beyond. There have been exhibitions every year, and money is going back to the communities – not a lot, but enough. There is peace with Na´apa, and Ömie art is now in public collections in the Museum Fünf Kontinente in Munich, the British Museum in London, the Fowler Museum, UCLA, Los Angeles, the Museum of Archaeology and Anthropology at the University of Cambridge, and the Museum of New Zealand, Te Papa Tongarewa in Wellington. This in addition to increased holdings in Australian private collections and public galleries.[76]

In the fjords the questions were different and at first, I thought, a good deal easier. It was mostly a matter of

school fees. Across PNG, David had dozens of children
in school. Were they to lose the opportunity now that
there was no sponsor? In case you think he had them
at fee-paying private schools, no; fees had been made
a condition of aid by the 1990s – a requirement of the
neo-liberal Washington Consensus – and are levied even at
ill-resourced schools in villages where families are usually
large and there is little or no access to cash. So I did a
whip-round of friends and colleagues, raising enough to
pay for the year that was upon us within two months of
David dying. It was a holding pattern, that's all, delaying
the inevitable. Individual sponsorship, as problematic
as it can be generous, is no solution. Even before David
died there'd been those whispers about which children
he sponsored, and the question of the girls who weren't
getting a look-in. While I was earning a university salary,
I could afford to sponsor more girls, and when I did
I found myself embarrassed by the attention I got from
the families, and the gifts of necklaces that'd come from
the relatives of others wanting fees for their girls. Worse
than embarrassed, I felt in bad faith, as if I was something
and someone I wasn't, feeding the notion that white
means rich, turning people I thought of as friends into
supplicants, distorting the relationship I'd thought I was
establishing – though I suppose I wasn't, or not entirely –
on other, more equal terms. They didn't need to read the
development literature to know the significance of literacy
and education; that's why those without sponsorship were
aggrieved. They understood what researchers tell people

like me, that education is a key to the future if they are to
protect their forests from the loggers and their reefs from
the pirate fishing boats; if they are to be in a position to
make meaningful contracts with those who wish to use their
resources; if they are to sustain their way of life, earn their
own money, enough to supplement lives rich in gardens
and forest resources. Let alone if their people, and people
from the many villages like theirs, are to have a voice in the
governing of their own district, their nation, and not leave
it to a self-perpetuating, all-too-often corruption-breeding
elite. Without these voices in the mix, without voices to
support the many working for good governance, how
else is change to come? This isn't my question. I might
be asking it here, but it's asked in many ways across the
country, in villages and markets, in universities and offices,
by bloggers and the rising generation of writers stepping
into the role of watchdog and witness. Naïve optimism,
you might say, and yes, maybe, when PNG is regarded as
a business opportunity by those with money and power to
know the value of its resources. In hotels in Moresby, I've
heard businessmen, drink in hand, boast of deals in the high
millions, while outside beyond the guards and the security
wire there are people living on a few kina a day. There's
a lot stacked against this new generation of writers, but
when one of them is also the governor of a once-corrupt
province, and with social media gathering pace, maybe it is
not entirely a false optimism.[77]

As to the matter of school fees and my small quandary,
a significant break came with the lifting of some, though

not all, fees – a change to the conditions of aid. When this happened, albeit in a piecemeal and uneven way, the teachers and the elders in the fjord villages were of the opinion that the community, the parents, the relatives, should pay the remaining fees, at least for primary school, which in PNG goes to Grade 8 (the equivalent of Grade 5 in Australia), when local education ends. That would eliminate the favouritism of sponsorship. But it left the matter of ill-resourced schools, and it did nothing for students who could, and should, go on to study at high school. Their options were either to go to town where the high schools are, or study by distance-learning. Village parents don't like sending their young to town with its very real risks of drugs and gangs – or pregnancy in the rare case of a girl getting there. Besides, there was the cost, and where would they stay? Everyone knew what happened when students dropped out, which – with so much stacked against them – they almost always did. It was the problem of boys again: boys returning to the village touched by town angers and town ways, the glimpse of a life that closed its door to them. Angry boys make dangerous men, I was told time and again, as if I didn't know, as if I didn't come from a world of angry and dangerous men, many of them concealed in smart suits and polished shoes. At least gangs declare themselves.

When it came to high school, the village preference was for distance-learning, which meant students could study from workbooks sent to villages from the Education Department. There were still fees to be paid, a charge for each subject, which makes it hard for parents who rely on fishing and gardening, but at least the boys were in sight. But where were these students to work each day, and how were they to maintain their focus, their study through four long years, with no supplementary resources and little supervision beyond that which could be given by already overstretched primary teachers not trained in the syllabus? And what about adult literacy, high on the list of priorities at every evening discussion after the meal was done and we sat talking, insects flying into the lamp, children leaning on the end of the table.

More than torches or even lamps, it was books I'd be asked to bring next time, and news magazines; books about other places, books about people like them, living in places like theirs; books for the school, books for the little ones. And so, around the table at night, from my earliest visits I'd ask the questions that had us imagining, conjuring up the possibility – the idea – of a *book house*. Imagine, just imagine if there was a place where the distance-learning students could study, and adults could learn to read, and the school could use the books. Imagine if there was a place where the old people could tell the stories of before, and the young ones could write them down, and the stories could live in that place, stories for the future. So much imagining, so much talk. And if anyone had told me five years ago that I'd set up a small foundation, I'd have laughed. Me? The writer who likes to say the best thing about writing is that you can do it in your pyjamas? And yet, the obvious, perhaps inevitable, outcome of all that talk was SEAM Fund, which came into being in 2012.[78] We'd raise the money to build that *book house* to support all forms of literacy, and work with the needs of the community.

But imagining is just that; there's a chasm between an idea, even an obvious one like this, and the realising of it. Yes, I'd hear from every side, the need is great, but be warned: many have failed. It's expensive getting materials in, and how will you resupply? Who will manage the resources and fix them when they need it, as inevitably they will? Who will teach? And if you do get something in place, will it still be going in a year's time? Daunted, I'd report back on the talks I'd had in Port Moresby with people from research centres and universities, from NGOs and the Education Department, with those I'd known back in our long-ago student days. There was almost always someone in the village with an answer for every contingency; if not, silence would fall and everyone would look at me. And then the talk would start again, and the imagining. Words are powerful drivers, which of course I well knew, and still I let them loose, conjuring up a literacy house for the village with the sigh of the night air around us, in the lamp light each face an unfolding story: Joseph the elementary teacher who saved from his pay for the tin roof that is now on the school's roof; Euphemia with the next baby in her bilum, who did Grade 11 in Alotau and longs for more; Jackson, who keeps his books safe in a plastic bag; Lancelot, who's teaching himself to read and is determined his boys get the education he didn't; fierce Barbara who's managed to get one of her sons to Grade 8, and now what? It was like wading into water that looks calm enough and finding yourself pulled along by the current. An irresistible current, sweeping me out of my depth.

And not only me, but friends I took there. Of the ones you've met in this book, Virginia, who I stayed with in Stoke Newington while Patrick was dying, came with her daughter Sylvie; I have photos of Sylvie, aged fourteen, jumping with the children from the low-hanging branches into the deep water of the fjord. It was seeing through Sylvie's eyes as well as her own that made Virginia co-founder of SEAM with me, and I couldn't have done it without her. Sophie came, and her daughter Jessie – who won an essay competition back in London with a story about an encounter with a pig. Martha was there that time, and Sylvie again. And then Martha went back on her own, spending hours at the school to which children from five villages canoe each day. She took photos of their paddles, big and small, leaning against the school wall during lessons. Dream children to teach, she said, and having taught in a school on the outskirts of Leeds, she knew what it was to work with children who were not easy to teach.[79] She also knew how much would depend on the training we could provide, the partnerships we could make, not only with the education authorities but with the new literacy projects that were starting up in the towns and settlements. She went back to PNG for a month and set to work. It was like a puzzle, she said, with many pieces needing to find a new shape. But to do the research, make the first steps towards turning talk into action, we'd need someone on the ground. And that would take money. And David was dead. And fundraising is tough, especially for a place so little understood.

I could have given up, and there were times in Sydney when I'd wake at night cold with the fear that I'd got myself, yet again, into a situation of raising expectations I wouldn't be able to meet. There were times when the obligations of exchange became onerous. It's a complex place, PNG – nothing's straightforward, I've barely skimmed the surface here – and it's easy to feel snared, overwhelmed. But I'd go back to the villages, hear the news of all that had happened since I last visited, and there'd be no way I was giving up. One time Joseph told me there'd been a village meeting, and guess what, they'd introduced gender equity. You have? How? In PNG, where violence against women is endemic – though it's not bad along that coast, nothing like in the Highlands and the towns. The women laughed when Joseph said some of the men had cooked one night, before their wives put a stop to it. The men were taking girls out on the canoes to learn to fish – that was still happening – and, Joseph said, it's been decided that when the *book house* is built, the girls must all go. He'd read a report on the education of girls; he'd got it from someone in the Education Department. Did I know, he asked, that a woman who is educated puts three times as much back into the community as a man? Yes, I said, I must have read the same report. Very good, the women said, literate and non-literate, young and old.

And although I haven't heard of gender equity since – it's not a term that's entered the vocabulary of the village – the participation of girls is rarely questioned now.

Another time the writer Russell Soaba flew across from Moresby to join Hilary and me. Russell had been at the Martyrs School outside Popondetta, and the boat he'd caught from his village further east along the coast had stopped at Tufi on its slow way from Alotau to Popondetta, and on to Lae. Also on that long-ago boat was John Wesley Vaso, then a schoolboy and now an elder from Uiaku on Collingwood Bay, an hour and a half in a dinghy east from the fjords. I'd got to know him when I was trying to understand what had happened there during the dispute with the loggers that had resulted in a victory for the landowners, hard-won in the National Court, only to have the loggers return, or try to return, in another guise.[80] John also joined us. He had his guitar with him. Russell had read the manuscript of *The Mountain*. An exemplary critic, and also a friend, he didn't protect me and every one of his comments stretched the manuscript in ways that were wholly good. He'd recognised an element of himself in the character Milton: Milton's writing, that is, not the fiction of the life I'd created for him. There in the fjords, where so much of the novel takes place, we enjoyed the play of fiction and character, moving between them, between the world of the imagination and the world around us.

With John and Russell in the villages, the idea for a resource centre became clearer. Hilary had recently returned from Jordan where, among many other things, she had visited a foundation working with students in the Palestinian refugee camps. The organisation gave scholarships for university students and in return they would work for the community a certain number of hours for each term they were supported. They'd work in the small library that had been set up, or with the school children; they'd paint rooms and knock windows into the walls of dark houses. It was a way of thinking, an exchange that the village responded to, listening, asking questions, not just about this particular project but about the Middle East. Why such bitter fighting? What was America doing? Why were they there at all? And Australia? Obama? Joseph had read about Iraq online in Popondetta, and he'd read about it in *Time*, but the more he read, the more questions there were. I knew the feeling. Hilary and Russell had a go at making some kind of sense of it, a conversation continuing the next morning when we stopped on our way up to the gardens for Hilary to draw a map on the ground with a stick.

On our last night together, the four of us stayed at the small resort overlooking the fjord near the airstrip, ready for the early plane out the next morning. On the terrace over a bottle of wine, maybe a beer too many, Russell reminisced about the student writers he had known and I'd read, a few of whom I remembered from back before Independence. Words had proved powerful then too, as the old colonial ways collapsed around the raised fists of student protestors. Newspaper editors had flown up from Melbourne to feature them; that's not what happens now, there's barely a flicker of interest in PNG unless it's for stories of violence and witchcraft. Was change easier back then, with enough political and economic interests running the way of those young anti-colonial writers? Of course, John said. It's all about money now, and no matter how you get it. No illusions there, yet despite all that he'd seen while fighting for his land, he is a man of humour. It bubbled up in him as Russell remembered lines from poems, and he strummed his guitar, picking up a theme here, a melody there, the familiar music of the Pacific. At the end of the evening when we were onto 'the sad crying of the midnight sun' – a line from John Kasaipwalova's rolling epic allegory, *Sail, the Midnight Sun* – John raised his voice over ours with *The House of the Rising Sun*.[81] That great Melanesian song, he joked, and it was, somehow, a fine finale to a fine visit.

By the time Libi, the anthropologist, was in Sydney at the beginning of 2014, there was still nothing on the ground and not much more than nothing in the bank. The other piece of advice we'd got from everyone was that if we were going to raise money for SEAM, the resource centre would have to be sustainable, affordable and *replicable*. Would one literacy house for one village, one school, not be another, larger, version of individual sponsorship? Why this village, this school, and not the next one in the fjords, or beyond, elsewhere along the coast? As for affordable – which also meant transportable – how was that to be achieved when getting tin roofs and building materials into remote villages and rugged terrain can cost considerably more than the educational and literacy materials themselves? Think helicopters, barges, cranes. Each step of the way the questions got harder, more complex. Was SEAM to be another fiction in my head, with no more reality than the box in my study marked with its name, sitting there next to the half-written, abandoned *Vanity*? At least when it's a book you don't write, the only person you let down is yourself.

While Libi was here, we walked and talked as we had in Milan, the fjords as present to us, this time, as the harbour of Sydney. Forest, rock, reef, waterfall: she knew them all. She knew the villages, she knew the currents and the tides; she knew the gossip in the township by the resort and the airstrip; she'd met Joseph and Euphemia. When it came to SEAM, she knew the need, and the dilemma. It was while she was in Sydney, staying with me, that I made a move – though I didn't realise it at the time – that proved critical. I invited an architect I'd had a short email exchange with, but had never met, to join us for lunch at a café close to my house. He'd written to me after reading *The Mountain*. He'd been born in Port Moresby in 1966, he told me, which meant he was two when Nick and I arrived at the university, too young to comprehend what was happening around him. He was ten when his family left Moresby after Independence. *The Mountain*, he said, had triggered 'clear and compelling memories of deep attraction (what I could describe as troubled love), yearning for what I was too young to see and actively take a part in, and for what I wish I could now be part of but feel (perhaps rightly) excluded from by dint of being white, and for the fact that PNG has remained at the rear margins of my thinking and identity for 30+ years.' Reading *The Mountain*, he said, had 'rekindled a desire' to know the place again, 'to know the people who are striving to make it strong'.

'I try to imagine whether I could overcome my own fears by returning there and making a contribution,' the email ended. 'Kind regards, Stephen Collier, Stephen Collier Architects.'

Well, I'd written back, as a matter of fact . . . And I told him about SEAM, without then realising that an architect was exactly what we needed. I thought of architects as urban and expensive, elevated far above the practical difficulties of getting tin roofs and sheets of fibro, or refitted containers, into remote communities. I didn't even realise it at lunch that day, though I liked Stephen at once, and so did Libi, and we talked as if we'd all known each other for a great deal longer than we had – which is often the way with people who share that 'troubled love' for PNG. Afterwards he walked back to my house with us; he looked at the mats and barkcloth Libi had with her from Tufi, at the Ömie barkcloth on my walls, at photos of the first tropical fjords he encountered.

'You should come up some time,' I said when he left late that afternoon.

'I will,' he said.

'Is April too soon?' I asked, telling him I was going up then with Alison Lester, the children's writer, to do a book-making project at the school. No, he said, and within a week, or maybe two, he'd booked his ticket.

Serendipity? Luck? An alignment of the stars? Sometimes things come our way and people walk into our lives, and at the time we don't realise their significance. Which is how it was with Stephen; how could it be otherwise after one short lunch? Besides, as soon as Libi left, I returned to the book – this book – that was insisting its way onto my desk and into my consciousness.

I have made a lot of SEAM here, catching you up with the years since David died, but during those first months of 2014 I kept it out of mind to the extent that I could. One more visit, and if something didn't happen then, I told myself, I'd have to face up to those raised expectations and find a way of telling the village how wrong I'd got it, that even in rich Australia I couldn't find a way to make it work. Not an encouraging prospect. So I put the SEAM box in a cupboard, out of sight, and wrote. A book as diversion? Maybe.

By May, one of Sydney's best months, with high skies and chill nights, the water still warm enough to swim, *Second Half First* was powering along, its shapes squaring up, when Lynne arrived from London. Lynne, the friend with whom there'd been that tangle thirty years earlier when she was here on a fellowship at Ross's university. You could say that it has something to do with feminism that we came back from that bad moment. Feminism gave us a framework, I suppose, a language for making sense of

what had happened. A critique of the roving man was easy
to agree on, but when it came to our part in it, the wounds
inflicted, the words spoken, the hurts, the angers – that
was a good deal harder. It was a long afternoon in the
kitchen at Lynne's house in London, with other people
living there coming in, putting on the kettle. For Lynne
it wasn't the wound it was for me; it had taken several
years before I could contemplate making that peace, but
I did, we did, and I am glad. The daughters of Simone de
Beauvoir truth-telling and responsibility-taking? Maybe.
Or maybe that is part of the feminist biographical illusion,
the truth being not so easily told, or agreed. But still, it
was a significant afternoon, and since then we always see
each other when we're in each other's cities, sharing as
we do that movement between north and south, England
and Australia.

Lynne has had a successful career since those distant
days, as an academic and a writer. Lynne Segal. She was in
Sydney that May for the writers' festival with *Out of Time*,
her book about ageing. When she'd been here for her
previous book, *Making Trouble* – feminist trouble, trouble
as a woman – I had done the onstage interview with her,
but this time I didn't. I'm not a good interviewer, another
skill I don't have; I talk too much, go off on tangents.
Sometimes I manage to pull it off, just, and I think I did
with Lynne, but sometimes I don't and it's a bad experience,
for me and – more importantly – for the writer who should
be shown to her or his best. One of the worst interviews
I have done was with Robert Dessaix; I don't know what

happened, for as an interviewer himself he is a good subject
for an interview, and it's not as if I didn't know him well, or
there weren't questions to ask about the book, *Arabesques*,
one of his best, about that perverse character André Gide.
It was in 2009, that bad year, and I haven't conducted a
public interview since. Lynne's onstage 'conversation' for
Out of Time was a success; I was glad to be an observer,
not a participant. The question she raised wasn't so much
how to survive ageing with its attendant decrepitudes, as
how to live well – on into the last years of our lives, until
eventually we must surrender to the challenge of dying.
It's a tough read, and though Lynne and I didn't agree on
sex and ageing, we argued amicably. I consider the easing
of the hormonal imperative a relief; she sees it more as a
cultural convenience that we've learned to accept, which
of course it also is, in a culture that doesn't like the face of
the post-fertile woman. Another inequity. At a market one
day, looking at clothes, I told her about the book I was
writing, and the strange night of remembering Ross, the
trigger that had had me writing these last five months.
Even with two weeks in PNG, I'd written the best part
of half of it, I thought, though with this book it was hard
to tell as it seemed less than usually under my command.
Our command. We laughed. What's that? Did we ever have
command?

The weekend before she left there was a farewell brunch
for her in a sprawling wooden house in Erskineville. It was
a fine day, a little chill in the air, wintry sunshine, Sunday
morning papers. Among the guests were people from the

long-ago 1960s, when Lynne was at Sydney University and libertarian meant not the economics of a neo-conservative right, but the social and sexual freedoms of a bohemian left. In some kind of weird time warp the women were gathered in the kitchen, while out in the courtyard were a few of those once-powerful men, now with bad backs and painful knees, struggling to lift themselves out of their chairs. I was surprised to find myself talking to them and enjoying it, the allure and the danger stripped away – frail bodies with still-sharp minds, talking with a disarming humour, including about their early sexual antics. Though of course the ability to recognise bad behaviour doesn't mean they weren't boasting. Still, I was not in a critical frame of mind. I went into the kitchen to refill their cups and their plates, and we chatted on in the winter sunlight, mostly about books. Ian Bedford, one of the kinder of the men back then, had taken to fiction, and somewhere in the conversation he invited me to the launch of his latest novel, *The Last Candles of the Night*, in which he thought I'd be interested – and I was. I already knew it was a further investigation into cross-cultural relationships in India, and after talking for a while about writing across cultures, he told me the date in June, and the bookshop where the launch was to be held. Would I like to come? Of course, I said.

'It should be a good evening,' Ian said. 'Ross will be here and is going to speak.'

'Oh,' I said, 'I'm not sure that's the way I want to re-encounter Ross.'

It was Ian's turn to say, Oh. Then, Ah, as memory came slowly. 'You were involved with him once,' he said – half-statement, half-question.

'Yes,' I said. 'It ended badly.'

'Ross didn't transition well.'

I laughed. 'You could say that.'

'Do you not want to see him at all?' This was the man with the bad knees who couldn't lever himself out of his chair. There was a woman in the kitchen, he said, who still wouldn't talk to him.

'No,' I said. 'It's not like that. I just don't want to encounter him in public, not for the first time.'

'Would you like his email?' Ian asked.

'No,' I said.

If Ross wanted to get in touch with me, that was one thing. But after what had happened – I used the word graceless – the move would need to come from him. But I did give Ian my email, and I knew Ian would give it to Ross.

And sure enough, a week or so after the launch I didn't go to, an email pinged into my inbox from Ross. It was polite, and slightly awkward. If I thought now was a good time to meet, he'd like that, he wrote. Despite being busy and leaving at the end of the month, he thought 'we could probably work something out'. What we worked out was lunch in the restaurant at the Art Gallery of New South Wales.

He was already at the table when I arrived. He stood up, put out his hand. He looked immediately familiar, and also distant as if he might be a stranger, a man in a darkish jacket at a table with a glass of white wine. The harbour was its sparkling winter self, and the old wharf that was once a working wharf and is now luxury accommodation was solidly there, a reproof to the foolish person – me – who said that if the developers did what they ended up doing, she'd leave Sydney. There were moored yachts and expensive cruisers. Ah well. Be careful what you promise.

I didn't have a glass of wine; I rarely drink in the middle of the day and it was easy to refuse. I knew I didn't need fortifying.

We enquired after each other's health. He is getting deaf, but otherwise okay. His hearing aid was new and not well adjusted. He told me of the bleakness around this journey back to Sydney. His brother was ill; an old friend and once lover was dying. He told me the title of the book he was working on, which I can't quite remember but which made me laugh, something to do with the past and its fingers into the present. He liked teaching his one course a term. He could bicycle to the university from the house in Brooklyn where he still lives with Elena. She didn't get a mention, not by name; but he spoke more of 'we' than of 'I'. As to our shared past, it hovered at the table but it too remained unspoken. I said something general – about the nadir being more about my mother's death, a deeper grief. Each decade, I said, which is true, has got better; each decade I am stronger and lighter. I'm not sure if he heard all or even most of what I had to say, as he didn't realise I still went to Papua New Guinea though I'd said it several times. He adjusted his hearing aid and was, I think, quite interested in SEAM, surprised even, as if it were beyond his expectation of me. Or maybe not. I don't know.

It might have ended there. He asked for the bill and when I reached for my bag he said, No, Let me – which I did. We said it was good to see each other, and how odd it is growing older, and the way we see the person who was in the person who is, so that age doesn't seem as it does for those we don't, or didn't, know. The vanity of age, I said. The curious thing was that the Ross sitting there at the table didn't look anything like as old as he had in that photo on the internet. The possibility of plastic surgery crossed my mind; that could explain why he looked like a stranger as well as familiar. Or maybe the change was in me and there's no need for surgery as an explanation; whatever that face had once done to me, or summoned up in me, it no longer did. I looked at my watch. Ten minutes until the next bus home. It was then that I said what had been waiting to be said for the hour or more we'd sat there. I made it a story, about Martha being here, and the slough I'd dropped into when she left, and the night I looked him up, the unexpected night when this unexpected book started. Not that it's about you, I said. You're the trigger, not the subject; the 'conceit' – in literary terms – that started it. It's about a whole lot of other things, my mother, psychoanalysis, reading, writing, New Guinea, living away from where I was born. At this point I felt a sweep of feeling. Was I dancing a dangerous dance? Would

I regret it in the morning? Or would I regret it more if I didn't say what needed saying? It wasn't that I feared being shamed for myself; if I feared, it was for the sake of a book, which at that moment in that restaurant sprang into its own life, no longer a private musing that might as well live beneath my bed. No! It was a book, insistent and real, for all that it was, in fact, only half-finished on my desk. Was I jeopardising it by telling Ross of its origin? But if I didn't would I be jeopardising it further when the day came that I'd have to tell him, or he'd hear about it, or read it and know the deceit? I put my bag back on the floor.

'Maybe I'll have a glass of wine after all,' I said.

It was then that we talked, carefully, tentatively, another half-hour at the table before we went to look at paintings before I caught another bus home. He walked to the front of the gallery with me, put out his hand, then an embrace, quick and cautious, a tear in his eye as well as mine, just possibly, a very small one. Or maybe not.

'It's been good,' he said.

'Yes,' I said. 'It's been good.'

'As to the book,' he said, 'do with me as you will.'

Of the talk that half-hour, only a little remains. I remember a few of the things he said. He used the word *extremis* of the state I'd been in, which was indeed the case. He said there was 'something powerful' about me and that he'd had to turn his back to survive. That surprised me, though I'm not sure he meant it as a compliment; powerful in my anger and grief, I suppose he meant. He said – and this also surprised me – that he hadn't known how to be honest with me, or what being honest with me would mean, what it would look like. And all these years I had thought it was his honesty that brought me undone; the confession of the penis, not the confession of the heart. When I said I was left with a sense of him as a chimera, he said he was left with a sense of himself as a man, in that regard, he didn't much like. No blame. No acrimony. That long-ago injury somersaulted into another shape at a table with a man in a dark jacket whom, in that present, I found I quite liked.

When I told Martha – who arrived from Singapore soon after for her term break – that Ross had said he hoped my seeing him wouldn't be destabilising, her hackles shot up. It was one of those moments when you realise that something has shifted and it's now the young, who are no longer so young, protecting us. The little girl who could once be picked up when she fell over in the sandpit, her face washed, an apple found, or a piece of chocolate, now rose in defence of me. On this occasion I didn't need it. He hadn't meant it with the vanity she ascribed to it, and all I needed to do was shake my head. The ground I stood on back then had been unstable, I said, and the air pressed down on me; but, as I'd told Ross, now and for a long time, though I couldn't quantify it, the ground beneath my feet was firm and the air around me light.

So there it was, the end of June, half a year gone, half a book written.

14

July. The salvia in the front garden cut back, neighbourhood cats taking advantage of the clear space to shit and
scratch. Vicks VapoRub, Helen read somewhere, keeps
them away. It doesn't, not entirely, but it helps. Other
than cats, there were no irritations, no interruptions.
Jeremy was in London. His elder sister had died – she'd
been ill for a long time and was ready to go – and as the
last surviving sibling, Jeremy went to sort out her house.
We had dinner before he left. He was sombre, and asked
if I'd *try again* when he returned. We can remain friends,
I said, but more than that, no, not if it meant returning to
the revolving door of dependence and resentment, habit
and reproach; it did neither of us any good. I could be
part of his support team, if there was a team to be a part
of, but that was all. Something needed to change, I said,
but change was not in Jeremy's repertoire. So he was
in London, ringing once a week, sounding morose but
otherwise not too bad, while here in Sydney my house was
quiet. I wrote each morning and walked each afternoon,

a drink or a meal with Helen up the road; that was the tenor of my days. It might sound boring, and maybe it's a symptom of age when I say that it wasn't. Sinking into a book, finding its shape, letting it build, chapter by chapter, is, for me, one of life's great satisfactions. Mostly. There are times, I admit, when I still wish I was an artist, and could lay it all out on the floor, an object in three dimensions that I could walk around and see from every angle. Gertrude Stein said the reason artists were mad and writers were not – a dubious proposition, but still – is that artists wake up every day to see it there in all its imperfection, hanging on the wall, balanced on studio tables, impossible to avoid. Janet Malcolm is closer to the mark when she writes:

> To the writer, the painter is a fortunate alter ego, an embodiment of the sensuality and exteriority that he has abjured to pursue his invisible, odourless calling. The writer comes to the places where traces of making can actually be seen and smelled and touched expecting to be inspired and enabled, possibly even cured.[82]

I don't expect to be cured, or even want to be, but it's true I invariably experience a hit of envy when in the studio of an artist friend – the physical nature of it all, their strong arms, their dirty aprons. All the way through the writing of this book, I've been able to see Helen's work as it's come into being in her studio. I saw the first of the vessels that were inspired by the blunt-backed boats in the bays at

Skopelos – an ancient shape, which, once rendered to its essence and etched onto metal plates, is part vessel, part boat. While I've been writing the last chapters of a book she knows about only in broad outline, Helen has made a series of three-dimensional bowls. Each began with a sheet of intaglio printed paper from plates 'etched' in salt water at a beach near the print workshop on Skopelos. Once printed, she moulds the paper, wet with a casting agent, into a vessel, a bowl which, when dry, changes shape from round to oval and back again according to the level of moisture in the air: a breathing, living container – a bowl, or a tiny boat. She has made eighty of them, and as she makes each next print the 'etched' surface of the plate wears down, resulting in lighter and lighter tones, so that when the bowls are assembled their colour fades from almost black to almost white, gradation within repetition. While I write on, they have been exhibited twice under the title 'earthen wear'. In her artist statement, Helen writes of the parallel she sees 'between the wearing down of the plates' in her use of them to make prints, 'and the wearing down of our earth in our use of it to sustain an ever demanding human habitation'.[83] I see that too, of course, but from the perspective of this book, for me they are also little boats of friendship floating together, a flotilla of possibility. Oh, to be able to do that – to accumulate those small living, breathing vessels, to see them there in front of me. Of course I'm envious! I can, and do, talk to her about this book, but I can't *show* her it – well, I can, and will, when it's finished. But while it is still on my desk I can't ask her what she thinks of this paragraph or that; would it be better here? I can't say, What about this semicolon, this comma, although it is a real question as my punctuation has changed with the writing of this book.

But even with Helen, even with the vision of those vessels sailing alongside each other, when I walk back down the hill to my house with its pens and paper – no smells, no heavy presses, no bottles of acid – there's a countervailing sense of relief. Imagine having to step around or over all those little objects; imagine if all my paragraphs, all those semicolons were actually there, tangible beings filling the house. Gertrude Stein is right; I'd go quite mad.

What I would like, though, is for a book when it is finished to transform itself into an object, a three-dimensional object that represents it, that I could put on the table or lay out on the floor and walk around. You can do that with a book, of course, once it's bound into an object, but you can't see its essence, its being, without reading the words, line by line. I don't want to *make* the object. I am well reconciled to my invisible, odourless calling. Artists make good friends and excellent companions, but when it comes to the way they create and work, they are another order of being.

And so are architects – fortunately.

It was in July that Stephen rang to say he thought he'd come up with a solution to SEAM's problem of how to get resources into those remote locations. Before the visit we'd made in April with Alison Lester, having only imagined the fjords from photos, Stephen had been attracted to the idea of a floating literacy centre that could move between the fjords, from one village to another; he'd seen photos of a barge on a lake in Africa, with a market on the deck and a school built above it. A neat concept, but impractical: expensive to build and maintain, and what would happen when the next cyclone – or even strong winds and high tides – pounded that usually peaceful coast?

Stephen had not been impressed by the school building where Alison Lester worked with the children. With an uninsulated roof, slatted sides preventing cross-ventilation, it was hot, hot, hot. I've been in those schools often enough not to notice, and anyway didn't have time to contemplate the absence of a ceiling beneath the tin. It was the first time Alison had been to PNG, and although she has run her book-making project many times in Australia, she didn't know what to expect, and I wanted everything to go as smoothly as it could for her. She was donating her time, and the materials we'd brought with us: wax crayons, paper, watercolours, stencils, scissors. Before we left, she'd said that fifty children was about all that was manageable, so I sent through a message to the school, to the teachers, and to the village. Fifty, I said, suggesting that this time we work with children from the middle grades. But when we arrived at the school and were drummed up the steps into the classroom, there

were at least a hundred children singing in welcome.
Who was going to send half of those expectant faces
out of the room? Not us. So we arranged the school's
two classrooms with the desks pushed together to make
working tables, each for six to ten children of similar
age. We then divided the materials among the tables,
crayons piled in the middle, watercolours, brushes and
pencils. Fortunately we'd brought extra paper, and
Alison's provisions were generous. In the heat of that
crowded school, she didn't miss a beat, no sign of dismay,
leading us all, showing the kids what could be done with
materials they hadn't encountered before – and within
minutes, it seemed, they were all drawing and writing
their stories. In the first moment of pause, not long in,
I was standing beside Alison when we glanced down
and saw rows of little eyes looking up at us though gaps
between the floorboards. These were the children from
the elementary class that was not part of the school,
along with some too young even for that, and others who
were not enrolled. So they all came in too: another thirty
children, or more, cross-legged on the floor. 'The tiny
school building at Tainabuna,' Alison wrote afterwards,
'was almost bursting with kids painting, drawing and
telling their stories. I'm sure if you'd looked down from
a cloud you'd have seen it glowing with creativity. It was
a hectic, wonderful, magical day.'[84] By the time we'd
finished, we had a painting or a drawing from each of
them: houses on stilts, fish, mountains, pigs, birds, trees,
canoes, pathways.

The next round of work was the following day with the
teachers back at the resort by the airstrip where there was
power. We transferred the images to Alison's computer
and printed them out into twenty-eight-page books; she
had even brought a laminator to do the covers. When we
returned to the village late that afternoon, the children
came running to see the books. Parents came from their
houses to shake our hands. On the table for the meal we
shared there was crayfish from the reef, sweet potato and
pumpkin from the gardens, the best bananas you're ever
likely to taste. The children were crowded round, turning
the pages of the books. They knew exactly who had drawn
which drawing, and they told us again the story of the
picture, the story of the child. Look, they said to each
other, to the adults and to us, we have made a book!
What would you write, Alison asked, if you wrote another
story for another book? One child would take a canoe out
past the rocks, along the pathways of the ocean, until she
knew every bird, every fish. Another would walk with his
friends through the forest to the highest peak where the
ancestors came from. And then he'd build a house. What
will your house look like? That was Stephen. What will
you keep in it? Books! Yes, he'd build a house just for the
books, all the books together, all our stories.

That night we fell asleep under our mosquito nets to
the sound of the children still talking, still looking at the
books. They would not go to sleep, the teacher said the
next morning. They were excited.

While we'd been at the school, Stephen had been looking at the village, talking to the men about their architecture, the materials they use, their methods of building. The school and the church were the only buildings not made by the men themselves from materials that came from the forest. Two buildings with tin roofs and neither had guttering for a tank, and neither had power. Near the school was a large community building with a sago-thatch roof, open sides and raised bamboo-slatted floors. Cool and beautiful. Why bring in tin when this was the way of the village?

In Moresby we'd visited children's libraries in the settlements, a project that started small and in less than a decade had grown to have twenty libraries catering to the least advantaged of urban children.[85] Most of the libraries are in refitted containers, which gives them power and water. But while the classes that take place inside are impressive indeed – there are kids lined up each morning waiting for the library to open – it was hot in there; again no cross-ventilation. While Alison and I were inside reading with the children, Stephen was outside with the caretaker having a good long look. Those building were cheap, serviceable, and they could be secured. They were also unimaginative, without charm, making no use of the breezes, no gesture towards a tradition of building that had been developed to combat the heat. Could a container be realigned somehow so that an entire side opened out, perhaps? Could it be combined with sago thatch to cool it down? These were the questions Stephen pondered back in the hotel with its security guards and businessmen. It seems parodic, but in the bar one night we were there, Thomas Piketty was on the television being interviewed about *Capital*, his book on rising inequality. Next to us another man talked to New York about immense sums of money, while Stephen and I contemplated the cost of refitted container.

And that's where I was up to with his thinking when he rang me that afternoon in July to say he thought he might have cracked it. What do you think of this? he asked, opening his laptop at my table and spreading out his drawings and diagrams. He showed me images and specifications of flexible roofing materials that can be combined with solar panels – enough to run a couple of computers and a printer – and with a water bladder to collect drinkable water. Why lug in heavy roofing material when this folds up like a tent and can be erected in a day? Rather than a refitted container, why not combine this roof with traditional building methods and practices: the best of the modern, the best of the traditional? Yes! But what about security? With those open sides where would the books go? The computers? Wouldn't we still need a building of some sort to put them in? And wouldn't that have to be made of those heavy materials if everything wasn't to vanish on the first night?

No, Stephen said, way ahead of me, and before he showed me the next part of the design, he reminded me of the giant open clam shell at the end of the peninsula where the canoes turn in to one of the villages. He had a photo of it, perched there on the rocks; it'd become, for

Stephen, a talisman. He'd found an off-the-shelf box used by the military, 1.4 metres square. My heart sank. Don't think military, he said. Think of that giant clam. Strong on the outside; beautiful inside. The box can be carried by a team of strong men; it can be secured into position; it is vandal-proof, and waterproof. Inside, there would be individual cabinets made of bamboo ply, that could be lifted out, each designed to be used from all four sides – with panels folding out as working surfaces for the computers, or lifting up as display boards, along with shelving, storage, a place for the printer, curriculum materials, art supplies. A modern version of the cabinet of curiosities. Stephen's cabinets are designed on Le Corbusier's system of form and proportion – the Modulor – a system itself based on the Golden Mean and the proportions of the human body. From whichever side you approached the cabinet, he explained, it would meet the scale of the human body. Clever. Although, as we looked at it that first day, I'm not sure I realised just how clever it was.

And a name? Stephen had that as well: *Schoolmate*, or *Wanskul*, to indicate that it is not a school – schools are the responsibility of the government – but a support for the school, a *book house* beside the school for all who want to learn, and to teach.

We tried the concept out on our advisors, who'd said we would only succeed if we found a way of housing the resources that would be replicable, sustainable and transportable. Yes, came the response, quietly at first; another look; more questions. Stephen had diagrams on his laptop and soon there was an animation. Yes, we heard from one person after another; if you can get it to work so the box can be carried and the cost can be kept down, you'll have done it. And then, after a pause, someone would say that while we were thinking of literacy and PNG, it was a design that could be adapted for other places, and for the delivery of other resources, medical aid, for instance.

As Stephen said, when the design concept became smaller, the possibilities became larger.

I'd have been grateful if we'd managed to get some sort of literacy support into the fjord villages; after years of talk and no action, my sights had shrunk. But in the second half of that year, 2014, with interest growing, and anthropologist friends saying, Yes, it would work well in the villages they knew, I was imagining again. And first among my imaginings was Ömie. The business was going well: the younger women were painting, the men were proud and busy. But there were few people on that mountain even with Grade 8, which is not surprising given there are only two primary schools for those widely separated villages. If children couldn't stay with relatives within walking distance of one of the schools, there was no way they could attend. The schools in the fjords might be under-resourced, but the teachers are committed and the students are in the classroom each day. The schools in Ömie have almost literally nothing in them, and teachers rarely stay, absent for weeks at a time, sometimes returning, sometimes not. It's a tough, isolated, unconducive posting. The art might be going well with Brennan to manage it, but in the long run, if it is to be sustainable into future generations, of course it was essential that the Ömie themselves had the education, the experience, the knowledge, to protect and manage their art, their business.

In September we launched SEAM and Stephen's *Wanskul* design in Melbourne. Martha came from Singapore. I met her at a café in a city lane not far from the gallery in Flinders Lane we'd been offered use of for the launch the next evening. It was the only moment we were able to talk of other things before Stephen arrived and we were swept into SEAM business, surrounded by the many people who were working to support this project. We had pro-bono design and construction of our website; we had invaluable pro bono accountancy. I don't know that SEAM would exist if it weren't for all this generosity, and the work of volunteers. But between us all, and with the support of writers and artists, with donations coming in, we raised enough to begin work on a prototype. For someone who'd been living a quiet life of writing, it was a radical shift of pace. Gone was that leisurely sense of days expanding. At first I managed to keep writing each morning – an insistent book this – limiting SEAM work to the afternoons and evenings. You need an uncluttered mind to push through to the end of a book, and as the days rushed by, uncluttered was not what my mind was.

And then there was Jeremy. He was finding it hard living in his sister's house on the outskirts of London, sorting out letters going back to their childhood, photos from earlier generations, stirring ghostly, unsettled memories. He'd ring to talk about his father, a figure I'd heard of over the years: a disapproving father, a tall man who cut a dashing figure on a motorbike, and who'd died in the car of his mistress of twenty years. No one in the family knew of her existence – what was her story? – until he died in this most awkward circumstance, a revelation made all the worse by the indignities that ensued when they had to get his large body out of a small car. Jeremy, who was still living in England then, was left to hold up his distraught mother, which proved an impossible task even for a beloved son. While his mother had pampered him – until he married and set sail for the other side of the world – he had always thought his father, a military man, had considered him weak, a bookish failure. That Jeremy wrote and published, that he was a well-regarded editor, was not – or Jeremy thought was not – enough for a man his father might have admired. Now that his sisters were both dead, there was no one to talk to about the past he was unearthing alone in that small, dark house. He had a young cousin in Wimbledon, and it was with this man's children that Jeremy found comfort, but for the rest, depression closed around him. At night he couldn't sleep, his body full of pain, his mind mired in dread. He'd ring me in the dark of his night and I picked up the phone in Sydney sunlight with a heavy heart. It was not easy listening, and there was nothing I could do, short of flying over, other than telling him to go to the hospital, which he did, but it turned out they couldn't admit him as a psychiatric patient. So he returned to his sister's house, alone with the past and a phone line to Australia. One night the pains were worse and he was more than usually frightened; the pain was too severe to ring, he said, it hurt to hold the phone. When, fortuitously, two friends of his sister came round the next morning to sort out her clothes, they took one look at him and called an ambulance. Jeremy was having a heart attack. The next call I received was from the hospital. Oliver had spoken to the doctor and I already knew that a stent was to be put in, that Jeremy had been told he must stop smoking and drinking, that the heart was damaged, but under the right conditions he should make a good recovery. Afterwards, he went to stay with the young cousin in Wimbledon, waiting to be well enough to come home. Home. After all those years away, England the lost ideal of home, when it came to the crunch it was Sydney where he wanted to be. Oliver arranged a flight; Jeremy had a panic attack on the way to the airport. Another flight was arranged. Jeremy was delivered into the care of the airline, and was taken in a wheelchair to board the plane.

On 1 October, his seventy-fourth birthday, Jeremy was in the air. I was at meetings about SEAM: a lawyer in the morning, a possible volunteer in the afternoon.

On the morning of 2 October, Jeremy arrived back in Sydney. The boys were to meet him at the airport. Stephen and I had a meeting that day with KTF, a small NGO run by 'a group of passionate and innovative problem solvers in PNG'. Working outwards from the Kokoda Track, they remind Australians that the people of PNG 'were there for us in our darkest hour . . . now it's our turn to lend a hand'.[86] As part of their education programme, KTF is developing an elementary and primary teacher-training curriculum, and it is in a community adjacent to their college not far from Kokoda that we are trialling our *Wanskul* prototype.

I didn't get home until late that afternoon. The anxiety I'd been holding at bay rushed in on me as I picked up the phone to dial Jeremy. It was not a good conversation. He was frightened, short of breath, and clearly very tired. He didn't want to die. They put a stent in, I said, they cleared you to fly, you're home. I wanted to be reassuring – for his sake, and also for mine. Instead I was short with him, anxiety turning into irritation at his stubborn, miserable insistence on gloom. He'd seen his GP that morning and she'd got him an appointment with a cardiologist for the next day. You're home, I said. Safe. But nothing would calm him; his anxiety morphed and spread. He was afraid to go to sleep. He was cold. He didn't know what to eat. The hospital in London had told him he must improve his diet. Would I help him? Tell him what was healthy?

'Jeremy,' I said, 'you've eaten my food for nearly twenty years, you know perfectly well what a good diet looks like.'

'Oh please. I need you. Be kind.'

'Have you stopped smoking?' I asked.

He sighed and huffed, noises that weren't an answer.

'Have you?'

'Well, no, but I'm smoking less.'

'Did you buy tobacco at Heathrow?'

'Well, um.' More noises. 'Well, yes. Just my allowance.'

'I thought you were being wheeled in a wheelchair.'

'I was.'

'So, how did you manage the tobacco?'

'I persuaded them to push me there.'

'Well, Jeremy,' I said. 'You stop smoking and we'll talk about diet.'

It was the last conversation we had.

He slept that night in his own bed, home again. In the morning he got up, went downstairs, saw his younger son who had a new job and was getting ready for the bus. The 8.20 bus. Later that morning his ex-wife, the boys' mother, came round to talk arrangements for their son, who was doing well, but would he remain stable with Jeremy returning in this bad state? Jeremy didn't answer the door. He didn't answer the phone. She found the spare key and let herself in. It was the middle of the day; she called out, walked upstairs and found Jeremy lying in his bed. She knew even before she entered the room that he was dead.

An hour or so later Oliver walked round to tell me. I'd had a bad morning, worrying about Jeremy, reproaching myself for not having gone to see him after that phone call. *Be kind.* I'd tried ringing; he didn't answer. I'd tried ringing Oliver and his phone was switched off. When I opened the door and saw him standing there on the step, sobbing, it took me a while to grasp what he was saying. And when I comprehended, there was numb disbelief, an emptying out of all feeling. Then shock: shock, with its attendant remorse, its deep, unquenchable sorrow. Oliver and I sat together, arms around each other. No, we kept saying. Not like this.

At Jeremy's house the officials had left, and Jeremy's body was still in his bed. Oliver and I went upstairs. Jeremy was lying on his back with no sign of disturbance, his hands on his chest as they were when he woke in the mornings. He looked calm; all that anguish, that twisted expression, the lines, the flush – all gone. It was as if ten years had fallen away. His fingers still bent when I slipped my hand into his.

I lay on the bed beside him. Oliver lay beside me. And it seemed to us both that the man we lay beside was the Jeremy of before: the Jeremy I'd slept beside for so many years; the father Oliver had got into bed with in the mornings when he was a boy. Peaceful. His right eye, the eye nearest to us as we lay beside him, kept opening – or rather the eyelid of that eye kept slipping up as if he were opening his eye to greet us. We sat up. Was he really dead? He didn't look dead. Tears. Our tears. The doors onto the roof were closed. Outside, the trees were moving in the wind, the view he loved; over to the side, the palms he'd never succeeded in persuading the neighbours to remove were more than usually ragged.

Heart disease was the verdict on the death certificate. The result of the stent going in? A clot from the flight? John, his friend and executor, a doctor, said it was probably the electrical system of the heart; it can short out and the heart just stops. A whopping heart attack, or a pulmonary embolism would probably have woken him, if only momentarily. From the way he lay undisturbed, he'd almost certainly have known nothing of it.

By the time the undertakers came at dusk, he was, as the cliché goes, as stiff as a board. They put him in a body bag and carried him down the steep, narrow stairs without a stretcher. That was waiting to wheel him out to the street and their unmarked van. They opened the body bag for us to have one last look. The jaw had dropped open, the skin had turned that terrible colour that only the dead have. The skin was cold, without resistance. The hands that had folded around mine only hours before were rigid. Dead. Very dead.

That is how I wrote of it in my diary: staccato, incomplete, minimal. Other than that, in the days that followed I was unable to write, even there. I'd try and the page closed, unwilling, resistant. Instead, I took out the photos that had accumulated over twenty years and made collages, cutting around the images, arranging and rearranging them, a tangible memorial, more immediate than words, more satisfying. Scissors and glue, discarded scraps piling up. It was a good way to mourn the man I'd loved for what he was, and could be, and became afraid to be. I backed the collages with stiff paper and pinned them

beside the table, lit candles and invited friends who'd
known him and me for a meal to mark the day Jeremy was
cremated. A memorial was to be held later, but that night,
when Jeremy had been reduced to ashes, I needed to mark
the occasion. We ate lasagne, and Jeremy was present at
that table as we remembered, and talked of him, and of
other things, life going on. The irony of it, Murray said,
was that Jeremy would have enjoyed the occasion; once,
when he still could enjoy such evenings, he would have
enjoyed it. You silly old bugger, I said to him as I cleared
up, gone though he was, and there in my head was that
image of him lying dead, looking more at peace than he
had for years. What was the point of all that anguish, that
fear? We end up dead anyway. A useless thought, I know,
but still I had it.

Death is strange in its absoluteness, its mystery, as if for
all that we see it before us, we do not believe it. We see that
eyelid move and we think he's not dead. Even when he
clearly is dead, in that body bag, still non-being makes no
sense. Disbelief. Shock. It was the same incredulity I'd felt
on seeing Poppy dead, and Patrick – and I remembered
it from David's dying, though I never saw his body. And
when the shock abates, and the disbelief, then there is
the mourning – and that is never straightforward. This
mourning was, for me, as much about the man long lost as
for the man who had died that day. I could weep at last for
the lover and companion I couldn't mourn while dealing
with the man he became. With that man I had been on the
narrow road of pity, a phrase that came to me after it was all

over, and which I was sure came from George Eliot – from *Middlemarch* when Dorothea realises the mistake she's made in her youthful marriage to Casaubon. I re-read the novel and couldn't find it; I downloaded the e-book so I could do one of those searches, and even then I couldn't find it. Still, it stayed with me, persistent. The narrow road of pity: a road that leads nowhere. Had Jeremy willed death in some strange way, getting himself back to Sydney, to his own bed? Or was I comforting myself from the stark reality of the depression that depleted the last years of his life? Can we ever accept that in the life of someone loved?

A cousin in England sent me a volume of Rumi's verse. 'This night will pass,' I read. 'Then we have work to do.' Rumi, I said to Martha on Skype from Singapore, and she reminded me of these lines:

> Out beyond ideas of wrongdoing and rightdoing,
> there is a field. I'll meet you there.[87]

That field is hard to reach, for any of us, and harder still from the long disablement of depression. What was it with Jeremy? Was it genetic? A brain chemical imbalance, that's all, as some of his psychiatrists said, an explanation Jeremy favoured? Or was it the emotional damage of a cold father? Being sent away to school too early, which I am sure had a lot to do with it? An adoring but domineering mother he never found a replacement for? Divorce? The sorrow of his son's illness? So many questions, and in their wake the harder question of my part in it. Would it have been different if I had gone round after that phone call? Could I have kept him alive if I'd fed him soup and slept beside him that night? And the darker, deeper question of whether it would have saved him had we separated as soon as it became clear that my life as a writer and his as a father were in some impossible collision? We did try to separate, several times, but we never managed it for long; there was love in the mix, not a lot by the end, but its traces remained, mixed in with habit, and those harsh patterns of dependence, guilt, exasperation. We moved further and further from that field, and if I'm left with regret, it is that in those final years we could so rarely reach again the grass of that field where 'the world is too full to talk about'.

For all of October and into November, I wrote nothing. I did not know – and still do not know – how to write of the recently dead when they are still too close for our entangled lives to have resolved into the past. Instead I read, and unlike the beginning of this book, which had taken me back to re-read the books of my youth, I read young writers, the ones who are starting out, finding a new voice for this disordered age. I read Eimear McBride's *A Girl is a Half-formed Thing*. Is she? Must she be, still? A *thing*? It is confronting for those of us in the affluent West with rooms of our own and the means to find our own shape to be reminded that even within our own societies, let alone beyond their borders, there are many who do not, and cannot, escape the deprivation of poverty, shame, abandonment. Eimear McBride's unnamed girl is a shattered, disassociated being whose only release is in a self-punishing sexuality. This is not the pornography of degradation; there is nothing titillating in this novel. It is a tough read, for its brutal truth is that this girl is indeed a half-formed thing. Yet there is nothing half-formed about the novel with its strong voice and dense fractured language of short, incomplete sentences. While so many of her contemporaries write of the past, or with an eye to the increasingly demanding and globalised market, she is uncompromising in a style that picks up the echoes of an earlier modernism, and points a way to something becoming formed, which I hope I live long enough to see.

In the meantime, there is work to do.

Come November, I was drawn back towards life by SEAM. We had another fundraiser already scheduled, in Sydney this time; we had documents and agreements to be drawn up and signed in order to take us forward. It's a complicated, highly regulated business working in this sector. I wrote what needed writing for SEAM, and was grateful for it; something to keep me from brooding. As to this book, which had been going so well, it stopped. Or rather, it was as if something inside, some resistant part of me, had stopped. Is this what happens when you insist on your writing life? People die and there you are, alone with it? Or was it a courtesy, this stopping, a last gesture of love made to a man I had all but ceased to love? Where did it all start, this unhappiness that had eclipsed so much of him? In childhood? School? Why can some people survive, and others not? Where had my own history of troubled love begun – for Jeremy and the lovers who had preceded him, for the troubled love, if that's what it was, for Papua New Guinea? Had one replaced another as if I need the challenge of something I think I can control, but can't? Or is it a reaction to growing up in a once-imperial country with great-uncles in the Indian Civil Service? Did everything derive from the contingency of birth: the ease with which I left England and barely a backwards glance? Was PNG that place between the pull of the tides, between north and south, England and Australia? These were questions that kept me from a book that had made its start at forty – as if that's where anything starts, even if in my case a lot had.

For all October and into November I'd venture out to see friends, or exhibitions, or movies, a semblance of life going on, and each time I'd return to a house cast in grief and a remorse made worse if I let myself feel the release that came creeping in with this death. So there I was reading the young and conversing with the dead, when one afternoon Robert Dessaix rang from Hobart where he lives. I told him about that last conversation with Jeremy and said to him that we should always be careful how we spoke to each other in case one of us was dead the next morning. Oh, no, he said. Think of the sentimental and pious nonsense we'd talk, none of our usual grit; it'd be as fake as those pearls you don't like. And when I said, here I was, at this late age, still tangled in those questions I'd been asking for years, about love and writing and independence, about memoir and its limits, questions I'd thought I'd got somewhere with, but clearly hadn't, he reminded me of Rilke. Live the question, he said. There are no answers. All we can do is live the question.

I put down the phone, went to the shelves and found Rilke's *Letters to a Young Poet*, and there it was in a letter written in 1903 from Worpswede in northern Germany – where I'd been, incidentally, with Jeremy on the trail of the artist Paula Modersohn-Becker. 'Have patience with everything unresolved in your heart,' Rilke wrote, 'and try to love the questions themselves . . . The point is, to live everything. Live the questions now.'[88] Now. Yes, now. Even now.

Thank you, Robert. That phone call was an act of friendship, and after it I let up on myself, and slowly remorse loosened its grasp. Looked at from another angle, the very end, the death itself, I came to see, was as good a death as one could hope for any of us. Is it so bad to say it was a release – for him, and for me? Sorrow, yes that will last, but also a sense of completion; a tentative opening out. In my tiny courtyard, the vines were sending out vigorous spring shoots.

December came, and with it the arrival in Sydney of my family: Jane and Nigel, Amy and her husband and two small boys on a summer break from wintry England, Tom for the ten brief days he could get off from work, and of course Martha. If there was any doubt where life lay, and the future, I had only to look around me. The house filled up with the sound of small boys running. For Christmas we were all in

Helen's garden: tables arranged in a large square, umbrellas to shade us, food contributed by everyone, plates and dishes carried up the hill, fish and prawns on the barbecue, cakes made by Jane. Both Helen's sons were home, Simon from Los Angeles and Nic from London. He'd had the previous Christmas, for which Martha had flown home, in Yorkshire at Jane and Nigel's house – another strand in the weaving of that day. Nic and Tom both work in architecture, like Stephen who, with his partner Matt, was also there at the table. And so was Max, a friend who's known me since before I was forty, and is now also a friend of Helen's. Even with everyone wearing those idiot paper hats that come out of crackers, for me, having left England so young and unformed, it was a powerful occasion, as if a pattern long in the making was drawing the threads of my life together in one place, at one time.

And so 2014 drew towards its close, that strange year, the now of this book, which I shall end by reeling back a few weeks to a warm December day, a house at the top of a hill above a small beach on the South Coast of New South Wales. The house is surrounded by a wall on three sides, enclosing discrete living spaces. On the fourth side it is open to the spotted gums, and through them is the shine of water. Two small boys stand looking down to the beach, they have new UV protective swimmers on, ready. We have just arrived, Amy, Gav and their boys fresh off the plane; we've chosen the rooms where we'll sleep; the car is unpacked. One of the boys gives a little leap. Look, he says, pointing through the trees. The other runs to his mother. Now? he asks. Soon, she says. And soon, yes, they are running ahead of us, down the hill through the trees. The undergrowth has been cleared, there's a carpet of eucalypt bark, no threat of snakes. The boys run across the sand, up to the water and stop. It's a small beach, a horseshoe-shaped cove with bush and rocky cliffs on either side. Because of its protected shape, the beach is usually calm, though on this day there are small waves. There is no one on the beach but us. The small boys are excited, and they're cautious. They haven't seen water quite like this. Their aunt, Martha, takes off her t-shirt and dives into the water. Look at Martha! the little one says. Then Amy, who first swam at this beach when she was only a few years older than her firstborn, does the same; she dives under, comes back to the boys, puts out her hands; Martha does too. Soon they are all in, their father as well, the boys holding on, not wanting to let go, running back onto the sand. They run to one end of this short beach, then to the other; they investigate the rocks, some flat, some tilted, waiting to be climbed. They climb, they step into a rocky pool, they get caught by a wave, and the next time they run into the water they are more confident. One kicks off towards his grandfather, who is standing in the water up to his waist. The other in his floaties throws himself alongside.

I stand on the beach beside my sister Jane. Look at them, we say, and it's not just the pleasure of seeing two London boys in the bright southern air, or that the journey has been safely made, gathering us together on this beach just over the headland from the house and the beach where we'd brought the girls and Tom when he was as small and round as the younger one. Are we in Australia? Tom would ask back then, and now it is for the next generation to marvel at the gift of travel.

And then Jane says, or maybe I do, She could have been here. We mean Poppy, our mother, who had she not died at fifty-nine would have been just ninety, the same age as Patrick's sister Betty, still going strong in England. The day will come when we will stop saying this, maybe this is the last year, for there will come a time when even Poppy would have been too old to make the journey. As we stand there watching the children, two generations of them absorbed in their moment, we are filled with memory and present both, as if the generations going back are there with us, and Jeremy too, who'd loved this beach, and Patrick who'd brought his watercolours here; all of them gathered in with us, on this day, in December 2014.

That evening Sam, the elder boy, draws a map of where we are. He draws the path winding down to the beach; he draws the trees, and the rocks. He draws the table where we sit when the day loses its lustre, the ocean a gleam of silver through dark trees. He draws the stars above our heads. There, he says. This is where we are.

How young it starts, that need to know where we are, and where we are going. And how long it lasts.

Notes

1 The book I was writing, commissioned by a small publisher, never eventuated. A version of the essay was published as part of the catalogue for Janet Laurence, *After Eden*, at Sherman Contemporary Art Foundation, Sydney, 2012. The quotation can be found on p. 45. A copy of it can be found on my website: www.drusillamodjeska.com/downloads/ DrusillaModjeska-TheGreenInGlass.pdf

2 Sophie Watson, *Inner Cities* (ed. Drusilla Modjeska), Penguin, Melbourne, 1989, p. 280.

3 Vera Brittain, *Testament of Youth*, first published 1933, Virago, London, 2004, p. 344. The gangrenous wound appears on p. 187; the dress on p. 206.

4 *Testament of Youth*, p. 413.

5 *Testament of Youth*, p. 585.

6 Virginia Woolf, *To the Lighthouse*, first published 1927, Penguin, Harmondsworth, 1992, p. 94.

7 Virginia Woolf, *Diary*, Vol. 3, 5 September 1925 (ed. Anne Oliver Bell), Harcourt Brace Jovanovich, London, 1980, p. 39.

8 Hermione Lee, *Virginia Woolf*, Chatto & Windus, London, 1996, p. 477, fn 13.

9 Virginia Woolf's dates are 25 January 1882 – 28 March 1941; Poppy's were 13 November 1924 – 16 January 1984.

10 Rebecca West, *The Return of the Soldier*, first published 1918, Virago, London, 1980, p. 187.

11 Victoria Glendinning, *Rebecca West: A Life*, Weidenfeld & Nicolson, London, 1987, p. 88.

12 Vera Brittain, *Testament of Youth*, p. 628; Vera Brittain's introduction, p. xxv.

13 Alison Clark, 'Unconscious Choice: Why writers and therapists do what they do', paper given to Sydney psychoanalytic interest group POPIG on 1 October 2014.

14 Portrait of Louise Bourgeois with *Fillette*, 1968, by Robert Mapplethorpe, 1982. www.artnet.com/magazineus/ features/saltz/the-heroic-louise-bourgeois6-4-10_detail. asp?picnum=1

15 Interview with Cecilia Blomberg, 16 October 1998. Quoted in Frances Morris and Marie-Laure Bernadec (eds), *Louise Bourgeois*, Tate Publishing, London, 2007.

16 First published in 1938. I read the subsequent revised and expanded edition, which was published as *Primitivism in Modern Art*, Harvard University Press, Massachusetts, 1986.

17 Doris Lessing, *The Golden Notebook*, first published 1962, Harper Perennial, New York, 1999, p. xiv.

18 Hazel Rowley, *Tête-à-Tête*, Vintage, Sydney, 2007, p. xiii.

19 Christina Stead, *The Beauties and Furies*, first published 1936, Virago Press, London, 1982, p. 159; Hazel Rowley, *Christina Stead*, Heinemann, Sydney, 1993, pp. vii-ix.

20 Virginia Woolf, *To the Lighthouse*, pp. 111–2.

21 Sophie Watson, 'Social Spatial Connections', *Inner Cities*, pp. 9–10.

22 Hazel Rowley, *Tête-à-Tête*, p.156.

23 *Tête-à-Tête*, p. 249. Hazel explains Sartre's temporary moral code on p. 246. Man is not responsible for the 'situation' in which he finds himself, though he is free in the response he makes. The problem comes when the *other* sticks to him and won't accept his views of freedom. 'What do you do if you are Sartre and you find yourself persecuted by the Other? You resort to a temporary moral code! That way, you wriggle out of the situation, and the huge moral edifice you have constructed remains intact.' She footnotes this (in a chapter called, incidentally, *Exiles at Home*, the title

I gave to my book published in 1980, a circularity I like) to a memoir, *Croquis de Mémoire* by Jean Cau.

24 Hazel Rowley, *Christina Stead*, p. ix.

25 There is a portrait of him in the National Portrait Gallery, and Amy's son Sam is named for him.

26 Virginia Woolf, *Diary*, Vol. 3, p. 273; December 1929.

27 Jacqueline Rose, 'Mothers', *London Review of Books*, 19 June 2014.

28 Adrienne Rich, 'Vesuvius at Home,' *Parnassus*, Vol. 5, No. 1, 1976.

29 Lee has an excellent chapter on Virginia Woolf's 'madness' which was a good deal more complicated than the point I make here about the conditions women suffered as psychiatric patients. Anyone interested in this aspect of Woolf would be well advised to start with this chapter of Hermione Lee, *Virginia Woolf*, pp. 175–200.

30 Virginia Woolf, *To the Lighthouse*, p. 91.

31 Frances Morris and Marie-Laure Bernadec (eds), *Louise Bourgeois*, p. 295.

32 Barack Obama, *Dreams from My Father*, first published 1995, Text Publishing, Melbourne, 2008, p. 320.

33 Hermione Lee, *Virginia Woolf*, p. 56.

34 *Virginia Woolf*, p. 68.

35 Statements from an interview with Donald Kuspit, 1988. Marie-Laure Bernadac and Hans-Ulrich Obrist, *Louise Bourgeois: Deconstruction of the Father/Reconstruction of the Father*, MIT Press, Cambridge, MA, 1998, p. 157.

36 Jacqueline Rose, 'Mothers', p. 22. This is an excellent article, reviewing several books and bringing together recent research and thinking about 'mothers'. I have drawn from it in thinking about this chapter.

37 Virginia Woolf, *To the Lighthouse*, p. 207.

38 Quoted in Hermione Lee, *Virginia Woolf*, p. 482.

39 Philip Roth, *Patrimony*, Vintage, New York, 1991, pp. 162; 217–8.

40 *Fathers, Granta, The Magazine of New Writing*, 104, London, 2008; my essay, 'The Death of the Good Father' was published

in *The Monthly*, September 2009. www.themonthly.com.au/ issue/2009/september/1274335721/drusilla-modjeska/ death-good-father

41 Barack Obama, *Dreams from My Father*, p. 539.

42 Quoted in Hermione Lee, 'Father and Son: Philip and Edmund Gosse', *Body Parts, Essays in Life-Writing*, Chatto & Windus, London, 2005, p. 100.

43 Edmund Gosse, *Father and Son*, (ed. and introduction James Hepburn), first published 1907, Oxford University Press, Oxford, 1974. The quotations are all taken from Chapter 5.

44 Siri Hustvedt, 'My Father/Myself', *Living, Thinking, Looking*, Picador, New York, 2012.

45 Sharon Olds, 'His Terror', *The Father: Poems*, Knopf, New York, 1992, p. 12.

46 Dave Eggers, *Your Fathers, Where Are They? And the Prophets, Do They Live Forever?* Hamish Hamilton, New York, 2014, pp. 210, 211.

47 The line removed from the draft of *To the Lighthouse* includes these words: 'she could not bear to be called, as she might have been called, had she come out with her views as a feminist'. Hermione Lee, *Virginia Woolf*, p. 479.

48 Knausgaard has, of course, done many interviews; the quotations in this paragraph are taken from the *Observer*, 2 March 2014, the *New York Times*, 21 May 2014, *Independent*, London, 7 July 2014. The comment by Lorin Stein appears in the *New York Times* profile listed here.

49 Doris Lessing, *The Golden Notebook*, p. xviii.

50 Barack Obama, *Dreams from My Father*, pp. 427, 429.

51 Zadie Smith, 'Speaking in Tongues,' New York Public Library, December 2008; *New York Review of Books*, 26 February 2009.

52 Paul Ham begins *Kokoda*, HarperCollins, Sydney, 2004 with this story.

53 Public Motor Vehicle.

54 Should anyone be interested in how the cloth and the dyes are made, there is a photo essay, mostly of shots taken on

that visit in 2004, in *The Wisdom of the Mountain*, National Gallery of Victoria, Melbourne, 2009.

55 Judith Ryan, 'Ömie nioge: Skin of Now', catalogue essay, *The Wisdom of the Mountain*. Nicholas Thomas, the Director of Cambridge University's Museum of Archaeology and Anthropology, calls the women of Ömie 'the most brilliant living exponents' of a great world art that once stretched across the Pacific from New Guinea to Hawaii. See www.seamfund.org

56 Quoted in Juhani Pallasmaa, *The Thinking Hand*, Wiley, Sydney, 2009, p. 82.

57 'The Fabric of Wisdom', *The Wisdom of the Mountain*, Also available at www.drusillamodjeska.com/other-writing/

58 *A Century of Women Artists: 1840s–1940s*, Deutscher Fine Art Gallery, Melbourne, 1993. The self-portrait is now held in the Art Gallery of South Australia, a gift from Stella Bowen's niece, Mrs Suzanne Brookman.

59 Drusilla Modjeska, *Stravinsky's Lunch*, Pan Macmillan, Sydney, 1999, p. 111.

60 *The Sock Knitter* can be seen at the Art Gallery of New South Wales. www.artgallery.nsw.gov.au/collection/works/OA18.1960/

61 This seminal text was first given as a lecture in Hawaii in 1993. It was published in expanded form in the essay 'Our Sea of Islands' along with responses in *Rediscovering Our Sea of Islands*, School of Social and Economic Development, University of the South Pacific, 1993.

62 The diaries of Mike Monsell-Davis are now held in the ANU archive.

63 Tok Pisin is the name given to the language once called Pidgin.

64 Martin Luther King Jr., 'I've Been to the Mountaintop'. It can be found at www.americanrhetoric.com/speeches/mlkivebeentothemountaintop.htm

65 Bob Connolly, *Making Black Harvest*, ABC Books, Sydney, 2005, p. 279. *Black Harvest* is the third in a trilogy of

films shot in the Highlands. *First Contact* is the story of the Leahy brothers gold prospecting into regions of the Highlands not previously contacted. *Joe Leahy's Neighbours* traces this next-generation Leahy and his relations with the Gangia people with whom he goes into a coffee plantation business that doesn't live up to expectations. *Black Harvest* traces the story into the war that erupts with the collapse of the coffee price.

66 This challenge is well articulated in all its complexity by, for instance, Regis Stella in 'PNG in the New Millennium: Some Troubled Homecomings', in David Kavanamur, Charles Yala and Quinton Clements, *Building a Nation in Papua New Guinea: Views of the Post-Independence Generation*, Pandanus Books, Canberra, 2003. For an Australian perspective, see, for instance, Ben Scott, *Reimagining PNG: Culture, Democracy and Australia's Role*, Lowy Institute, Sydney, 2005.

67 Jo Chandler, 'Manus in the Balance', *The Monthly*, February 2015, pp 34–39. Written after visiting Manus, this is a very good introduction to the island, its history and the impact of the detention centre.

68 You can see some of this footage at www.ngv.vic.gov.au/multimedia/wisdom-of-the-mountain-songs-1/

69 Regis Tove Stella, *Imagining the Other*, Pacific Islands Monograph Series 20, University of Hawaii Press, Honolulu, 2007. Highly recommended to anyone interested in a critical analysis by a fine PNG critic of outsider fiction of the Pacific.

70 Stella Bowen, *Drawn from Life*, first published 1941, Pan Macmillan, Sydney, 1999, p. 104.

71 'Childless by Choice', *Sydney Morning Herald*, 1 December 2012, www.smh.com.au/lifestyle/childless-by-choice-2012 1130-2a25u

72 In 2013, I wrote about the experience of this diagnosis, and the women doctors who treated me, and the huge strides that have been taken in the diagnosis and treatment of breast cancer for which we should be grateful. *Good*

Weekend, 6 April 2013. www.theage.com.au/lifestyle/the-harsh-light-of-day-20130405-2h231.html

73 I have written elsewhere of the impact on my writing of Pauline's question and David's death. See 'The Informed Imagination', *Meanjin*, Vol. 74, No. 2, Melbourne University Press, Melbourne, June 2015.

74 Virginia Woolf, *Diary*, Vol. 3, September 1926, p. 112. My italics.

75 Elizabeth Bishop, 'Three Valentines', *Elizabeth Bishop: Poems, Prose and Letters*, Library of America, 2008, p. 195. I have made a different use of this phrase than she made in the poem. I think, and hope, she would forgive me.

76 www.omieartists.com/about/about-us/collections/

77 The Crocodile Awards for PNG writers, established in 2010, has been an important spur to the resurgence of local writing. I have reviewed two of the annual Crocodile anthologies for the *Australian*. These reviews can be found on www.drusillamodjeska.com/other-writing/. Gary Juffa, writer and governor of Oro, makes his first appearance in the 2014 anthology. There's been a groundswell of support for Juffa, as well as disappointment that he hasn't achieved more; there have also been moves against him by those who stand to lose from his protection of the forests and land.

78 SEAM – Sustain Education Art Melanesia – has a website, built for us pro bono, by Involved in Melbourne. www.seamfund.org

79 www.seamfund.org/our-people/. There's a photo of Martha in the water with the children at Jebo village.

80 The transcript of an interview I did with John Wesley Vaso in 2007 can be found on my website: www.drusillamodjeska.com/downloads/DrusillaModjeska-JohnWesleyVason.pdf

81 You can read this magnificent poem, and a whole lot more besides, in Albert Wendt (ed.), *Nuanua: Pacific Writing in English since 1980*, University of Hawaii Press, Honolulu, 1995.

82 Janet Malcolm, 'Forty-one false starts', 1994, in *Forty-one False Starts: Essays on Artists and Writers*, Text Publishing, Melbourne, 2013, p. 13.

83 Helen Mueller shows at the Brenda May Gallery, Danks Street, Waterloo, Sydney. While I've been writing this book, she has had two exhibitions and appeared in several group shows, there and in other galleries. www.brendamaygallery. com.au/artworks.php?artistID=89-Helen-Mueller. In 2015 'earthen ware' was exhibited at both Brenda May Gallery and at the Hazelhurst Art on Paper Award, Hazelhurst Gallery.

84 Alison Lester made this comment for SEAM's website. You can see photos there of the day and of the children's work, and the books we made: www.seamfund.org/news-and-updates.

85 I interviewed the founder of *Buk bilong Pikinini* for *Meanjin*, Vol. 72, No. 1, March 2013. The interview can also be found at www.drusillamodjeska.com/downloads/DrusillaModjeska-BukbilongPikinini.pdf

86 KTF (Kokoda Track Foundation). To read about KTF and its programmes in sustainable education, health, livelihood and leadership, see www.ktf.ngo/

87 The first quotation is from *Unseen Rain: Quatrains of Rumi*, translated by John Moyne and Coleman Barks, Shambhala Publications, Massachusetts, 1986, p. 18. The second is from *The Essential Rumi*, translated by Coleman Barks, HarperCollins, Sydney, 1995, p. 36.

88 Rainer Maria Rilke, *Letters to a Young Poet*, first published 1929. Letter 4.

Acknowledgements

This book is published with thanks to friends and family and all whom I've loved, and known, and worked beside.

Since the first publication of this book in October 2015, SEAM has made major advances, thanks to the generosity of readers and writers. A book house is in place at Tainabuna village in the fjords of Cape Nelson.

Six more books have been made with the teachers and children.

Through the generosity of a donor, there is now a PNG graduate project co-ordinator to develop and extend, monitor and evaluate the roll-out of *Wanskul*.

SEAM thanks them all.

**If you would like to support SEAM's work,
you can donate at**

www.seamfund.org

Also by Drusilla Modjeska

Drusilla Modjeska is one of Australia's most acclaimed writers. Her books include the award-winning memoir of her mother, *Poppy*, *The Orchard* and *Stravinsky's Lunch*. Her first novel, *The Mountain*, was shortlisted for the 2013 Miles Franklin Award. *Second Half First* was shortlisted for the Kibble Award, the Victorian Premier's Award and the ALS Gold Medal Award. Drusilla co-founded SEAM Fund – Sustained Education Art Melanesia – in 2011, which supports community-based projects in Papua New Guinea. She lives in Sydney.